高等学校试用教材

建筑类专业英语
给水排水与环境保护

第二册

傅兴海　褚羞花　　主编
耿建琴　张　萍　　　编
史长远　刘　澍
迟国基　　　　　　主审

中国建筑工业出版社

《建筑类专业英语》编审委员会

总 主 编　徐铁城
总 主 审　杨匡汉
副总主编　（以姓氏笔画为序）
　　　　　王庆昌　乔梦铎　陆铁镛
　　　　　周保强　蔡英俊
编　　委　（以姓氏笔画为序）
　　　　　王久愉　王学玲　王翰邦　卢世伟
　　　　　孙　玮　李明章　朱满才　向小林
　　　　　向　阳　刘文瑛　余曼筠　孟祥杰
　　　　　张少凡　张文洁　张新建　赵三元
　　　　　阎岫峰　傅兴海　褚羞花　蔡慧俭
　　　　　濮宏魁
责任编辑　刘茂榆

前　言

　　经过几十年的探索，外语教学界许多人认为，工科院校外语教学的主要目的，应该是："使学生能够利用外语这个工具，通过阅读去获取国外的与本专业有关的科技信息。"这既是我们建设有中国特色的社会主义的客观需要，也是在当前条件下工科院校外语教学可能完成的最高目标。事实上，教学大纲规定要使学生具有"较强"的阅读能力，而对其他方面的能力只有"一般"要求，就是这个意思。

　　大学本科的一、二年级，为外语教学的基础阶段。就英语来说，这个阶段要求掌握的词汇量为2400个（去掉遗忘，平均每个课时10个单词）。加上中学阶段已经学会的1600个单词，基础阶段结束时应掌握的词汇量为4000个。仅仅掌握4000个单词，能否看懂专业英文书刊呢？还不能。据统计，掌握4000个单词，阅读一般的英文科技文献，生词量仍将有6%左右，即平均每百词有六个生词，还不能自由阅读。国外的外语教学专家认为，生词量在3%以下，才能不借助词典，自由阅读。此时可以通过上下文的联系，把不认识的生词猜出来，那么，怎么样才能把6%的生词量降低到3%以下呢？自然，需要让学生增加一部分词汇积累。问题是，要增加多少单词？要增加哪一些单词？统计资料表明，在每一个专业的科技文献中，本专业最常用的科技术语大约只有几百个，而且它们在文献中重复出现的频率很高。因此，在已经掌握4000个单词的基础上，在专业阅读阶段中，有针对性地通过大量阅读，扩充大约1000个与本专业密切有关的科技词汇，便可以逐步达到自由阅读本专业科技文献的目的。

　　早在八十年代中期，建设部系统院校外语教学研究会就组织编写了一套《土木建筑系列英语》，分八个专业，共12册。每个专业可选读其中的三、四册。那套教材在有关院校相应的专业使用多年，学生和任课教师反映良好。但是，根据当时的情况，那套教材定的起点较低（1000词起点），已不适合今天学生的情况。为此，在得到建设部人事教育劳动司的大力支持，并征得五个相关专业教学指导委员会同意之后，由建设部系统十几所院校一百余名外语教师和专业课教师按照统一的编写规划和要求，编写了这一套《建筑类专业英语》教材。

　　《建筑类专业英语》是根据国家教委颁发的《大学英语专业阅读阶段教学基本要求》编写的专业阅读教材，按照建筑类院校共同设置的五个较大的专业类别对口编写。五个专业类别为：建筑学与城市规划；建筑工程（即工业与民用建筑）；给水排水与环境保护；暖通、空调与燃气；建筑管理与财务会计。每个专业类别分别编写三册专业英语阅读教材，供该专业类别的学生在修完基础阶段英语后，在第五至第七学期专业阅读阶段使用，每学期一册。

　　上述五种专业英语教材语言规范，题材广泛，覆盖相关专业各自的主要内容：包括专业基础课，专业主干课及主要专业选修课，语言材料的难易度切合学生的实际水平；词汇以大学英语"通用词汇表"的 4000 个单词为起点，每个专业类别的三册书将增加 1000～1200 个阅读本专业必需掌握的词汇；本教材重视语言技能训练，突出对阅读、翻译和写作能力的培养，以求达到《大学英语专业阅读阶段教学基本要求》所提出的教学目标："通过指导学生阅读有关专业的英语书刊和文献，使他们进一步提高阅读和翻译科技资料的能力并能以英语为工具获取专业所需的信息。"

《建筑类专业英语》每册 16 个单元，每个单元一篇正课文（TEXT），两篇副课文（ReadingMaterialA&B），每个单元平均 2000 个词，三册 48 个单元，总共约有十万词，相当于原版书三百多页。要培养较强的阅读能力，读十万词的文献，是起码的要求。如果专业课教师在第六和第七学期，在学生通过学习本教材已经掌握了数百个专业科技词汇的基础上，配合专业课程的学习，再指定学生看一部分相应的专业英语科技文献，那将会既促进专业课的学习，又提高英语阅读能力，实为两得之举。

本教材不仅适用于在校学生，对于有志提高专业英语阅读能力的建筑行业广大在职工程技术人员，也是一套适用的自学教材。

建设部人事教育劳动司高教处和中国建设教育协会对这套教材的编写自始至终给予关注和支持；中国建筑工业出版社第五编辑室密切配合，参与从制定编写方案到审稿各个阶段的重要会议，给了我们很多帮助。在编写过程中，各参编学校相关专业的许多专家、教授对材料的选取、译文的审定都提出了许多宝贵意见，谨此致谢。

《建筑类专业英语》是我们编写对口专业阅读教材的又一次尝试，由于编写者水平及经验有限，教材中不妥之处在所难免，敬请广大读者批评指正。

《建筑类专业英语》
编审委员会

Contents

UNIT ONE
    Text   Historical Development of Municipal Water Systems in the United States 1

    Reading Material A   Groundwater and Surface-water Supplies 7
    Reading Material B   Water Transmission 9

UNIT TWO
    Text   Measurement of Water Quality 11
    Reading Material A   Biochemical Oxygen Demand 16
    Reading Material B   Bacteriological Measurements 18

UNIT THREE
    Text   Water Processing 21
    Reading Material A   Methods for Removal of Wastes and Odours 26
    Reading Material B   Magnetic Water Treatment 28

UNIT FOUR
    Text   Filtration 31
    Reading Material A   Rapid Gravity Filtration 36
    Reading Material B   Backwashing 38

UNIT FIVE
    Text   Collection of Wastewater 40
    Reading Material A   Storm Sewer System 45
    Reading Material B   Sanitary Sewer System 47

UNIT SIX
    Text   Composition of Wastewater 49
    Reading Material A   Primary Treatment 54
    Reading Material B   Secondary Treatment 56

UNIT SEVEN
    Text   Biological Treatment System 58
    Reading Material A   Biological Towers 63
    Reading Material B   Biological Aeration 64

UNIT EIGHT
    Text   Characteristics of the Sludges 66
    Reading Material A   Sludge Stabilization 71
    Reading Material B   Sludge Dewatering 73

UNIT NINE
    Text   Pumps and Pumping Stations 75

Reading Material A	Choice of Pumps	80
Reading Material B	Pump Station Buildings	82

UNIT TEN
Text	Classification of Water Pollutants	84
Reading Material A	Regulations Concerning Water Pollution	89
Reading Material B	Sources of Water Pollution	91

UNIT ELEVEN
Text	Potential Impact of Air Contaminants on Water Quality	93
Reading Material A	The Need for Water Quality Studies	98
Reading Material B	Water Quality Standards	99

UNIT TWELVE
Text	Hazardous Waste	102
Reading Material A	Treatment of Hazardous Waste	107
Reading Material B	Radioactive Waste Management	109

UNIT THIRTEEN
Text	Air Pollution	111
Reading Material A	Meteorological Effects and Changes	116
Reading Material B	Causes of Air Pollution	118

UNIT FOURTEEN
Text	Health Effects of Noise	120
Reading Material A	Measurement and Control of Noise	125
Reading Material B	Noise Control	127

UNIT FIFTEEN
Text	Resource Recovery	130
Reading Material A	Disposal of Solid Waste-Landfilling	135
Reading Material B	Solid Wastes	137

UNIT SIXTEEN
Text	Removal of Organic Vapour from Effluent Gases	140
Reading Material A	Managing Climatic Change	145
Reading Material B	Pollution Prevention or Cure	147

Appendix I Vocabulary 149

Appendix II Translation for Reference 156

Appendix III Key to Exercises 178

UNIT ONE

Text   Historical Development of Municipal Water Systems in the United States

[1]   Today Americans use approximately 150 to 200 gpcd of water (including commercial usage) and domestic use is approximately 60 gpcd. ①On the average, over 37 bil gal of water daily are consumed in this country, most of it treated by a public water utility. ②

[2]   The story of the development of the public water-supply systems in the US is not only the story of the water-supply field, but the story of a growing country as well; water and its many uses have been integral facets of the growth and expansion of the US. As a matter of record, the transformation of the US from a rural, agricultural nation to an urban, industrialized world power has in fact depended to a large degree on the water supply and the engineering needed to provide large amounts of water for domestic use, industry, and that of commerce. ③

[3]   The earliest recorded public water-supply system in the US is credited to the City of Boston, Mass., in 1652. In these early days, people saw little need for a public water-supply system because the service offered did not appear to be as good as people could get from a private well or cistern. Water was "good" if it looked clean—sparkling, clear, cool, and free from foreign taste or odor. Such water was readily available from the backyard well. Most never stopped to think that typhoid, dysentery, cholera, and "summer complaint" could be caused by the water, which all too frequently came from a well not too distant from the family outhouse.

[4]   It was not until after 1875 that scientific knowledge established for certain that waterborne germs caused typhoid and cholera, and it wasn't until after 1900 that the general public realized the danger of using impure water-regardless of how it looked or tasted. Unfortunately, until the 1800s and early 1900s, when filtration became relatively common, the public supplies were usually no safer than the private sources. It was common practice in early systems to take water directly from creeks and rivers, with little or no effort to treat it before the water was pumped into the distribution system. ④

[5]   In 1800, there were only sixteen public water-supply systems in the US, most of them originally built for "fire protection and the laying of dust", with little thought given to domestic service. Most of these were in New England, or among the larger cities on the Atlantic seaboard.

[6]   By 1850, the number of community systems had grown to 83, none of which had installed any purification processes with the exception of some basic turbidity control in the form of settling basins. However, the period around 1900 became known as the "New Era" in public water supply, primarily because treatment processes began to deliver better

water and better domestic service than could be realized from the private supply, such as a well or cistern. ⑤In 1880 only 600 water systems were in existence, but by 1897 nearly 3,350 public water-supply systems were in existence—1400 of which were built between 1891 and 1897!

[7]   By 1950, public water systems had reached their maturity. The fears and trepidation of the early years had vanished with the advent of technology, and in the 50 year period between 1900 and 1950 the success of public water supply became evident. In 1950, there were over 17,000 urban water systems in the US, and treatment techniques using coagulation, rapid filtration, and chlorination had changed the role of the public water supply from a "fire protection and laying of the dust" concept to a multi-million dollar industry.

[8]   The technological advances of the past 200 years in the US water-supply field have possibly been the most important in the entire history of public water supply. Waterborne disease has been reduced to almost nothing, and the abundance of relatively inexpensive potable water has created a unique problem for the industry—the average customer has taken his public water supply for granted! New research and technology, needed to provide even more and better water, may prove to be expensive.

[9]   Although water-supply service is one of the oldest industries in the nation and, in terms of volume, the largest supplier of a single commodity in the US, it is faced with several other areas of concern. Water quality problems are surfacing in many areas of the US. News reports flow in daily of pollution of the country's water by heavy metals. ⑥Chlorine-resistant viral organisms threaten grave health concerns by rendering currently applied disinfection technologies impotent. Present facilities in many communities are totally incapable of handling contamination from accidental industrial or transportation spillages. Cross-connection and backflow potentials continue to haunt water systems because of insufficient regulation and inspection procedures. ⑦

[10]   Despite these obstacles, the water-supply field as a whole seems confident that it can overcome the problems, and rise to the challenge of the future. Using the tools of research, advancing technology, and plain hard work, water men are showing the grit and determination for which America is famous, and they are confident that they can continue to provide the best water available to the citizens of the US.

New Words and Expressions

utility [juːˈtiliti]	n.	公用事业公司，公用事业设备
integral * [ˈintigrəl]	a.	主要的，必备的，构成整体所必要的
facet [ˈfæsit]	n.	方面
cistern [ˈsistən]	n.	蓄水池，储水器
backyard [ˈbækjɑːd]	n.	后天井，后院

typhoid ['taifɔid]	n.	伤寒
dysentery ['disəntəri]	n.	痢疾
cholera ['kɔlərə]	n.	霍乱
outhouse ['authaus]	n.	（户外）厕所
all too		可惜太，过于
waterborne ['wɔːtəbɔːn]	a.	水传播的，水生的
creek [kriːk]	n.	小溪，小河
distribution [ˌdistri'bjuːʃən]	n.	传输
lay [lei]	v.	消除
seaboard ['siːbɔːd]	n.	海岸线，沿海地区
turbidity [təːbiditi]	n.	混浊度
settle ['setl]	v.	（使）沉淀
basin ['beisn]	n.	水池，流域，排水区域
trepidation [ˌtrepi'deiʃən]	n.	惊恐，惶恐
advent * ['ædvənt]	n.	到来，出现
with the advent of		随着……的到来
coagulation [kəuˌægju'leiʃən]	n.	絮凝，混凝
chlorination [ˌklɔːri'neiʃən]	n.	氯化处理，氯气灭菌
potable ['pəutbl]	a.	可饮用的
surface ['səːfis]	v.	暴露出来
chlorine * ['klɔːriːn]	n.	氯（气）
viral ['vaiərəl]	a.	病毒的
disinfection [diˌsin'fekʃən]	n.	消毒，灭菌
impotent ['impətənt]	a.	不起作用的，软弱无能的
contamination * [kənˌtæmi'neiʃən]	n.	污染
spillage ['spilidʒ]	n.	泄漏，溢出
backflow ['bækfləu]	n.	回流，倒流
grit [grit]	n.	勇气和耐力

Notes

①gpcd = gallons per capita per day

②bil = billion

③As a matter of record,···depended to a large degree on···the engineering needed···domestic use, ···and that of commerce.

句首，As a matter of record 作状语，修饰全句；短语动词 depended on 被介词短语 to a large degree 所分隔；needed 引出的分词短语作 engineering 的后置定语；that 替代 the use。

④It was common practice···to take···rivers, with little or no effort to treat it···.

句首 it 为形式主语，真正的主语为 to take…rivers；句末的 with 结构作状语，用以补充说明。

⑤…and better domestic service than could be realized from the private supply，…

此处的 than 为连接词，引导比较状语从句，省略了主语部分，这种结构多用于正式文体。

⑥介词短语 of pollution…heavy metals 修饰主语 News reports，被谓语所分隔。

⑦Cross-connection 指在监督下的饮用供水和未经监督又不知其可否饮用的供水之间的连接。

backflow 指由压差引起的流动状况，使水流从预定的水源以外的一处或数处来源进入饮用供水配水管。

Exercises

Reading Comprehension

Ⅰ. Say whether the following statements are true (T) or false (F) according to the text.

1. Water and its many uses have played a vital part in the development of the US. ( )

2. According to the author, water was good if it looks clean—sparkling, clear, cool and free from foreign taste or odor. ( )

3. The early public water-supply systems in the US were originally built not only for fire protection and the laying of dust, but for domestic use, industry and that of commerce. ( )

4. During the period around 1900, which was known as the "New Era" in public water supply, treatment processes began to deliver better water and better domestic service than could be realized from the private supply. ( )

5. Despite the problems surfacing in the water-supply field, American water men are confident that they can continue to provide the best water available to the citizens of the US. ( )

Ⅱ. Choose the best answer for each of the following.

1. Which of the following statements is the topic sentence of Para. 2?

   A. The story of the development of the public water-supply systems in the US is not only the story of the water-supply field, but the story of a growing country as well.

   B. Water and its many uses have been integral facets of the growth and expansion of the US.

   C. The transformation of the US from a rural, agricultural nation to an urban, industrialized world power has depended to a large degree on the water supply.

   D. The engineering is needed to provide large amounts of water for domestic use, industry, and that of commerce.

2. The true reason that in those early days, people saw little need for a public water-supply system is that _____ .
   A. the water from the system was not so good as people could get from a private well or cistern
   B. the water from the system was as good as people cold get from a private well or cistern
   C. most never stopped to think that typhoid, dysentery, cholera, and "summer complaint" could be caused by the water from a well not too distant from the family outhouse
   D. it was not so convenient to get water from a public water-supply system as from a private well or cistern.
3. What has been the most important in the entire history of public water supply in the US?
   A. The success of making the general public realize the danger of using impure water.
   B. The success of public water supply.
   C. The scientific knowledge that established for certain that waterborne germs caused typhoid and cholera.
   D. The technological advances of the past 200 years in the water-supply field.
4. Why, according to the author, has the average customer taken his public water supply for granted?
   A. Because it is easy to get the potable water.
   B. Because the potable water is abundant and inexpensive.
   C. Because new research and technology prove to be inexpensive.
   D. Because waterborne disease has been reduced to almost nothing.
5. What problems is the US water-supply field faced with?
   A. Water quality problems.
   B. Cross-connection and backflow potentials.
   C. New research and technology, needed to provide even more and better water, may prove to be expensive.
   D. Both A) and B) .

Vocabulary

I. Fill in the blanks with the words given below, changing the form where necessary.

settle	surface	pump
install	establish	

1. Industry will be required to _____ new equipment and meet tougher emission limits.
2. Once the link between waste disposal and disease in the population through drinking water supplies had been _____ , steps were being taken to break this cycle.

3. As a result of the increase of the population and the contribution from municipal discharges, new problems have _____ in the water-supply field.
4. At the headworks sewage is screened and _____ before discharge into the Thames Estuary (河口).
5. The company used two steam engines to _____ the well water to elevated reservoirs and then to the distribution system.

Ⅱ. Match the words in Column A with their corresponding definitions or descriptions in Column B.

Column A	Column B
1. advent	a. necessary (to complete something)
2. creek	b. coming or arrival
3. integral	c. the destruction of disease germs
4. utility	d. a small stream
5. disinfection	e. a public service

Translation　　　　　　　　词义选择

　　英语词汇也具有一词多义、一词多类的特点。正确选择一个词的意义是翻译中首先要解决的问题。选择词义一般从三方面着手：1. 根据词类确定词义；2. 根据上下文选择词义；3. 根据词的搭配习惯确定词义。

例 1. The service offered did not appear to be as good as people could get from a private (a.) well or cistern.
所提供的服务似乎还不如人们用自家的水井或水池方便。

例 2. He looked at me, as a colonel might look at a private (n.) whose bootlaces were undone.
他看着我，就象一位上校看着一位没有系好鞋带的列兵。

例 3. Scientific knowledge established for certain that waterborne germs caused typhoid and cholera.
科学知识确凿地证实了水生细菌可导致伤寒和霍乱。

例 4. He has been established in New York as a physician.
他已在纽约开业行医了。

例 5. In 1950, there were over 17,000 urban water systems in the US.
1950 年，美国城市供水系统已超过 17,000 个。

例 6. The social system in China is quite different from that in the US.
中国的社会制度同美国的大不相同。

Translate the following sentences into Chinese, paying attention to the underlined words.

1. A large portion of the flow to streams is derived from subsurface water.

2. Any notion of "safe yield" must consider each factor.
3. Water can be transported from either a ground or surface supply source directly to a community or, if water quality considerations indicate, initially to a water treatment facility.
4. Service reservoirs are also necessary in the transmission system to help level out peak demands.
5. Groundwater is an important direct source of supply which is tapped by wells.

Reading Material A

Groundwater and Surface-water Supplies

Groundwater is both an important direct source of supply which is tapped by wells and a significant indirect source of supply since a large portion of the flow to streams is derived from subsurface water.

Near the surface of the earth in the zone of aeration soil pore spaces contain both air and water. This zone, which may have a zero thickness in swamplands and be several hundred feet thick in mountainous regions, contains three types of moisture. ①Gravity water is in transit after a storm through the larger soil pore spaces. Capillary water is drawn through small pore spaces by capillary action, and is available for plant uptake. *Hygroscopic moisture* is water held in place by molecular forces during all except the driest climatic conditions. Moisture from the zone of aeration cannot be tapped as a water supply source.

On the other hand, the zone of saturation offers water in a quantity that is directly available. In this zone, located below the zone of aeration, the pores are filled with water, and this is what we consider groundwater. The stratum which contains a substantial amount of groundwater is called an aquifer. At the surface between the two zones, labeled the water table or phreatic surface, the hydrostatic pressure in the groundwater is equal to atmospheric pressure. An aquifer may extend to great depths, but because the weight of overburden material generally closes pore spaces, little water is found at depths greater than 600 m (2000ft). The water readily available from an aquifer is that which will drain by gravity. Each soil type thus has a specific yield,② defined as the volume of water, expressed as a percent of the total volume of water in the aquifer, which will drain freely from the aquifer.

Groundwater supplies are often tapped by drilling wells into the ground and pumping the water up and out.

Many factors help determine the "safe yield" of a given well or a selected aquifer:③
- precipitation (P)

- net groundwater flow to the area (G_N)
- evapotranspiration (E_T)
- surface flow out of the area (S_0)
- change in groundwater storage (G_s)
- change in surface water storage (S_s)
- cost of pumping.

Any notion of "safe yield" must consider each factor, and must reference a given time period. If we focus on the quantity of water available for a year, for example, and neglect cost, we can define safe yield S_F as:

$$S_F = P + G_N - E_T - S_0 - S_s - G_s$$

Other factors in the determination of safe yields include the transmissibility of the aquifer[④] (can the aquifer transmit the water to the well (s) at a rate great enough to sustain the demand) and the location of contaminated bodies of water (including salt water intrusion possibilities from the oceans and chemical migrations from disposal or spill sites).

Besides offering a source of well water, aquifers also combine with precipitation to feed surface water courses. Surface water supplies are not as reliable as groundwater sources since quantities often fluctuate widely during the course of a year or even a week, and qualities are restricted by various sources of pollution. If a river has an average flow of 10 cubic feet per second (cfs), it means often the flow is less than 10 cfs. If a community wishes to use this for a water supply, its demands for the water should be considerably less than 10 cfs in order to be assured of a reasonably dependable supply.

The variation in the river flow can be so great that even a small demand cannot be met during dry periods in many parts of the nation, and storage facilities must be constructed to hold the water during wet periods so it can be saved for the dry ones. The objective is to build these reservoirs sufficiently large to have dependable supplies.

Notes

①这一通气层中含有三种类型的水分。在沼泽地，该通气层的深度可能是零，在山区其深度可达几百英尺。

"this zone" 指 "the zone of aeration（通气层）"。

② "specific yield" 单位产水量。

③许多因素有助于确定某一水井或某一选定的含水层的可靠出水量。

"safe yield" 可靠出水量。

④Other factors in the determination of safe yields include the transmissibility of the aquifer…决定可靠出水量的其他因素包括含水层的输水率……。

"transmissibility" 含水层的输水率。

Reading Material B

Water Transmission

Water can be transported from either a ground or surface supply source directly to a community or, if water quality considerations indicate, initially to a water treatment facility, by different types of conduits, including:
- Pressure conduits: tunnels, aqueducts and pipelines
- Gravity-flow conduits: grade tunnels, grade aqueducts and pipelines

The location of the well field or river reservoir defines the length of the conduits, while the topography indicates whether the conduits are designed to carry the water in open-channel flow or under pressure. The profile of a water supply conduit must generally follow the hydraulic grade line to take advantage of the forces of gravity and thus minimize pumping costs.

Service reservoirs are also necessary in the transmission system to help level out peak demands. In practice, intermediate reservoirs close to the city, or water towers, are sized to meet three design constraints:
- hourly fluctuations in water consumption within the service area
- short-term shutdown of the supply network for servicing
- back-up water requirements to control fires.

These distribution reservoirs are most often constructed as open or covered basins, elevated tanks, or, in the past, standpipes. If the service reservoirs are adequately designed to meet these capacity considerations, then the supply conduits leading to them generally must only be designed to carry approximately 50% in excess of the average daily demand of the system or subsystem.

Before discussing flow, it might first be useful to review some important fluid properties.

The *density* of a fluid is its mass per unit volume. In common units, density is expressed as slugs per cubic foot, or as lb. sec^2/ft^4. Density in the metric system is in terms of grams per cubic centimeter. The density of water under standard conditions is 1.94 in common units and unity in the metric system. [1]

Specific Weight represents the force exerted by gravity on a unit volume of fluid and therefore must be in terms of force per unit volume, such as pounds per cubic foot. The specific weight is related to density as

$$w = \rho g$$

where w = specific weight, lb/ft^3

ρ = density, lb. sec²/ft⁴

g = gravitational constant, ft/sec².

The specific weight of water is 62.4 pounds per cubic foot.

Specific gravity of a liquid is the ratio of its density to that of pure water at a standard temperature.② In the metric system the density of water is one gram per cubic centimeter and hence the specific gravity has the same numerical value as the density.

The *viscosity* of a fluid is a measure of its resistance to shear or angular deformation and is defined as the proportionality constant relating the shear stress τ to the rate of deformation du/dy. This proportionality constant is usually written as

$$\tau = \mu(du/dy)$$

The assumption inherent in this definition is that the shear stress is directly proportional to the rate of deformation.③ Such a definition holds for many fluids, which are known as Newtonian fluids. Fluids for which the shear stress is not proportional to the shear rate are known as non-Newtonian fluids. An example of a non-Newtonian fluid is biological sludge. The term viscosity, when applied to biological sludge, is therefore significant only if either the rate of deformation or the shear stress is also specified.

In the metric system, a unit of viscosity is a poise, with units of grams per centimeter-second. Most fluids have low viscosity and a more convenient unit is the centipoise or 0.01 poise. The viscosity of water at 20℃ (68.4℉) is 1 centipoise. In the English system the unit of viscosity is pound seconds per square foot. One lb. sec/ft² equals 479 poise.

Kinematic viscosity is defined as the absolute viscosity, μ, divided by the density of the fluid, or $\nu=\mu/\rho$. The dimensions of kinematic viscosity are square centimeters per second.

Notes

①标准条件下水的密度以英制单位计算为1.94，公制为1。

　common units 此处指英制单位。

②to that of pure water = to the density of pure water

③该定义中原有的假设是：剪应力与形变率成正比。

　inherent in this definition 为形容词短语作定语，修饰 assumption。

UNIT TWO

Text   Measurement of Water Quality

[1]　Quantitative measurements of pollutants are obviously necessary before water pollution can be controlled. Measurement of these pollutants is, however, fraught with difficulties.

[2]　The first problem is that the specific materials responsible for the pollution are sometimes not known. The second difficulty is that these pollutants are generally at low concentrations, and very accurate methods of detection are therefore required.

[3]　Only one of the many analytical tests available to measure water pollution is discussed here. A complete volume of analytical techniques used in water and wastewater engineering is compiled as *Standard Methods*. This volume, now in its 15th edition, is the result of a need for standardizing test techniques. ①It is considered definitive in its field and has the weight of legal authority.

[4]　Many of the pollutants are measured in terms of milligrams of the substance per liter of water (mg/l). This is a weight/volume measurement. In many older publications pollutants are measured as parts per million (ppm), a weight/weight parameter. If the liquid involved is water these two units are identical, since 1 milliliter of water weighs 1 gram. Because of the possibility of some wastes not having the specific gravity of water, the ppm measure has been scrapped in favor of mg/l. ②

[5]　A third commonly used parameter is percent, a weight/weight relationship. Obviously 10,000 ppm = 1 percent and this is equal to 10,000 mg/l only if 1ml = 1g.

[6]　Probably the most important measure of water quality is the dissolved oxygen. Oxygen, although poorly soluble in water, is fundamental to aquatic life. Without free dissolved oxygen, streams and lakes become uninhabitable to most desirable aquatic life. Yet the maximum oxygen that can possibly be dissolved in water at normal temperatures is about 9 mg/l, and this saturation value decreases rapidly with increasing water temperature. The balance between saturation and depletion is therefore tenuous.

[7]　The amount of oxygen dissolved in water is usually measured either by an oxygen probe or the old standard wet technique, the Winkler Dissolved Oxygen Test. ③The Winkler test for dissolved oxygen, developed more than 80 years ago, is the standard to which all other methods are compared.

[8]　Chemically simplified reactions in the Winkler test are as follows:

　　1. Manganese ions added to the samples combine with the available oxygen

$$Mn^{++} + O_2 \longrightarrow MnO_2 \downarrow$$

　　forming a precipitate.

　　2. Iodide ions are added, and the manganous oxide reacts with the iodide ions to

form iodine

$$MnO_2 + 2I^- + 4H^+ \longrightarrow Mn^{++} + I_2 + 2H_2O$$

3. The quantity of iodine is measured by titrating with sodium thiosulfate, the reaction being

$$I_2 + 2S_2O_3^= \longrightarrow S_4O_6^= + 2I^-$$

[9]　Note that all of the dissolved oxygen combines with Mn^{++}, so that the quantity of MnO_2 is directly proportional to the oxygen in solution. Similarly, the amount of iodine is directly proportional to the manganous oxide available to oxidize the iodide. Although the titration measures iodine, the quantity of iodine is thereby directly related to the original concentration of oxygen.

[10]　The Winkler test has obvious disadvantages, such as chemical interferences and the necessity to either carry a wet laboratory to the field or bring the samples to the laboratory and risk the loss (or gain) of oxygen during transport. ④All of these disadvantages are overcome by using a dissolved oxygen electrode, often called a probe.

[11]　The principle of operation of the simplest (and historically the first) probe is that of a galvanic cell. If lead and silver electrodes are put in an electrolyte solution with a microammeter between, the reaction at the lead electrode would be

$$Pb + 2OH^- \longrightarrow PbO + H_2O + 2e^-$$

[12]　At the lead electrode, electrons are liberated which travel through the microammeter to the silver electrode where the following reaction takes place:

$$2e^- + 1/2O_2 + H_2O \longrightarrow 2OH^-$$

[13]　The reaction would not go unless free dissolved oxygen is available, and the microammeter would not register any current. The trick is to construct and calibrate a meter in such a manner that the electricity recorded is proportional to the concentration of oxygen in the electrolyte solution.⑤

[14]　In the commercial models the electrodes are insulated from each other with nonconducting plastic and are covered with a permeable membrane with a few drops of an electrolyte between the membrane and electrodes. ⑥The amount of oxygen that travels through the membrane is proportional to the DO concentration. A high DO in the water creates a strong push to get through the membrane, while a low DO would force only limited O_2 through to participate in the reaction and thereby create electrical current. Thus the current registered is proportional to the oxygen level in solution.

New Words and Expressions

quantitative *	[ˈkwɔntitətiv]	a.	定量的，(数)量的
fraught (with)	[frɔːt]	a.	充满……的，伴随着……的
parameter *	[pəˈræmitə]	n.	参数[量，项]，系数

specific [spi'sifik]		a.	比（率）的，单位的
scrap * [skræp]		vt./n.	废弃；废料，碎片
aquatic [ə'kwætik]		a.	水生［产，上，中］的
uninhabitable ['ʌnin'hæbitəbl]		a.	不适于居住的
saturate ['sætʃəreit]		vt.	使饱和
depletion [di'pli:ʃən]		n.	消［损］耗，减少，降低
tenuous ['tenjuəs]		a.	薄［脆］弱的
probe * [prəub]		vt./n.	探测，探查；探测器，（试）探（电）极
manganese * [mæŋgə'ni:z]		n.	锰
ion * [ain]		n.	离子
precipitate * [pri'sipitit]		v./n.	（使）沉淀；沉淀物
iodide ['aiədaid]		n.	碘化物
manganous ['mæŋgənəs]		a.	（亚，二价，含）锰的
oxide * ['ɔksaid]		n.	氧化物
iodine ['aiədi:n]		n.	碘
titrate ['taitreit]		v.	滴定
thiosulfate [θaiə'sʌlfeit]		n.	硫代硫酸盐
solution [sə'lu:ʃən]		n.	溶液；溶解（状态）
electrode * [i'lektrəud]		n.	电极；电焊条
galvanic [gæl'vænik]		a.	（流）电的，（电池）电流的
electrolyte * [i'lektrəulait]		n.	电解（溶）液，电解［离］质
microammeter ['maikrəu'æmitə]		n.	微安计，微安表
calibrate * ['kælibreit]		vt.	校准［正］，标定
insulate ['insjuleit]		vt.	使绝缘（热）
permeable ['pə:miəbl]		a.	可渗［穿］透的，渗透性的
membrane * ['membrein]		n.	（薄，隔）膜片［状物］
oxygen level			含氧量

Notes

①…, now in its 15th edition, …
  两逗号之间部分为插入语。
②…be scrapped in favor of…。
  意为"……被放弃而采用……。"
③The amount of…the old standard wet technique, the Winkler Dissolved Oxygen Test.
  the Winkler Dissolved Oxygen Test 为 the old standard wet technique 的同位语。
  此法即测定溶解氧的碘量滴定法。
④The Winkler test…disadvantages, such as…the necessity to either carry…or bring…and risk…during transport.

such as 至句末为同位语。either…or…引导两个并列的不定式短语作 the necessity 的定语。bring 和 risk 前均省略不定式符号。

⑤The trick is to construct and calibrate a meter in such a manner that….

in such a manner that 引导一方式状语从句，修饰的 to construct and calibrate。

⑥In the commercial models…with nonconducting plastic…covered with…with a few drops …between the membrane and electrodes.

句中，第一个 with 意为"使用"，第二个 with 为 covered 所要求，第三个 with 构成的短语表示伴随状况。

⑦A high DO…the membrane, while…would force…and thereby create….

while 连接两个并列的句子，表示对比。第二分句有并列谓语 would force 和（would）create，用 and 连接。

Exercises

Reading Comprehension

I. Say whether the following statements are true (T) or false (F) according to the text.

1. Very accurate methods are necessary in detecting pollutants at low concentrations. ( )

2. The volume, *Standard Methods*, is considered deficient in its field. ( )

3. The ppm, mg/l and percent are three different parameters used for quantitative measurements of pollutants. ( )

4. Without pollution, any stream or lake is inhabitable to aquatic life. ( )

5. The principle of operation of the probe is similar to that of a cell. ( )

II. Choose the best answer for each of the followings.

1. The expression "one of the many analytical tests" that appears at the beginning of Para. 3 refers to _____ .

   A. ppm   B. the Winkler test

   C. percent measure   D. dissolved oxygen

2. The ppm measure has been got rid of in favor of mg/l, because _____

   A. it is a weight/weight parameter

   B. it is not so good as the measure of mg/l

   C. it is too old to be used

   D. it is a weight/weight parameter and some wastes may not have the same specific gravity as water has.

3. _____ is (are) probably the most important measure of water quality.

   A. Pollutants   B. The quantity of pollutants

   C. Oxygen   D. The dissolved oxygen

4. The higher the water temperature is, _____.
   A. the lower the saturation value of the dissolved oxygen is
   B. the lower the concentration of the dissolved oxygen is
   C. the higher the saturation value of the dissolved oxygen is
   D. the higher the concentration of the dissolved oxygen is
5. Which of the following statements is NOT true?
   A. It is not easy to destroy the balance between dissolved oxygen saturation and depletion.
   B. Both an oxygen probe and the Winkler test serve to measure the amount of the dissolved oxygen.
   C. There is the risk of getting an incorrect result, if we use the Winkler test for dissolved oxygen.
   D. A dissolved oxygen probe is more advanced than the Winkler test.

Vocabulary

I. Fill in the blanks with the words given below, changing the form where necessary.

| precipitate | solution | saturate |
| permeable | specific | |

1. A _____ solution is one which cannot dissolve the same solute as in it any more.
2. Inorganic chemicals may _____ out in lakes, reservoirs, and, under certain conditions, in flowing streams.
3. _____ gravity of a liquid is the ratio of its density to that of pure water at a standard temperature.
4. As the concentration of the solute increases, the mass of the _____ also increases.
5. The _____ of a rock is its capacity for transmitting a fluid under the influence of a hydraulic gradient.

II. Match the words in Column A with their corresponding definitions or descriptions in Column B.

Column A   Column B

1. ion   a. to correct or mark degrees and dividing points on (the scale of a measuring instrument)

2. insulate   b. of, concerning, or using analysis

                c. electrically charge particle formed by losing or gaining electrons

3. calibrate   d. to cover or separate (sth.) so as to prevent the passing or losing of electricity, heat, or sound

4. analytical   e. full of (something that has or gives warning of a probable unpleasant result)

5. fraught

Translation　　　　　　　　词义的引申

英语和汉语的表达习惯不同，因此在汉译时，必须对一定的上下文中的英文词义作适当的引申，使其符合汉语的表达习惯；切忌照搬英汉词典中的中文释义直译。

例 1. The specific materials <u>responsible for</u> the pollution are sometimes not known.

有时<u>有些造成污染</u>的特殊物质不得而知。

例 2. Oxygen, although <u>poorly</u> soluble in water, is fundamental to aquatic life.

氧，虽<u>难</u>溶于水，对水生生物来说却十分重要。

Translate the following sentences into Chinese, paying attention to the underlined Words.

1. A very low rate of oxygen use would indicate either clean water or that the available microorganisms <u>are uninterested</u> in consuming the available organics.
2. The <u>difference</u> in the oxygen levels was the BOD, or oxygen demand, in milligrams of oxygen used per liter of sample.
3. Light is also an important variable since most natural waters contain algae and oxygen can be replenished in the bottle if light is <u>available</u>.
4. A number of diseases can be transmitted by water, <u>among them</u> typhoid and cholera.
5. It is a perfect example of the proverbial <u>needle in a haystack</u>.

Reading Material A

Biochemical Oxygen Demand

Perhaps even more important than the determination of dissolved oxygen is the measurement of the rate at which this oxygen is used. A very low rate of use would indicate either clean water or that the available microorganisms are uninterested in consuming the available organics. A third possibility is that the microorganisms are dead or dying. (Nothing decreases oxygen consumption by aquatic microorganisms quite so well as a healthy slug of arsenic.[①])

The rate of oxygen use is commonly referred to as *biochemical oxygen demand* (BOD). It is important to understand that BOD is not a measure of some specific pollutant. Rather, it is a measure of the amount of oxygen required by bacteria and other microorganisms while stabilizing decomposable organic matter.

The BOD test was first used for measuring the oxygen consumption in a stream by filling two bottles with stream water, measuring the DO in one and placing the other in the stream. In a few days the second bottle was retrieved and the DO measured. The difference in the oxygen levels was the BOD, or oxygen demand, in milligrams of oxygen used per liter of sample.

This test had the advantage of being very specific for the stream in question since the water in the bottle is subjected to the same environmental factors as the water in the stream,② and thus the result was an accurate measure of DO usage in that stream. It was impossible, however, to compare the results in different streams, since three very important variables were not constant: temperature, time and light.

Temperature has a pronounced effect on oxygen uptake (usage), with metabolic activity increasing significantly at higher temperatures. The time allotted for the test is also important, since the amount of oxygen used increases with time. Light is also an important variable since most natural waters contain algae and oxygen can be replenished in the bottle if light is available. Different amounts of light would thus affect the final oxygen concentration.

The BOD test was finally standardized by requiring the test to be run in the dark at 20℃ for five days. This is defined as five-day BOD, or BOD_5, or the oxygen used in the first five days. Although there appear to be some substantial scientific reasons why five days was chosen, it has been suggested that the possibility of preparing the samples on a Monday and taking them out on Friday, thus leaving the weekend free, was not the least important of these reasons.③

The BOD test is almost universally run using a standard BOD bottle (about 300 ml volume). It is of course also possible to have a 2-day, 10-day, or any other day BOD. One measure used in some cases is <u>ultimate BOD</u> or the O_2 demand after a very long time.

If we measure the oxygen in several samples every day for five days, we may obtain curves such as Figure 2-1. Referring to this figure, sample A had an initial DO of 8 mg/l, and in five days this has dropped to 2 mg/l. The BOD therefore is $8-2=6$ mg/l.

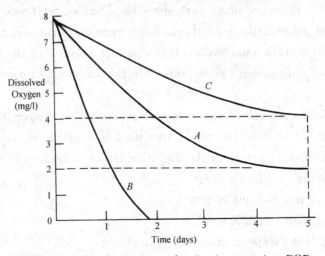

Figure 2-1 Typical oxygen uptake (use) curves in a BOD test

Sample B also had an initial DO of 8 mg/l, but the oxygen was used up so fast that it dropped to zero. If after five days we measure zero DO, we know that the BOD of sample B was more than 8−0＝8 mg/l, but we don't know how much more since the organisms might have used more DO if it were available. For samples containing more than about 8 mg/l, dilution of the sample is therefore necessary.

Suppose sample C shown on the graph is really sample B diluted by 1∶10. The BOD of sample B is therefore

$$(8-4)/0.1 = 40 \text{mg/l}$$

Notes

① 用水生微生物降低氧气消耗以砷的效果为最好，但其用量以不影响人的健康为宜。
② 这一检测法最适用于上面所提及的河流，因为瓶中的水与该河流中的水经受的环境因素是相同的，……
③ 尽管选用五天看来具有某些充分的科学道理，但它表明星期一准备水样，星期五取出，以便周末自由支配，有可能是一个不可忽视的理由。

Reading Material B

Bacteriological Measurements

From the public health standpoint the bacteriological quality of water is as important as the chemical quality. A number of diseases can be transmitted by water, among them typhoid and cholera. However, it is one thing to declare that water must not be contaminated by pathogens (disease-causing organisms) and another to determine the existence of these organisms. First, there are many pathogens. Each has a specific detection procedure and must be screened individually. Second, the concentration of these organisms can be so small as to make their detection impossible. It is a perfect example of the proverbial needle in a haystack. And yet only one or two organisms in the water might be sufficient to cause an infection.

How then can we measure for bacteriological quality? The answer lies in the concept of indicator organisms. The indicator most often used is a group of microbes called *coliforms* which are organisms normal to the digestive tracts of warm-blooded animals.[①] In addition to that attribute, coliforms are:

- plentiful, hence not difficult to find
- easily detected with a simple test
- generally harmless except in unusual circumstances
- hardy, surviving longer than most known pathogens.

Coliforms have thus become universal indicator organisms. But the presence of coliforms does not prove the presence of pathogens. If a large number of coliforms are present, there is a good chance of recent pollution by wastes from warm-blooded animals, and therefore the water *may* contain pathogenic organisms.

This last point should be emphasized. The presence of coliforms does not mean that there are pathogens in the water. It simply means that there *might* be. A high coliform count is thus suspicious and the water should not be consumed (although it may be perfectly safe).

There are three ways of measuring for coliforms. The simplest is to filter a sample through a sterile filter, thus capturing any coliforms. The filter is then placed in a Petri dish containing a sterile agar which soaks into the filter and promotes the growth of coliforms while inhibiting other organisms. After 24 or 48 hr of incubation the number of shiny black dots, indicating coliform colonies, is counted. If we know how many milliliters were poured through the filter, the concentration of coliforms can be expressed as coliforms/ml.

The second method of measuring for coliforms is called the most probable number (MPN), a test based on the fact that in a lactose broth coliforms will produce gas and make the broth cloudy. The production of gas is detected by placing a small tube upside down inside a larger tube so as not to have air bubbles in the smaller tube. After incubation, if gas is produced, some of it will become trapped in the smaller tube and this, along with a cloudy broth, will indicate that the tube had been inoculated with at least one coliform.

And here is the trouble. One coliform can cause a positive tube just as easily as a million coliforms can. ②Hence it is not possible to ascertain the concentration from just one tube. We get around this problem by inoculating a series of tubes with various quantities of sample, the reasoning being that a 10-ml sample would be more likely to contain a coliform than a 1-ml sample. ③

For example, if we take three different inoculation amounts, 10, 1 and 0.1 ml of sample, and inoculate three tubes with each amount, after incubation we might have an array such as follows. The plus signs indicate a positive test (cloudy broth with gas formation) and the minus sign represent tubes where no coliforms were found.

Amount of sample,	Tube Number		
ml put in test tube	1	2	3
10	+	+	+
1	−	+	−
0.1	−	−	+

Based on these data we would suspect that there is at least 1 coliform per 10 ml, but we still have no firm number.

The solution to this dilemma lies in statistics. It can be proven statistically that such an array of positive and negative results will occur most probably if the coliform concentration was 75 coli/100ml. A higher concentration would most probably have resulted in more positive tubes while a lower concentration would most probably have resulted in more negative tubes. This is how MPN is established.

A third way of measuring coliforms is by a proprietary device called a "Coli-Count." A sterile pad with all the necessary nutrients is dipped into the water sample, incubated, and the colonies counted. The pad is designed to adsorb exactly 1 ml of sample water so that the colonies counted give a coliform concentration per ml.

Notes

①最常使用的指示剂是一群称为大肠菌的微生物，它们是能在温血动物消化道内正常存活的有机体。
②一个大肠菌就能象一百万个大肠菌那样很容易地使试管（水样）呈现出阳性。
③通过给一系列试管接种不同量的水样，我们便可解决这一问题，其理由是，10-mL 水样往往比 1-mL 水样含大肠菌的可能性更大。

UNIT THREE

Text Water Processing

[1] The objective of municipal water treatment is to provide a potable supply——one that is chemically and bacteriologically safe for human consumption. ①For domestic uses, treated water must be aesthetically acceptable—— free from apparent turbidity, color, odor, and objectionable taste. Quality requirements for industrial uses are frequently more stringent than domestic supplies. Thus additional treatment may be required by the industry. For an example, boiler feed water must be demineralized to prevent scale deposits.

[2] Common water sources for municipal supplies are deep wells, shallow wells, rivers, natural lakes, and reservoirs. Well supplies normally yield cool, uncontaminated water of uniform quality that is easily processed for municipal use. Processing may be required to remove dissolved gases and undesirable minerals. The simplest treatment is dsinfection and fluoridation. Deep well supplies are chlorinated to provide residual protection against potential contamination in the water distribution system. In the case of shallow wells recharged by surface waters, chlorine both disinfects the groundwater and provides residual protection. Fluoride is added to reduce the incidence of dental caries. Dissolved iron and manganese in well water oxidizes when contacted with air, forming tiny rust particles that discolor the water. ②Removal is performed by oxidizing the iron and manganese with chlorine or potassium permanganate, and removing the precipitates by filtration. Excessive hardness is commonly removed by precipitation softening. Lime and, if necessary, soda ash are mixed with raw water, and settleable precipitate is removed. Carbon dioxide is applied to stabilize the water prior to final filtration. Aeration is a common first step in treatment of most groundwaters to strip out dissolved gases and add oxygen.

[3] Pollution and eutrophication are major concerns in surface water supplies. Water quality depends on agricultural practices in the watershed, location of municipal and industrial outfall sewers, river development such as dams, season of the year, and climatic conditions. ③Periods of high rainfall flush silt and organic matter from cultivated fields and forest land, while drought flows may result in higher concentrations of waste-water pollutants from sewer discharges. ④River temperature may vary significantly between summer and winter. The quality of water in a lake or reservoir depends considerably on season of the year. Municipal water quality control actually starts with management of the river basin to protect the raw water supply. Highly polluted waters are both difficult and costly to treat. Although some communities are able to locate groundwater supplies, or alternate less polluted surface sources within feasible pumping distance, the majority of the nation's population draw from nearby surface supplies. ⑤The challenge in waterworks operation is to process these waters to a safe, potable product acceptable for domestic use.

[4]   The primary process in surface water treatment is chemical clarification by coagulation, sedimentation, and filtration. Lake and reservoir water has a more uniform year-round quality and requires a lesser degree of treatment than river water. Natural purification results in reduction of turbidity, coliform bacteria, color, and elimination of day-to-day variations. On the other hand, growths of algae may cause increased turbidity and may produce difficult-to-remove tastes and odors during the summer and fall. Chlorination is commonly the first and last steps in treatment, providing disinfection of the raw water and establishing a chlorine residual in the treated water. Excess prechlorination and activated carbon are used to remove taste-and odor-producing compounds. The specific chemicals used in coagulation depend on the character of the water and economic considerations. River supplies normally require the most extensive treatment facilities with greatest operational flexibility to handle the day-to-day variations in raw water quality. The preliminary step is often presedimentation to reduce silt and settleable organic matter prior to chemical treatment. Many river water treatment plants have two stages of chemical coagulation and sedimentation to provide greater depth and flexibility of treatment. The units may be operated in series, or by split treatment with softening in one stage and coagulation in the other. As many as a dozen different chemicals may be used under varying operating conditions to provide a satisfactory finished water.

[5]   The two primary sources of waste from water treatment processes are sludge from the settling tank, resulting from chemical coagulation or softening reactions, and wash water from backwashing filters. These discharges are highly variable in composition, containing concentrated materials removed from the raw water and chemicals added in the treatment process. The wastes are produced continuously, but are discharged intermittently. Historically, the method of waste disposal was to discharge to a watercourse or lake without treatment. This practice was justified from the viewpoint that filter backwash waters and settled solids that were thus returned to the watercourse added no new impurities, but merely returned material that had originally been present in the water.⑥This argument is not now considered valid, since water quality is degraded to the extent that a portion of the water is withdrawn, and chemicals used in processing introduce new pollutants.⑦ Therefore, more stringent federal and state pollution control regulations have been enacted requiring treatment of waste discharges from water purification and softening facilities.

New Words and Expressions

bacteriologically [bæktiəriəˈlɔdʒikəli]	ad.	按细菌学的观点
aesthetically [iːsˈθetikəli]	ad.	从审美角度看
odor [ˈoudə]	n.	气味
objectionable [əbˈdʒekʃənəbl]	a.	不能采用的,不好的,有害的
stringent * [ˈstrindʒənt]	a.	严格的,精确的

demineralize [di'minərəlaiz]		vt.	脱〔去〕矿质，除盐，软化
scale ['skeil]		n.	结〔锅，管〕垢，水垢〔锈〕
uncontaminated [ˌʌnkən'tæmineitid]		a.	未被污染的，无杂质的
fluoridation [ˌfluəri'deiʃən]		n.	氟化作用〔反应〕，加氟作用
residual * [ri'zidjuəl]		a./n.	剩余的，残余〔留〕的；剩余，残余（物）
disinfect [ˌdisin'fekt]		vt.	（给……）消毒，杀菌，洗净，清除
fluoride ['fluəraid]		n.	氟化物
incidence * ['insidəns]		n.	发生（率）；影响（范围，程度，方式）
caries ['kɛəriːz]		n.	龋，骨疡
potassium * [pə'tæsjəm]		n.	钾
permanganate [pəːˈmæŋgənit]		n.	高锰酸盐
soften * ['sɔfn]		v.	软化；使〔弄，变〕软
stabilize * ['steibilaiz]		vt.	使稳定
eutrophication [juːˌtrɔfi'keiʃən]		n.	富（营）养化，水体加富过程
flush * [flʌʃ]		v./n.	（强液体流）冲〔清〕洗，冲水〔砂〕
silt [silt]		n.	淤泥，泥沙
alternate * [ɔːl'təːnit]		v./a.	（使）交替，（使）轮流；交替的，轮流的
challenge ['tʃælindʒ]		n.	（提出的，复杂）问题，（造成的）困难
waterworks ['wɔːtəwəks]		n.	供水设备〔系统〕；自来水厂
sludge [slʌdʒ]		n.	污泥，泥状沉积物
disposal [dis'pəuzəl]		n.	处理〔置〕，清〔消〕除
watercourse ['wɔːtəkɔːs]		n.	水道，渠道，河道
degrade * [di'greid]		v.	降低，下降；褪化，恶化
enact [i'nækt]		vt.	制定，颁布

Notes

①The objective of…a potable supply-one that is….
  one 为支撑词，为 supply 的同位语。
②Dissolved iron…when contacted…forming tiny rust particles that….
  when 后省略了 they are。forming 引起的分词短语作结果状语，其中还套有 that 引导的定语从句修饰 particles。
③Water quality depends on agricultural practices…location…river development such as dams, season…and climatic conditions.
  depend on 后有五个并列的宾语，其中第三个宾语 river development 后有 such as dams 作同位语，用来例举。
④Periods of high rainfall…while drought flows….
  periods of 对中心词 high rainfall 修饰，和其共同构成句主语。while 用作连词，对比前后两种情况。

⑤Although…able to locate…or alternate…the nation's population….
在 although 引导的让步状语从句中，able 后有 or 连接的并列不定式短语，alternate 前省略了不定式符号。the nation 指美国。

⑥This practice was…the viewpoint that…and settled solids that…material that….
句中第一个 that 引导同位语从句，具体说明 the viewpoint，第二个 that 引导定语从句修饰 settled solids，第三个 that 从句修饰 material。

⑦This argument…since water quality…to the extent that…, and chemicals….
since 引导两个并列原因状语从句，它们的主语分别为 water quality 和 chemicals。第一从句又含有 to the extent that 引导的程度状语从句。

Exercises

Reading Comprehension

I. Say whether the following statements are true (T) or false (F) according to the text.
1. Water for domestic uses needs additional treatment. ( )
2. Water processing may be required to remove dissolved oxygen. ( )
3. Fluoride is added to some water supplies, because it is helpful in strengthening young children's teeth against decay. ( )
4. Precipitation softening means separating the solid substance from the water by chemical action to soften it. ( )
5. During water treatment processes, since no new impurities are added, we can say that waste discharge from water treatment plants is harmless. ( )

II. Skim through the text and find out the phrase that is closest in meaning to the given words.
1. discolor (Para. 2)
   A. lighten the color of   B. spoil the color of   C. reduce the color of
2. strip out (Para. 2)
   A. squeeze out   B. take off   C. remove
3. locate (Para. 3)
   A. discover the position of   B. show the position of   C. fix the position of
4. extensive (Para. 4)
   A. far-reaching   B. covering a large surface   C. comprehensive
5. finished (Para. 4)
   A. ended   B. properly treated   C. washed-up

Vocabulary

Ⅰ. Fill in the blanks with the words given below, changing the form where necessary.

> soften   sludge   alga
> disinfect   stabilize

1. There are two different methods available for changing a hard water into a _____ water.
2. The third commonly employed method of sludge _____ is anaerobic digestion.
3. When plant nutrients spill over in large amounts into water, they act as fertilizers, stimulating the growth of water plants, such as _____ and water weeds.
4. Raw _____ is generally of odoriferous and full of water, two characteristics which make its disposal difficult.
5. In treatment stations, water is _____ with agent that kills harmful bacteria and microorganisms.

Ⅱ. Match the words in Column A with their corresponding definitions or descriptions in Column B.

Column A   Column B

1. basin   a. sand, mud, etc., carried by running water and left (at the mouth of a river, in a harbour, etc.)
2. degrade   b. to arrange or perform by turns; cause to take place, appear, one after the other
3. alternate   c. to lower in value, price, quality, etc.
4. silt   d. area drained by a river and its tributaries
5. flush   e. to clean or wash with a rush of water

Translation   词量增减

英译汉时，由于两种语言内部结构不同，表达方式也不尽相同，因此，不可能要求二者在词的数量上绝对相等。而往往要根据汉语的习惯适当增加，省略或重复一些词。

词的增加：

例1. The primary process in surface water treatment is chemical clarification by coagulation, sedimentation and filtration.

地表水的一级处理是用混凝、沉淀和过滤<u>等方法</u>对水进行化学澄清。

例2. Chlorination is commonly the first and last steps in treatment.

按常规，加氯既是水处理中的第一<u>步</u>，也是最后一<u>步</u>。

词的减少：

例1. The quality of water in a lake or reservoir depends on considerably on season <u>of the year</u>.

湖泊或水库的水质与季节有相当大的关系。

例 2. Highly polluted waters are both difficult and costly <u>to treat</u>.

污染严重的水，既难处理，成本又高。

Translate the following sentences into Chinese, paying attention to the underlined words.

1. A water which <u>behaves like this</u> is said to be "hard".
2. We see that calcium and magnesium are the <u>cause</u> of hardness, the bicarbonates producing temporary hardness, the sulphates and chlorides permanent hardness.
3. Hardness can be measured by the "soap destroying power" of a water, but more precisely by the total of the hardness producing <u>constituents</u> expressed in the chemically equivalent amount of calcium carbonate ($CaCO_3$).
4. Chloramine is <u>a way of preventing</u> taste troubles arising from the presence of free chlorine.
5. <u>As</u> the bed becomes dirtier the loss of head through it increases.

Reading Material A

Methods for Removal of Wastes and Odours

Of the methods suggested below each has its place according to the character of the water being supplied. Where chlorine is suspected as being the agent giving rise to the complaint the first attempt should consist of raising the initial dosage of chlorine to ensure that all organic and vegetable matter in the water is properly oxidized, and this may then be followed by removing the excess chlorine as much as is desired by the addition of sodium thiosulphate. Aeration is only useful in certain circumstances. Ozonisation is useful in practically all circumstances and would be used specifically to improve the palatability of a poor water. The addition of activated carbon is a sound standby treatment to use in conjunction with filtration. The methods in more detail are:

(a) *Super-chlorination*. This remedy is simple and cheap, if it works. It has been found by experience that, if sufficient chlorine is added to a water to give an excess of free chlorine over and above that absorbed by organic and vegetable matter in the water, tastes and odours are reduced.①

(b) *Chloramine*, which is a combination of ammonia and chlorine obtained by adding ammonia to the water in proportions varying from 1 : 2 to 1 : 4 of ammonia to chlorine according to the type of water is a way of preventing taste troubles arising from the presence of free chlorine.②

(c) *Chlorine dioxide*, formed by adding sodium chlorite to chlorine solution is a stronger oxidizing agent than chlorine and is sometimes found more effective than super chlorination.

(d) *Dechlorination*, by the addition of sodium thiosulphate for small supplies, and sulphur dioxide (as a gas) for large supplies, is again a negative way of avoiding taste troubles by removing any free chlorine from a water. As a result there is no sterilising agent left in the water.

(e) *Aeration* will normally improve the appearance of a water which is poor in palatability, or stagnant. The particular use of aeration is to get rid of sulphuretted hydrogen smells found in deep well water. If iron is present in the water this may precipitate out as a result of the aeration, and filtration will then be necessary. Aeration is seldom effective when tastes are caused by organic pollution.

(f) *Ozonisation* is highly effective but costly. It is a more powerful source of oxygen than chlorine and has no after-taste troubles. Ozone will improve the appearance of a water, remove traces of colour, and should remove all smells and odours if applied in sufficient quantity. It is an excellent finishing treatment to a poor quality water, its effects being wholly positive with no residual to cause trouble.

(g) *Activated carbon* will remove or reduce all kinds of tastes and odours by adsorption of the materials producing them. Carbon has been used in individual household filters since the nineteenth century in the form of charcoal. The 'activated' carbon is a very finely divided carbon which presents a high surface area for adsorption. It can be added to the water in powder form, or as a slurry, or in granular form. Good mixing with the water is necessary. The point of addition is either before any mixing and sedimentation tanks,[3] or just before water passes on to rapid gravity filters. The dosage can be intermittent at 8 to 20 ppm., or else continuous at about 3 ppm. When the water is filtered the carbon is left on the top of the beds and is removed by backwashing. If the granular form is used it is placed as a definite layer over a rapid gravity filter bed, and if it has not been contaminated more than a certain amount it may be removed and regenerated when its adsorptive powers have been exhausted.[4] This can only occur if the water is clear. For effective use the dose must be adequate, the mixing thorough, and the time of contact long enough for the material to carry out its work. The water should preferably be slightly acid, with a pH value of between 5 and 6.

(h) *Flushing of mains*. Many complaints of taste come from water which has been left to stagnate in the ends of mains and the flushing out of dead ends of mains is one of the commonest methods of preventing taste troubles. This should be a carefully controlled routine operation in a waterworks distribution system; if it is not, complaints will certainly arise.

Notes

①经验表明，如果向水中加入足够的氯，使之产生超过水中有机物和植物性物质所能吸收的过量游离氯，就会大大减轻异味和气味。

②氯胺法是防止因游离氯存在而产生不良味道的一种方法。氯胺是氨和氯的化合物，可按不同类型的水以氨氯之比为 1:2 到 1:4 的比例向水中加氨获得。

③the point of addition 加入点。

④当其吸附力耗尽时，如果污染程度不超过一定量，可以将其去除并使之再生。

Reading Material B

Magnetic Water Treatment

In hard water areas, incrustation of water tubing, boilers, coils, jets sprinklers, cooling towers, heat exchangers, or wherever industry uses heated hard water, can no longer be considered a hidden problem.

Water hardness is due to various dissolved salts, mainly carbonates and sulphates such as those of calcium and magnesium, which when heated produces an insoluble precipitate of scale-forming crystals. ①Crystals grow by bonding to each other and to water contact surfaces to form scale. ②

Scale formation affects performance. Just 1mm of scale adds 7.5% to energy costs, 1.5mm adds 15% and 12mm adds a staggering 70% cost increase. But the problem of energy costs is only part of the story. There are all the additional problems and maintenance costs of scale removal, anything from inconvenience to total plant shutdowns in severe cases. ③

Water softeners

The traditional method of combating scale build-up is to use water softening compounds such as sodium carbonate, sodium phosphate, or hydrated silicates of calcium and aluminium known as zeolites to remove or sequester the metallic ions.

Most problems of scale build-up can be controlled, if not always totally overcome, by using water softeners. But the cost of chemicals has to be included as an ongoing charge to overheads of the service or production process. Also, care must be exercised to avoid contaminating drinking water.

Magnetic water treatment

The cost-effective alternative to water softening chemicals is magnetic water treatment. Water passing through a powerful magnetic field changes the crystal pattern of growth. Instead of bonding to each other to form aggregated clumps, or to the walls of tubing and equipment, crystals remain discrete and separate, so are able to pass through and out of the system.

When correctly processed, magnetically-treated water has no disadvantages. No chemicals are needed, so it retains its original quality, because nothing is added or subtracted. If the water was potable before magnetic treatment, it remains so afterwards.

There are many designs of equipment claiming to treat water magnetically. Some use permanent magnets, others use electromagnets. Not all will handle commercial or industrial water volumes. Also, permanent magnet and some electromagnet types require frequent attention to remove internal scale. Most are unable to handle mains water at a single pass. An exception is the patented Hydromag.

How it works

For an explanation of how magnetic water treatment works it helps to be aware of established laws such as Coulombs Law and Flemings left hand rule. Hydromag patents are based on designs incorporating these and other laws.

Law 1 states that in all pipework systems which contain water and which have not been manipulated, there will be a positive (+VE) charge. Normally, this charge is minute but can theoretically reach a maximum of 1500 gauss. Therefore, Hydromag has to produce lines of force greater than this to overcome any theoretical force exerted by the pipework.

By experimentation, it was found that the most efficient conditioning effect was achieved by generating force or power lines of 2500 gauss. A magnetic field is required to produce these lines of force, then concentrate the magnetic field into lines of force as described by Coulombs Law.

In Hydromag, the magnetic field strength of its embedded circular electrical coil is controlled by the voltage supplied by the control unit, and both are matched to ensure the lines of force produced are at the optimum level.

Notes

① 水的硬度是由水中各种溶解盐类，主要是碳酸盐和硫酸盐引起，如钙和镁的碳酸盐和硫酸盐，加热时，这些盐类会产生一种结成水垢结晶的不溶沉淀物。

②晶体互相粘结生长，并附着在水接触面上，从而结成水垢。

③它（水垢）带来另外许多问题以及除垢的保养费用问题；它能引起诸多不便，以致严重时使整个工厂停产。

④hydrated silicates of calcium and aluminium known as zeolites 称为沸石的钙和铝的水化硅酸盐。

UNIT FOUR

Text Filtration

[1]   Filtration is used to separate nonsettleable solids from water and wastewater by passing it through a porous medium. The most common system is filtration through a layered bed of granular media, usually a coarse anthracite coal underlain by a finer sand. [①]

[2]   Gravity filtration through beds of granular media is the most common method of removing colloidal impurities in water processing and tertiary treatment of wastewater.

[3]   The mechanisms involved in removing suspended solids in a granular-media filter are complex, consisting of interception, straining, flocculation, and sedimentation. Initially, surface straining and interstitial removal results in accumulation of deposits in the upper portion of the filter media. Because of the reduction in pore area, the velocity of water through the remaining voids increases, shearing off pieces of captured floc and carrying impurities deeper into the filter bed. The effective zone of removal passes deeper and deeper into the filter. Turbulence and the resulting increased particle contact within the pores promotes flocculation, resulting in trapping of the larger floc particles. [②]Eventually, clean bed depth is no longer available and breakthrough occurs, carrying solids out in the underflow and causing termination of the filter run.

[4]   Microscopic particulate matter in raw water that has not been chemically treated will pass through the relatively larger pores of a filter bed. On the other hand, suspended solids fed to a filter with excess coagulant carry-over from chemical treatment produces clogging of the bed pores at the surface. [③]Optimum filtration occurs when impurities in the water and coagulant concentration cause "in-depth" filtration. The impurities neither pass through the bed nor are all strained out on the surface, but a significant amount of flocculated solids is removed throughout the entire depth of the filter.

[5]   A typical procedure for processing surface supplies to drinking-water quality consists of flocculation with a chemical coagulant and sedimentation prior to filtration. Under the force of gravity, often by a combination of positive head and suction from underneath, water passes downward through the media that collect the floc and particles. When the media become filled or solids break through, a filter bed is cleaned by backwashing where upward flow fluidizes the media and conveys away the impurities that have accumulated in the bed. Destruction of bacteria and viruses depends on satisfactory turbidity control to enhance the efficiency of chlorination.

[6]   Filtration rates following flocculation and sedimentation are in the range of 2—10 gpm/ft^2 (1.4—6.8l/m^2 · s), with 5 gpm/ft^2 (3.4l/m^2 · s) normally the maximum design rate.

[7]   The process of direct filtration does not include sedimentation prior to filtra-

tion. The impurities removed from the water are collected and stored in the filter. Although rapid mixing of chemicals is necessary, the flocculation stage is either eliminated or reduced to a mixing time of less than 30 min. Contact flocculation of the chemically coagulated particles in the water takes place in the granular media. Successful advances in direct filtration are attributed to the development of coarse-to-fine multimedia filters with greater capacity for "in-depth" filtration, improved backwashing systems using mechanical or air agitation to aid cleaning of the media, and the availability of better polymer coagulants.④

[8]　Surface waters with low turbidity and color are most suitable for processing by direct filtration. Based on experiences cited in the literature, waters with less than 40 units of color, turbidity consistently below 5 units, iron and manganese concentrations of less than 0.3 and 0.05 mg/l, respectively, and algal counts below 2000/ml can be successfully processed. Operational problems in direct filtration are expected when color exceeds 40 units or turbidity is greater than 15 units on a continuous basis. Potential problems can often be alleviated during a short period of time by application of additional polymer. Tertiary filtration of wastewaters containing 20-30 mg/l of suspended solids following biological treatment can be reduced to less than 5 mg/l by direct filtration. For inactivation of viruses and a high degree of bacterial disinfection, filtration of chemically conditioned wastewater precedes disinfection by chlorine.

[9]　The feasibility of filtration without prior flocculation and sedimentation relies on a comprehensive review of water quality data. The incidence of high turbidities caused by runoff from storms and blooms of algae must be evaluated. Often, pilot testing is valuable in determining efficiency of direct filtration compared to conventional treatment, design of filter media, and selection of chemical conditioning.⑤

[10]　Filtration rates in direct filtration are usually 1—6 gpm/ft² (0.7-4.1 l/m² · s), somewhat lower than the rates following traditional pretreatment.

New Words and Expressions

granular ['grænjulə]	a.	粒状 [面] 的，晶 [颗] 粒的
anthracite ['ænθrəsait]	n.	无烟煤
interception [ˌintə'sepʃən]	n.	截流，拦截，阻断
strain [strein]	v.	粗 [过] 滤
interstitial [ˌintə'stiʃəl]	a.	间 [缝，填] 隙的，隙间的
pore * [pɔː]	n.	细 [毛，微，气] 孔，孔隙
void * [vɔid]	n./a.	空隙，孔隙；空的，空虚的
turbulence * ['təːbjuləns]	n.	湍流，紊流，涡流
breakthrough * [ˌbreikθruː]	n.	渗漏，穿透
underflow ['ʌndəfləu]	n.	潜 [底，下层] 流；地下水流
termination * [ˌtəːmi'neiʃən]	n.	终止，结束

filter run			过滤周期，过滤循环
clog [klɔg]		v.	阻［堵，填］塞，障［妨］碍
optimum * ['ɔptiməm]		a./n.	最佳的（值，点，状态）
in-depth ['in'depθ]		a.	深入的，深层的，彻底的
suction * ['sʌkʃən]		n.	吸力；吸入；空吸
fluidize ['fluidaiz]		vt.	使液体化，使流（体）化，使变成流体
virus ['vaiərəs]		n.	（过滤性）病毒，毒素
enhance * [in'hɑːns]		vt.	增［加］强，提高，增加
multimedia [mʌlti'miːdjə]		n.	多层滤料
agitation * [ˌædʒi'teiʃən]		n.	搅动（作用），搅拌（作用）
polymer * ['pɔlimə]		n.	聚合物［体］，多［高］聚物
alleviate * [ə'liːvieit]		vt.	（使）减轻，（使）缓和
inactivation [inˌækti'veiʃən]		n.	灭活，失活，纯化（作用）
bloom [bluːm]		n.	大量增殖，旺发
pilot ['pailət]		a.	中间规模的
pilot testing			中间试验
conditioning [kən'diʃəniŋ]		n.	调理［节，整，解］

Notes

①The most common system···a layered bed of granular media, usually a coarse anthracite coal underlain by···.

a coarse anthracite coal 为前面成分的同位语，其后由过去分词短语修饰，该短语意为"由···置于其下"。

②Turbulence and the resulting in creased particle contact···resulting in···.

Turbulence 和 contact 为并列主语。名词 contact 前有多级修饰。resulting in···particles 为分词短语作结果状语。

③···suspended solids fed to a filter with excess coagulant carry-over from chemical treatment···.

fed to a filter 和 with···chemical treatment 分别为主语的修饰和连带成分。carry-over 为由短语动词转化成的复合名词。

④Successful advances···are attributed to the development···, improved backwashing systems···, and the availability···

attributed to 后有三个并列宾语，由两个逗号和 and 连接，它们的后面都有修饰成分。"in-depth"指滤床深层。

⑤Often, pilot testing···compared to conventional treatment···.

compared to 为短语介词，它引导的短语作状语。

Exercises

Reading Comprehension

I. Say whether the following sentences are true (T) or false (F) according to the text.
1. When solids break through the filter bed, it suggests the end of a filter run. ( )
2. A typical procedure for processing surface supplies to drinking-water involves flocculation with two steps. ( )
3. Rapid mixing of chemicals is one of the steps in the flocculation stage. ( )
4. According to the text, surface water is most suitable for processing by direct filtration. ( )
5. Compared to conventional treatment, design of filter media and selection of chemical conditioning, direct filtration is most in need of pilot testing. ( )

II. Choose the best answer for each of the following.
1. Which of the following statements is true?
   A. A layered bed of granular media usually consists of a layer of rough anthracite coal and a layer of finer sand.
   B. A layered bed of granular media usually is a mixture of some anthracite coal and sand.
   C. A layered bed of granular media usually consists of a rough anthracite coal with a finer sand under it.
   D. A layered bed of granular media usually consists of a finer sand with a coarse anthracite coal under it.
2. Flocculation is promoted by _____ .
   A. turbulence
   B. the velocity of water
   C. the increased particle contact within the pore caused by turbulence
   D. both a and c
3. What is the problem in optimum filtration?
   A. Microscopic particulate matter in raw water that has not been chemically treated will pass through the relatively larger pores of a filter bed.
   B. Suspended solids fed to a filter with excess coagulant carry-over from chemical treatment produces clogging of the bed pores at the surface.
   C. The impurities neither pass through the bed nor are all strained out on the surface.
   D. Both a and b.
4. The phrase "satisfactory turbidity control" in Para. 5 means _____ .
   A. low turbidity

B. turbidity neither low nor high
C. high turbidity
D. higher turbidity

5. Surface waters are suitable for processing by direct filtration _____ .
   A. when the water color is more than 40 units
   B. when the water turbidity keeps being greater than 15 units
   C. when neither a nor b is true
   D. when both a and b are true

Vocabulary

I . Fill in the blanks with the words or expressions given below, changing the form where necessary.

| strain | porous | filter run |
| fluidize | virus | |

1. Filtration is defined as the passage of a fluid through a _____ medium to remove matter held in suspension.
2. At the beginning of a _____ nearly all of the floc particles lodge in the sand within 1/2 in. of the surface.
3. Screens and racks _____ out floating and suspended solids larger in size than their openings.
4. Living agents that can pollute water include bacteria, _____, and other microorganisms that can cause disease.
5. The sand cleans itself when the bed has been _____ by the rising water.

II . Match the words in Column A with their corresponding definitions or descriptions in Column B.

Column A   Column B
1. optimum   a. the act of drawing air or liquid away
2. suction   b. to increase (the value, power, price, efficiency, etc.)
3. underflow   c. best or most favourable
4. alleviate   d. an undercurrent
5. enhance   e. to remove in part; to lessen, mitigate or make easier to be endured

Translation　　　　　　　　否定形式

英语中否定形式的表示方法很多，大致可分为：全部否定、部分否定、双重否定、意义否定等。这里着重介绍部分否定和双重否定的译法。

部分否定是指英语中 all, both, every 等不定代词与否定词 not 连用时，无论前置或后置都译成"不都是"，"并非全是"等。

例1. Actually <u>not all</u> biodegradable organic matter can be classed into these three simple grouping.

实际上，<u>并非所有</u>的可生物降解的有机物都可被分成这三种简单的类别。

例2. <u>Both</u> of the dams are <u>not</u> gravity dams.

这两座水坝<u>并不都是</u>重力坝。

例3. <u>Every</u> river in our country is <u>not</u> polluted.

我们国家的河流<u>并没有全部</u>受到污染。

双重否定通常由 no (not) 等与某些表示否定意义的词连用而构成，一般译成肯定。

例1. <u>No</u> flow of water occurs <u>unless</u> there is a difference in pressure.

<u>没有</u>压差，水<u>就不</u>会流动。

例2. There is <u>no</u> river in this African country <u>but</u> is polluted more or less.

这个非洲国家的河流<u>多少都</u>受到了污染。

Translate the following sentences into Chinese, paying attention to the underlined words.

1. <u>Until</u> enough soap has been dissolved to react with all these materials, <u>no</u> lather can be formed.
2. The reaction would <u>not</u> go <u>unless</u> free dissolved oxygen is available.
3. Coliforms are generally <u>harmless</u> except in <u>unusual</u> circumstances.
4. <u>Both</u> of the substances do <u>not</u> dissolve in water.
5. <u>Not</u> <u>every</u> minute difference is noted.

Reading Material A

Rapid Gravity Filtration

'Rapid' gravity filters are so called because the rate of flow through them is about twenty times as fast as with the slow sand filter. Rapid filters work on principles which are greatly different from those of a slow sand filter. There is no schmutzdecke film acting as a strainer on their surface; the sand bed is cleaned regularly by forcing air and water upwards through the bed and discharging the dirty wash water to waste; also the incoming water must be chemically treated so that impurities existing in colloidal state are induced to coagulate and a suitably sized floc has been formed for the rapid gravity filter to deal with. Although the rapid gravity filter acts more of a 'strainer in depth' than the slow sand filter, the process of water purification is not wholly one of straining.[①] As with the slow sand filter, certain complex biological and chemical changes are induced in the water as it passes through the bed and these——as far as they are known——are believed to be the chief mode of action of the filter.

The sand bed is usually between 1 ft 6 in. and 2 ft 6 in. thick, and the sand grains are as uniform as can be practically arranged,②of a size between 0.5 mm and 1 mm. The actual size of sand grain used depends upon the type of water to be filtered but, on the whole, a large variety of different waters are treated by sand grains of normal size, the depth of the bed varying for individual waters. Thus a heavily polluted water would be passed through a deeper sand bed than a relatively pure water. The filtering sand is supported upon graded layers of gravel, the coarsest at the bottom, the finest at the top supporting the sand, each layer being 3 in. to 4 in. thick. The gravel layers permit water to filter downwards evenly through the sand without the sand grains passing into the collector pipes below. The collector system of pipes, or ducts, or perforated plates below the gravel is usually a proprietary innovation and may take any one of a number of forms.③The aim of any collector system, however, is to collect the water from the underside of the sand bed in an even and uniform manner. The collecting pipes join to a common header pipe which discharges to the front of the filter where control and measurement of the quantity discharged can take place.

The usual size of a rapid gravity filter bed is up to 30 ft wide by 40 ft long, a 'normal' size being 15 ft wide by 20 to 25 ft long. The limiting factor for size is the difficulty of maintaining an even flow over large areas and the large quantity of water required for 'backwashing' such filters in order to clean them. The total thickness of sand bed and supporting gravel is some 3 to 4 ft, but the concrete tank containing the bed will be about 10 to 12 ft in depth to allow for 6 to 8 ft water depth over the bed.

When a cleaned bed is put into supply the loss of head through it will be small and an outlet controller will throttle the discharge so as to maintain a flow which does not exceed the permitted maximum. As the bed becomes dirtier the loss of head through it increases and the outlet controller will adjust for this, permitting a larger hydraulic head to be applied across the sand bed. The limit of operation of the bed is reached when the outlet control valve is wide open, the head upon the bed is a maximum and the output of the filter will still not reach the design flow. When this occurs the filter must be taken out of service and washed.④

Notes

①与慢速砂滤池相比，虽然快速重力滤池更象一个'深层过滤器'，但水的净化过程并不全是过滤过程。

②the sand grains are as uniform as can be practically arranged 砂粒大小要均匀，以达到实际上能够对之进行排列的程度

③砾石下面的水管、导管或多孔板集水系统通常是一种专利发明，可在若干形式中采用任

何一种。

④take out of service 停止使用。

Reading Material B

Backwashing

A rapid gravity filter is washed by sending air and water upwards through the bed. The first operation is to allow the sand bed to drain until the water lies just a few inches above the top of the bed. Air is then blown back through the collector pipes at the rate of about 3 to 5 cubic feet per minute per square foot of sand bed, for about 2 to 3 minutes. The surface of the sand bed should show an even spread of bursting air bubbles coming through the sand. The water over the bed quickly becomes very dirty as the agitation of the sand grains breaks up any surface scum or dirt, and dirt is loosened from the surface of the sand grains. Following this an upward flow of water is sent through the bed. This water is at a carefully designed high velocity, sufficient to expand the bed and cause the sand grains to be agitated together so that surface deposits are washed off them, but not so high that the sand grains are carried away bodily in the rising upflush of water. It is particularly important to see that both air scour and backwash are uniformly spread, otherwise strong jets of air or water will split the bed into lumps, and overturn parts of it, so that dirty sand, instead of being washed, is taken down into the bed. Backwashing at exactly the right rates of flow, and visual inspection of the bed while air scouring are important matters for the maintenance of beds in good condition. Sometimes, after a long run of life, sand beds need a prolonged steady backwashing or treatment with an acid for better cleaning.

Upward washwater rates are usually of the order of 18 in./min., ①which is about 10 gals/min. per sq. ft of bed area. In America rates up to 3 ft/min. may be used, but the use of air scour in America is infrequent. At 3 ft/min., upward velocity the thickness of the sand bed may expand up to 50 per cent; at 18 in. upward rate the expansion will be of the order of 30 per cent. The efficacy of the air scour has been called into question by Key who, conducting some experiments with a model, believed that some silt tended to penetrate the bed instead of being washed away and that only the top 1/2 in. or so of the sand bed received any effective agitation. ②There has not, however, been a change in British Practice as a result of his observations and air scour continues to be used and found effective. Air scour also has the advantage that it replenishes the filter bed with oxygen and thereby increases the biological activities in the filter bed. In America, though air scour is but little used, ③it has been found necessary in some plants to add to the effectiveness of water backwashing by directing water jets on to the surface of the sand bed so as to agitate and clean those layers which are usually the dirtiest.

The backwash water, being very dirty, must be discharged to waste. Even so, the water standing in the bed after the first flush of backwashing is usually also dirty and this cannot be taken into supply when normal downward filtering is resumed. A common practice is to discharge the first amount of effluent to waste. An alternative method, now widely used, is to arrange for a 'slow start' to the filter run. This initial start at a slow rate of filtering allows the suspended impurities in the remaining washwater to settle out on top of, or within, the sand bed and the output of the filter can then be increased so that no impurities are discharged into the effluent. This initial slow start can be arranged to take place automatically, full discharge rate not being reached until some 15 to 20 minutes have elapsed.

Wash water is nearly always filtered and sterilized water, i.e. not the raw water, though evidence that the use of raw water for backwashing would be harmful is lacking. Manufacturers of filter plant are usually prepared to guarantee that the amount of wash water sent to waste will not exceed or2 per cent of the treated water output. It should not exceed 3 per cent.

Notes

①冲洗水的上冲速度通常约为 18 英寸每分钟。
②The efficacy of the air scour has been called into question by Key
  Key 对空气冲洗的效力表示怀疑……
  call…into question 对……表示怀疑。
③but little 几乎没有。

UNIT FIVE

Text   Collection of Wastewater

[1] In old cities, drainage ditches were constructed for the sole purpose of moving stormwater out of the cities. Eventually, these ditches were covered over and became what we now know as *storm sewers*.

[2] As water supplies developed and the use of the indoor water closet increased, the need for transporting domestic wastewaters, called sanitary wastes, became obvious. This was accomplished in one of two ways: (1) discharge of the sanitary wastes into the storm sewers, which then carried both sanitary wastes and storm-water, and were known as *combined sewers*, and (2) construction of a new system of underground pipes for removing the wastewater, which became known as *sanitary sewers*. ①

[3] Newer cities, and more recently built (post-1900) parts of older cities almost all have separate sewers for sanitary wastes and stormwater. In this text, storm sewer design is not covered in detail. Emphasis here is on estimating the quantities of domestic and industrial wastewaters, and in the design of the sewerage systems to handle these flows. ②

[4] The term *sewage* is used here to mean only domestic wastewater. In addition to sewage, however, sewers also must carry industrial wastes, infiltration and inflow.

[5] The quantity of industrial wastes can usually be established by water use records. Alternatively, the flows can be measured in manholes which serve only a specific industry, using a small flow meter in a manhole. Typically, a Parshall flume is used, and the flow rate is calculated as a direct proportion of the flow depth. ③Industrial flows often vary considerably throughout the day and continuous recording is mandatory.

[6] Infiltration is the flow of groundwater into sanitary sewers. Sewers are often placed under the groundwater table and any cracks in the pipes will allow water to seep in. Infiltration is the least for new, well-constructed sewers, and can go as high as 500 m^3/km-day (200,000 gal/mi-day). Commonly, for older systems, 700 m^3/km-day (300,000 gal/mi-day) is used in estimating infiltration. This flow is of course detrimental since the extra volume of water must go through the sewers and the wastewater treatment plant. It thus makes sense to reduce this as much as possible by maintaining and repairing sewers, and keeping sewerage easements clear of large trees which could send roots into the sewers and cause severe damage. ④

[7] The third source of flow in sanitary sewers is called *inflow*, and represents stormwater which is collected unintentionally by the sanitary sewers. A common source of inflow is a perforated manhole cover placed in a depression, so that stormwater flows into the manhole. Sewers laid next to creeks and drainageways which rise up higher than the manhole elevation, or where the manhole is broken, are also a major source. ⑤Lastly, ille-

gal connections to sanitary sewers, such as roofdrains, can substantially increase the wet weather flow over the dry weather flow. Commonly, the ratio of dry weather to wet weather flow is between 1 : 1.2 and 1 : 4.

[8]　Domestic wastewater flows vary with season, day of the week and the hour of the day. The three flows of concern when designing sewers are the average flow, the peak or maximum flow, and the extreme minimum. The ratios of average to both the maximum and minimum flows is a function of the total flow, since a higher average daily discharge implies a larger community in which the extremes are evened out.

[9]　Sewers that collect wastewater from residences and industrial establishments almost always operate as open channels, or gravity flow conduits. Pressure sewers are used in a few places, but these are expensive to maintain and are useful only when there either are severe restrictions on water use, or the terrain is such that gravity flow conduits cannot be efficiently constructed.⑥

[10]　Building connections are usually made with clay or plastic pipe, 6 in. in diameter, to the *collecting sewers* which commonly run under the street. Collecting sewers are sized to carry the maximum anticipated peak flows without surcharging (filling up) and are commonly made of clay, asbestos, cement, concrete or cast iron pipe. They discharge in turn into intercepting sewers, known colloquially as *interceptors*, which collect large areas and discharge finally into the wastewater treatment plant.

[11]　Collecting and intercepting sewers must be placed at a sufficient grade to allow for adequate velocity during low flows, but not so great as to promote excessively high velocities when the flows are at their maximum. In addition, sewers must have manholes, commonly every 120—180 m (400—600ft) to facilitate cleaning and repair. Manholes are also necessary whenever the sewer changes grade (slope), size or direction.

[12]　In some cases it becomes either impossible or uneconomical to use gravity flow, and the wastewater must be pumped.

New Words and Expressions

closet ['klɔzit]	n.	盥洗室，厕所
sanitary waste		生活废水，生活废物，卫生设备排出的废物
sewerage ['sjuəridʒ]	n.	污水［排水］工程；排水系统；污水
sewage ['sjuːidʒ]	n.	污水；下水道（系统）
inflow ['infləu]	n.	流入物，流入（量），进水［气］
manhole ['mænhəul]	n.	人孔，检查［修］孔，探［检查］井
flume [fluːm]	n.	水［渡］槽
mandatory ['mændətəri]	a.	必须遵循的，强制性的
detrimental * [ˌdetri'mentl]	a.	有害的，不利的
easement ['iːzmənt]	n.	附属建筑物

keep clear of			避开，不接触
perforate ['pə:fəreit]		v.	穿［钻，打，冲］孔
elevation * [ˌeli'veiʃən]		n.	高程［度，地］；上升，提高
even ['iːvən]		vt.	使平均［平衡］
conduit ['kɔndit]		n.	水［输送］管，水道，水［沟］渠
terrain ['terein]		n.	地带，地形，场所
collecting sewer			污水支管
size [saiz]		n./vt.	尺寸，大小；依一定尺寸制造，（管材，轧管）定径
surcharge [sə:'tʃɑ:dʒ]		vt.	超［过］载，（使负担）过重
asbestos * [æz'bestəs]		n.	石棉
intercept * [intə'sept]		vt.	截取［断，击］，拦截
colloquially [kə'ləukwiəli]		ad.	口语地，通俗地
interceptor [ˌintə'septə]		n.	截流管，截水沟

Notes

①This was…two ways：(1) …the storm sewers, which…carried…, and were known as…, and (2) …the wastewater, which….

(1) 和 (2) 并列，对 two ways 加以解释，由 and 连接。两者结构相似，都带有 which 引导的非限定性定语从句。

②Emphasis here is on estimating…wastewaters, and in the design….

on 引起的分词短语作表语，on 为 emphasis 所要求。in 前面可看作省略了 on estimating…wasewaters。

③a Parshall flume 帕歇尔发明的测量明渠中液体流量的一种校准装置。

④It thus makes sense to reduce this…by maintaining…, and keeping…large trees which…severe damage.

It 为形式主语，真正主语为 to reduce…damage。this 指上文提到的"渗流"，by 后有两个并列的动名词短语，用逗号和 and 连接。

⑤Sewers laid…drainageways which…, or where…a major source.

drainageways 后有并列的定语从句，分别由关系代词 which 和关系副词 where 引导，它们由 or 连接。

⑥Pressure sewers…, but…are useful only when there either…, or the terrain is such that …be efficiently constructed.

but 连接两个并列的句子，第二分句含两个 when 引导的状语从句，由 either…or…并列连接。or 后的从句又套有 such that 引出的结果状语从句。

Exercises

Reading Comprehension

I. Say whether the following statements are true (T) or false (F) according to the text.
 1. Sewers for both sanitary waste and stormwater can be found in almost all new cities and many parts of old cities. ( )
 2. There are altogether three sources of flow in sanitary sewers. ( )
 3. When a Parshall flume is used, we can get the flow rate from the flow depth without any calculation. ( )
 4. We have three ways to measure the quantity of industrial wastes. ( )
 5. Inflow mainly refers to the stormwater which comes into the sewers from the manholes. ( )

II. Choose the best answer for each of the following.
 1. In this text, _____ is (are) emphasized.
    A. only the estimation of the quantities of domestic and industrial wastewaters
    B. both the estimation of the quantities of domestic and industrial wastewater and the design of the sewerage systems to handle these flows
    C. only the estimation of the quantities of domestic and industrial wastewater, especially that in the design of the sewerage systems to handle these flows
    D. only the design of the sewerage systems to handle these flows
 2. According to Para. 6, which of the following is NOT true?
    A. New sewers must have the least infiltration.
    B. The least infiltration can go as high as 500 m3/km-day.
    C. The sewers which have the least infiltration must be not only new, but also well-constructed.
    D. We think the flow of infiltration is harmful because it is an extra load for sewers and the wastewater treatment plant.
 3. In order to reduce the flow of infiltration, _____.
    A. the sewers ought to be well maintained and repaired
    B. the sewers ought to be kept far away from large trees
    C. The manholes should be well covered and have a high elevation
    D. Both A and B
 4. Illegal connections to sanitary sewers can substantially increase the wet weather flow over the dry weather flow. Which of the following can take the place of the word, over?
    A. comparing with   B. as compared with
    C. higher than   D. faster than

5. The phrase "to allow for adequate velocity during low flows" means _____ .
   A. to get an adequate velocity during low flows
   B. to take adequate velocity into consideration
   C. to permit adequate velocity during low flows
   D. to promote high velocity during low flows

Vocabulary

I. Fill in the blanks with words or expressions given below, changing the form where necessary.

| keep…clear of | sewerage | detrimental |
| sanitary waste | collecting sewer | |

1. To extend their life, pumps must be _____ acid.
2. Higher water temperature may have a direct _____ effect on fish and aquatic life.
3. The modern trend is to build separate drainage systems for stormwater and for _____ .
4. _____ gather flows from individual buildings and transport the wastes to an interceptor or main sewer.
5. In combined _____ systems, a single set of sewers collects both domestic and industrial wastewater and surface runoff from rainfall.

II. Match the words in Column A with their corresponding definitions or descriptions in Column B.

Column A   Column B
1. seep   a. soft, fibrous, grey, mineral substance that can be made into fire-proof fabrics and used as a heat-insulating material
2. depression   b. height (esp. above sea-level); lifting up, raising
3. asbestos   c. to stop and usu. seize (a person or thing moving from one place to another)
4. intercept   d. (of a liquid) to flow slowly through small openings in a material
5. elevation   e. a part of a surface lower than the other parts

Translation　　　　　　　　　　词类转换

英译汉时，有时必须把词类适当地加以转换。如：把英语中的动词译成汉语中的名词，名词译成动词，形容词译成副词等。

例1. Illegal connections to sanitary sewers, such as roofdrains, can substantially increase the wet weather flow <u>over</u> the dry weather flow.
　　生活污水管的非法连接物，如屋顶雨水管，可明显增加雨季流量和旱季流量<u>之比</u>。

例2. Collecting sewers are <u>sized</u> to carry the maximum anticipated peak flows without surcharging.

污水支管<u>口径</u>要大到足以输送可能出现的最大高峰流量而不至超载。

Translate the following sentences into Chinese, paying attention to the underlined words.

1. Ease of maintenance <u>dictates</u> many of the design criteria for wastewater collection system.
2. Street grade, curb design, and gutter depression define the best type of inlet to <u>select</u>.
3. Pipeline gradients follow the general slope of the ground surface <u>such that</u> water entering can flow downhill to a convenient point for discharge.
4. Sanitary sewers are <u>designed</u> and constructed to prevent surcharging.
5. Special provision must be made to protect the pipe and manholes <u>against</u> displacement by erosion and shock hydraulic loadings.

Reading Material A

Storm Sewer System

Surface waters enter a storm drainage system through inlets located in street gutters or depressed areas that collect natural drainage. Cooling water from industries and groundwater seepage that enters footing drains are pumped to the storm sewer, since the pipes are usually set too shallow for gravity flow; furthermore, direct connections would be subject to backflow when the pipe surcharges. The curb inlet has a vertical opening to catch gutter flow. Although the gutter may be depressed slightly in front of the inlet, this type offers no obstructions to traffic. The gutter inlet is an opening covered by a grate through which the drainage falls. The disadvantage is that debris collecting on the grate may result in plugging of the gutter inlet. Combination inlets composed of both curb and gutter openings are also common. Street grade, curb design, and gutter depression define the best type of inlet to select; nevertheless, minimizing traffic interference and eliminating plugging often take precedence over hydraulic efficiency.[①]

Catch basins under street inlets are connected to the main storm sewer located in the street right-of-way, often along the center line, by short pipelines. Manholes are placed at curb inlets, intersections of sewer lines, and at regular intervals to facilitate inspection and cleaning. Pipeline gradients follow the general slope of the ground surface such that water entering can flow downhill to a convenient point for discharge. Sewer pipes are set as shallow as possible to minimize excavation while providing 0.6 to 1.2 m of cover above the pipe to reduce the effect of wheel loadings. Sewer outlets that terminate in natural channels subject to tides or high water levels are equipped with flap gates to prevent back-flooding into the sewer system. Backwater gates are also used on combined sewer outfalls and effluent lines from treatment plants where needed.

The rational method is used to calculate the quantity of runoff for sizing storm sewers. Climatic conditions are incorporated by using local rainfall intensity-duration formulas or curves. In dry regions, sewers may be placed only in high-value districts, while streets and roadside ditches serve as surface drains in sparsely populated areas. On the other hand, in regions of the country having intense thunderstorm weather, lined open channels are often found to be more economical compared with large buried conduits; sewers leading from small drainage areas terminate in grassed or concrete-lined ditches that discharge to surface watercourses.

Flowing full velocities used in design of storm sewers are a minimum of 0.90 m/s and a maximum of about 3.0 m/s. The lower limit is set so that the lines are self-cleansing to avoid deposition of solids, and the upper limit is fixed to prevent erosion of the pipe by grit transported in the water.

A major difference in design philosophy between sanitary and storm sewers is that the latter are assumed to surcharge and overflow periodically. For example, a storm drain sized on the basis of a 10 year rainfall frequency presumes that one storm every 10 years will exceed the capacity of the sewer. Sanitary sewers are designed and constructed to prevent surcharging. Where backup of sanitary sewers does occur, it is more frequently attributable to excess infiltration of groundwater through open pipe joints and unauthorized drain connections.② A second easily recognizable difference between sanitary and storm sewers is the pipe sizes that are needed to serve a given area. Storm drains are many times larger than the pipes collecting domestic waste water. Consequently, only a small amount of infiltrating rain water results in overloading domestic sewers.

Notes

①minimizing traffic interference and eliminating plugging often take precedence over hydraulic efficiency 将交通干扰减至最低程度并消除堵塞，常常要优先于对水力效率的考虑。

②如果当真发生卫生污水管阻塞，常常是由地下水过量渗入造成的，而地下水是通过明露的管道接头和不合格的排水管接头渗入的。

Reading Material B

Sanitary Sewer System

Sanitary sewers transport domestic and industrial wastes by gravity flow to treatment facilities. A lateral sewer collects discharges from houses and carries it to another branch sewer, and has no tributary sewer lines. Branch or submain lines receive waste water from laterals and convey it to large mains. A main sewer, also called trunk or outfall sewer, carries the discharge from large areas to the treatment plant. A force main is a sewer through which waste water is pumped under pressure rather than by gravity flow.

Design flows for sewer systems are based on population served, using the following per capita quantities: laterals and submains 1500 l/person · d, main and trunk 950 l/person · d, and interceptors 350 percent of the estimated average dry-weather flow.[1]These figures include normal infiltration and are based on flowing full capacity. Excluded are industrial wastes and excessive infiltration.[2]Sewer slopes should be sufficient to maintain self-cleansing velocities; this is normally interpreted to be 0.60 m/s, when flowing full. Table 5-1 lists sewer size, minimum slope for 0.60 m/s, and the corresponding quantity of flow. Slopes slightly less than those listed may be permitted in lines where the design average flow provides a depth of flow greater than one third the diameter of the pipe. Where velocities are greater than 4.5 m/s, special provision must be made to protect the pipe and manholes against displacement by erosion and shock hydraulic loadings.

Table 5-1 Minimum Slopes for Various Sized Sewers at a Flowing Full Velocity of 0.60m/s and Corresponding Discharges, Based on Manning's For-mula with n = 0.013

Sewer Diameter (mm)	Minimum Slope (m/km)	Flowing Full Discharge (l/s)
200	3.30	18.8
250	2.45	29.5
300	1.92	42.4
375	1.43	66.3
450	1.12	95.4
525	0.912	130
600	0.763	170
675	0.652	215
750	0.567	265
900	0.444	382

Sanitary sewers are placed at sufficient depth to prevent freezing and to receive waste water from basements. As a general rule, laterals placed in the street right-of-way are set at a depth of not less than 3.5 m below the top of the house foundation. To provide economical access to the sewer after street construction, service connections are generally extended from laterals to outside the curb line at the time of sewer placement. ③An alternative is to place the sanitary sewer behind the curb on one side of the street, making it readily accessible for service connections on that side. Pipe connections from the opposite side of the street are accomplished by excavating working pits on each side and by jacking the house sewer into position for connection to the lateral on the opposite side. In jacking, pipe sections are pushed beneath the roadway by hydraulic jacks. For hard soils, boring machines are used to cut an opening through which the pipeline is pushed. The cutter head operates in front of the first pipe section and an auger pulls the excavated material out through the pipe to the jacking pit.

Ease of maintenance dictates many of the design criteria for waste-water collection systems. The minimum recommended size for laterals is 200 mm diameter. Manholes located at regular intervals allow access to the pipe for inspection and cleaning. Pipes laid on too flat a grade require periodic flushing and cleaning to remove deposited solids and to prevent pipe plugging. Sewers less than 600 mm should be laid on a straight line between manholes. Although in recent years curves have been permitted on smaller lines, this is a questionable practice that can interfere with sewer cleaning. For example, a cable riding on the inside wall of the pipe around a curve may damage the pipe interior. ④Because of the high cost and problems associated with maintenance of pumping stations in the collection system, they are used only when it is impracticable to continue the sewer by gravity flow.

Notes

①interceptors 350 percent of the estimated average dry-weather flow 截留管的设计流量是估计平均旱季流量的 350%。
②工业废水和过量渗入水不包括在内。
③为了减少道路建好后接通污水管的费用，在铺设污水管时，通常将用户连接管从污水支管处延伸至路缘线的外侧。
④例如，处于弯道处水管的内壁如有缆索在上面拉动，会损害管子内部。

UNIT SIX

Text　　　　Composition of Wastewater

[1]　　The data in Table 6-1 represent the approximate composition of domestic wastewater before and after primary sedimentation. BOD and suspended solids (nonfiltrable residue) are the two most important parameters used to define the characteristics of a domestic wastewater. [1]A suspended-solids concentration of 240 mg/l is equivalent to 0.24 lb of suspended solids in 120 gal, and 200 mg/l of BOD is equivalent to 0.20 lb of BOD in 120 gal. Reduction of suspended solids and BOD in primary sedimentation is approximately 50% and 35%, respectively. Approximately 70% of the suspended solids are volatile, defined as those lost upon ignition at 550℃. [2]

[2]　　Total solids (residue on evaporation) include organic matter and dissolved salts; the concentration of the latter is dependent to a considerable extent on the hardness of the municipal water. The concentration of nitrogen in domestic waste is directly related to the concentration of organic matter (BOD). Approximately 40% of the total nitrogen is in solution as ammonia. If raw wastewater has been retained for a long time in collector sewers, a greater percentage of ammonia nitrogen results from deamination of the proteins and urea in wastewater. Ten milligrams per liter of phosphorus is approximately equivalent to a 3-lb phosphorus contribution per capita per year. About 2 lb of this is from phosphate builders used in synthetic detergents.

TABLE 6-1　　Approximate composition of an Average Domestic Wastewater (mg/l)

	Before Sedimentation	After Sedimentation	Biologically Treated
Total solids	800	680	530
Total volatile solids	440	340	220
Suspended solids	240	120	30
Volatile suspended solids	180	100	20
BOD	200	130	30
Ammonia nitrogen as N	15	15	24
Total nitrogen as N	35	30	26
Soluble phosphorus as P	7	7	7
Total phosphorus as P	10	9	8

[3]　　The surplus of nitrogen and phosphorus in biologically treated wastewater reveals that domestic wastewater contains nutrients in excess of biological needs. The approximate BOD/nitrogen/phosphorus (BOD/N/P) weight ratio required for biological treatment is 100/5/1. The exact BOD/N/P ratio needed for treatment depends on the process and the biological availability of the nitrogen and phosphorus compounds in the wastewater. A minimum of 100/6/1.5 is commonly related to treatment of unsettled sanitary wastewater,

while 100/3/0.7 is generally adequate for wastewater where the nitrogen and phosphorus are in soluble forms. The average domestic wastewater listed in Table 6-1 has a ratio of 100/17/5 before sedimentation and 100/19/6 after sedimentation, both of which are in excess of the minimum 100/6/1.5. ③For biological treatment of industrial wastewaters deficient in nutrients, soluble phosphorus can be supplied by adding H_3PO_4 and soluble nitrogen by adding NH_4NO_3.

[4] Biodegradable organic matter in wastewater is generally classified in three categories: carbohydrates, proteins, and fats. *Carbohydrates* are hydrates of carbon with the empirical formula $C_nH_{2n}O_n$ or $C_n(H_2O)_n$.

[5] *Proteins* in simple form are long-chain molecules composed of amino acids connected by peptide bonds and are important in both the structural (e.g., muscle tissue) and dynamic aspects (e.g., enzymes) of living matter. ④Twenty-one common amino acids when linked together in long peptide chains form a majority of simple proteins found in nature. A mixture of proteins as a bacterial substrate is an excellent growth medium, since proteins contain all the essential nutrients. On the other hand, pure carbohydrates are unsuitable as a growth medium since they do not contain the nitrogen and phosphorus essential for synthesis.

[6] *Lipids*, together with carbohydrates and proteins, form the bulk of organic matter of living cells. The term refers to a heterogeneous collection of biochemical substances having the mutual property of being soluble to varying degrees in organic solvents (e.g., ether, ethanol, hexane, and acetone) while being only sparingly soluble in water. ⑤Lipids may be grouped according to their shared chemical and physical properties as fats, oils, and waxes. A simple fat when broken down by hydrolytic action yields fatty acids. In sanitary engineering, the word fats in current usage apparently conveys the meaning of lipids. The term grease applies to a wide variety of organic substances in the lipid category.

[7] Actually not all biodegradable organic matter can be classed into these three simple groupings. Many natural compounds have structures that are combinations of carbohydrates, proteins, and fats, such as lipoproteins and nucleoproteins.

[8] Approximately 20%—40% of the organic matter in wastewater appears to be nonbiodegradable. Several organic compounds, although biodegradable in the sense that specific bacteria can break them down, must be considered by sanitary engineers as partially biodegradable because of time limitations in waste treatment processes. ⑥For example, lignin, a polymeric noncarbohydrate material associated with cellulose in wood fiber, is for all practical purposes nonbiodegradable. Cellulose itself is not readily available to the general population of domestic wastewater bacteria. Saturated hydrocarbons are a problem in treatment because of their physical properties and resistance to bacterial action.

New Words and Expressions

residue * ['rezidjuː]	n.	剩余（物），残余（物）；滤［余，残］渣
volatile * ['vɔlətail]	a.	挥发（性）的，易挥发［发散］的
ignition [ig'niʃən]	n.	点火，引燃，起爆
ammonia * [ə'məunjə]	n.	氨（水）
deamination [diːæmi'neiʃən]	n.	脱氨基（作用）
urea ['juəriə]	n.	尿素
phosphorus * ['fɔsfərəs]	n.	磷；磷光体，发光物质
phosphate ['fɔsfeit]	n.	磷酸盐［酯］
detergent [di'təːdʒənt]	n./a.	洗涤［净］剂，去污剂；清洁［除］的；
surplus * ['səːpləs]	n.	剩余（物，额），过剩
biodegradable [ˌbaiəudi'greidəbl]	a.	生物可降解的
hydrate ['haidreit]	n./v.	水合［化］物，水合［化］作用；（使成）氢氧化物
empirical * [em'pirikəl]	a.	实验（上）的，以实验为根据［基础］的
amino ['æminəu]	a.	氨基的
peptide ['peptaid]	n.	肽，缩氨酸
bond [bɔnd]	n.	键，链
enzyme ['enzaim]	n.	酶，酵素
substrate ['sʌbstreit]	n.	基质，被（酶作）用物
synthesis * ['sinθisis] (pl. syntheses)	n.	合成（法）
lipid (e) ['laipaid]	n.	类脂（化合）物
heterogeneous * ['hetərəu'dʒiːnjəs]	a.	不［非］均匀的，多相的，非均质的
solvent * ['sɔlvənt]	n./a.	溶剂（的）
ether ['iːθə]	n.	醚，乙醚
ethanol ['eθənɔl]	n.	乙醇，酒精
hexane ['heksein]	n.	己烷
acetone ['æsitəun]	n.	丙酮
sparingly ['spɛəriŋli]	ad.	有节制地，缺乏地，少量地
grease * [griːs]	n.	油［动物］脂
lipoprotein [ˌlipə'prəutiːn]	n.	脂（肪）蛋白
lignin ['lignin]	n.	木质素，木质
polymeric [ˌpɔli'merik]	a.	聚合的

Notes

①BOD＝biochemical oxygen demand 生化需氧量。

②Approximately 79% of the suspended solids…defined as those….

defined as…为过去分词短语作状语,用来补充说明。其中,those 替代前面的 the suspended solids。

③The average domestic wastewater…, both of which are….

逗号后 both of which are…为非限制性定语从句,which 的先行词为主句中所说的两种比例的废水。

④Proteins in simple form…molecules composed of amino acids connected by peptide bonds and are…in both the structural and living matter.

proteins, molecules 和 amino acids 分别被介词短语和两个过去分词短语所修饰。第一个 and 连接两个并列表语,第二个 and 和 both 一起连接并列定语。

⑤The term…biochemical substances having…of being soluble…while being only sparingly soluble….

having…为分词短语,修饰它前面的名词;其中,being soluble…和 being only sparingly soluble 为 of 的并列宾语,用连词 while 连接。

⑥Several organic compounds, although biodegradable in the sense that…as partially biodegradable….

although 引导的让步从句省略了主语和系动词 they are,the sense 后跟 that 引导的同位语从句。as 短语为主句主语的补足语。

Exercises

Reading Comprehension

I. Say whether the following statements are true (T) or false (F) according to the text.

1. The greater the hardness of the municipal water is, the bigger the concentration of dissolved salt in it. ( )

2. Deamination of the proteins and urea in wastewater results in an increase in ammonia nitrogen content, if raw wastewater has been kept for a long time in collector sewers. ( )

3. In order to reduce the phosphorous content of domestic wastewater, synthetic detergents ought to be used as little as possible. ( )

4. Lipids can be classed into fats, carbohydrates and proteins. ( )

5. According to the text, the difference between the two words, fats and lipids, can be neglected. ( )

II. Choose the best answer for each of the following.

1. Find out the true statement according to Para. 1.

   A. Volatile suspended solids have the property of starting to burn at 550℃.

   B. Suspended solids will become volatile at 550℃.

   C. About 70% of the suspended solids can be lost at any temperature.

D. Nearly 70% of the suspended solids can be lost by burning at 550℃.
2. What is mainly discussed in Para. 3?
   A. The surplus of nitrogen and phosphorus in biologically treated wastewater.
   B. How to determine the exact BOD/N/P ratio.
   C. How to supply soluble phosphorus and nitrogen for biological treatment of industrial wastewater deficient in nutrients.
   D. The weight ratio of BOD/N/P needed for biological treatment.
3. As a bacterial substrate, _____ is an excellent growth medium.
   A. bacteria   B. a mixture of proteins
   C. carbohydrates   D. protein
4. For synthesis, _____ are necessary.
   A. hydrates   B. nitrogen
   C. ammonia   D. both nitrogen and phosphorus
5. Biodegradable organic matter means that _____.
   A. the organic matter can be grouped
   B. the organic matter consists of carbohydrates, proteins and fats
   C. the organic matter is able to be broken down into harmless products by the action of living things
   D. the organic matter will be lost at 550℃

Vocabulary

Ⅰ. Fill in the blanks with the words given below, changing the form where necessary.

| phosphate | nutrient | polymer |
| solvent | grease | |

1. The two principal water polluting elements in plant _____ are nitrogen and phosphorus.
2. The _____ in most wastewater sludges are small in amount (1 to 3%), and potash is even smaller (0.1 to 0.3%).
3. A highly polar _____ such as water will tend to readily dissolve ionic or polar solutes.
4. Because these compounds have the characteristics of both polymer and electrolyte, they have been called "_____ electrolytes".
5. Sand and other heavy solids from cellars or yards are kept out of the drainage system by sand interceptors, _____ by grease interceptors, and oil by oil interceptors.

Ⅱ. Match the words in Column A with their corresponding definitions or description in Column B.

   Column A   Column B
   1. volatile   a. what is left, esp. (in science) after chemical treatment

2. hydrate   b. (of a liquid or oil) easily changing into a gas
3. residue   c. chemical compound of water with another substance
4. lipoprotein   d. any of a group of proteins combined with a lipid
5. phosphorus   e. a poisonous yellowish waxlike simple substance that shines faintly in the dark and starts to burn when brought out into the air

Translation   成分转换

句子成分的转换就是把句子的某一成分译成另一成分。因为英汉两种语言的表达习惯和修辞特点不尽相同，通顺的译文与英语原文在句法成分上不可能一一对应，需要做适当的改变。

例 1. Reduction of suspended solids and BOD in primary sedimentation is approximately 50% and 35%, respectively.
在初步沉淀中，悬浮固体和生化需氧量分别减少约50%和35%。

例 2. Domestic wastewater contains nutrients in excess of biological needs.
生活污水中，营养物的含量 超过了生物的需求。

Translate the following sentences into Chinese, paying attention to the underlined words.

1. Mechanical cleaning equipment is used in almost all new plants.
2. The settling tank which follows preliminary treatment such as screening and grit removal is known as a primary clarifier.
3. The water leaving the primary clarifier has lost much of the solid organic matter but still contains a high demand for oxygen.
4. A very active biological growth forms on the rock.
5. Raw sludge is generally odoriferous and full of water, two characteristics which make its disposal difficult.

Reading Material A

Primary Treatment

The most objectionable aspect of discharging raw sewage into watercourses is the floating material. It is only logical, therefore, that *screens* were the first form of wastewater treatment used by communities,[①] and even today, screens are used as the first step in treatment plants. Typical screens consist of a series of steel bars which might be about 2.5 cm (1 in.) apart. The purpose of a screen in modern treatment plants is the removal of materials which might damage equipment or hinder further treatment. In some older treatment plants screens are cleaned by hand, but mechanical cleaning equipment is used in almost all new plants. The cleaning rakes are automatically activated when the screens get sufficiently clogged to raise the water level in front of the bars.

In many plants, the next treatment step is a *comminutor*, a circular grinder designed to grind the solids coming through the screen into pieces about 0.3 cm (1/8 in.) or smaller. Many designs are in use.

The third treatment step involves the removal of grit or sand. This is necessary because grit can wear out and damage such equipment as pumps and flow meters. The most common grit chamber is simply a wide place in the channel where the flow is slowed down sufficiently to allow the heavy grit to settle out. Sand is about 2.5 times as heavy as most organic solids and thus settles much faster than the light solids. The objective of a grit chamber is to remove sand and grit without removing the organic material. The latter must be further treated in the plant, but the sand can be dumped as fill without undue odor or other problems.

Following the grit chamber most wastewater treatment plants have a settling tank to settle out as much of the solid matter as possible. Accordingly, the retention time is kept long and turbulence is kept to a minimum. ②The solids settle to the bottom and are removed through a pipe while the clarified liquid escapes over a V-notch weir, a notched steel plate over which the water flows, promoting equal distribution of liquid discharge all the way around a tank. ③Settling tanks are also known as *sedimentation tanks* and often as *clarifiers*. The settling tank which follows preliminary treatment such as screening and grit removal is known as a *primary clarifier*. The solids which drop to the bottom of a primary clarifier are removed as *raw sludge*, a name which doesn't do justice to the undesirable nature of this stuff. ④

Raw sludge is generally odoriferous and full of water, two characteristics which make its disposal difficult. It must be both stabilized to retard further decomposition and dewatered for ease of disposal. In addition to the solids from the primary clarifier, solids from other processes must similarly be treated and disposed. The treatment and disposal of wastewater solids (sludge) is an important part of wastewater treatment.

Primary treatment then is mainly a removal of solids, although some BOD is removed as a consequence of the removal of decomposable solids. Typically, the wastewater which was described earlier might now have these characteristics:

	Raw Wastewater	Following Primary Treatment
BOD mg/l	250	175
SS mg/l	220	60
P mg/l	8	7

A substantial fraction of the solids has been removed, as well as some BOD and a little P (as a consequence of the removal of raw sludge).

In a typical wastewater treatment plant, this would now move on to secondary treatment.

Notes

①因此，格栅过去被用在居民区污水处理的第一道工序上是很有道理的，……
②所以，持水时间要长，紊流要维持到最低限度。
③promoting equal distribution of liquid discharge all the way around a tank 自始至终促使滤池从四周均衡往外排水。
④doesn't do justice to the undesirable nature of this stuff 与这种废物的不良性质不相称

Reading Material B

Secondary Treatment

The water leaving the primary clarifier has lost much of the solid organic matter but still contains a high demand for oxygen; i.e., it is composed of high-energy molecules which will decompose by microbial action, thus creating a biochemical oxygen demand (BOD). This demand for oxygen must be reduced (energy wasted) if the discharge is not to create unacceptable conditions in the watercourse. The objective of secondary treatment is thus to remove BOD while, by contrast, the objective of primary treatment is to remove solids.

Almost all secondary methods use microbial action to reduce the energy level (BOD) of the waste. Although there are many ways the microorganisms can be put to work, the first really successful modern method of secondary treatment was the *trickling filter*.

The trickling filter consists of a filter bed of fist-sized rocks over which the waste is trickled. A very active biological growth forms on the rocks, and the organisms obtain their food from the waste stream dripping through the bed of rocks. Air is either forced through the rocks or, more commonly, air circulation is obtained automatically by a temperature difference between the air in the bed and ambient temperature. In the older filters the waste is sprayed onto the rocks from fixed nozzles. The newer designs utilize a rotating arm which moves under its own power, like a lawn sprinkler, distributing the waste evenly over the entire bed. Often the flow is recirculated, thus obtaining a higher degree of treatment. The name trickling filter is obviously a misnomer since no filtration takes place.

It took some time before a more advanced process became established as what we now call the *activated sludge system*.①The key to the activated sludge system is the reuse of microorganisms. The system consists of a tank full of waste liquid (from the primary clarifier) and a mass of microorganisms. Air is bubbled into this tank (called the *aeration tank*) to provide the necessary oxygen for the survival of the aerobic organisms. The microorganisms come in contact with the dissolved organics and rapidly adsorb these organics on their surface. In time, the microorganisms decompose this material to CO_2, H_2O, some stable compounds and more microorganisms. ②The production of new organisms is relatively slow, and most of the aeration tank volume is in fact used for this purpose.

Once most of the food has been utilized, the microorganisms are separated from the liquid in a settling tank, sometimes called a *secondary* or *final clarifier*. The liquid escapes over a weir and can be discharged into the recipient. The separation of microorganisms is an important part of the system. In the settling tanks, the microorganisms exist without additional food and become hungry. They are thus activated; hence the term *activated sludge*.

The settled microorganisms, now known as return *activated sludge*, are pumped to the head of the aeration tank where they find more food (organics in the effluent from the primary clarifier) and the process starts all over again. The activated sludge process is a continuous operation, with continuous sludge pumping the clean water discharge. ③

When the sludge does not settle, the return activated sludge becomes thin (low suspended solids concentration) and thus the concentration of microorganisms in the aeration tank drops. This results in a higher F/M ratio (same food input, but fewer microorganisms) and a reduced BOD removal efficiency.

Secondary treatment of wastewater then usually consists of a biological step such as activated sludge, which removes a substantial part of the BOD and the remaining solids. Looking once again at the typical wastewater, we now have the following approximate water quality:

	Raw Wastewater	Following Primary Treatment	Following Secondary Treatment
BOD mg/l	250	175	15
SS mg/l	220	60	15
P mg/l	8	7	6

The effluent, in fact, meets our previously established effluent standards for BOD and SS. Only the phosphorus remains high. The removal of inorganic chemicals like phosphorus is accomplished in tertiary (or advanced) wastewater treatment.

Notes

①过了一段时间，产生了一种更先进、我们今天称为活性污泥系统的处理方法。
②in time 过了一定时间以后。
③活性污泥工艺是一连续操作过程，随着污泥的连续作用泵送出净水。

UNIT SEVEN

Text   Biological Treatment System

[1]　Biological processing is the most efficient way of removing organic matter from municipal waste waters. These living systems rely on mixed microbial cultures to decompose, and to remove colloidal and dissolved organic substances from solution. The treatment chamber holding the microorganisms provides a controlled environment; for example, activated sludge is supplied with sufficient oxygen to maintain an aerobic condition. Waste water contains the biological food, growth nutrients, and inoculum of microorganisms. Persons who are not familiar with waste-water operations often ask where the "special" biological cultures are obtained. The answer is that the wide variety of bacteria and protozoa present in domestic wastes seed the treatment units. ①Then by careful control of waste-water flows, recirculation of settled microorganisms, oxygen supply, and other factors, the desirable biological cultures are generated and retained to process the pollutants. The slime layer on the surface of the media in a trickling filter is developed by spreading waste water over the bed. Within a few weeks the filter is operational, removing organic matter from the liquid trickling through the bed. Activated sludge in a mechanical, or diffused-air, system is started by turning on the aerators and feeding the waste water. Initially a high rate of recirculation from the bottom of the final clarifier is necessary to retain sufficient biological culture. However, within a short period of time a settleable biological floc matures that efficiently flocculates the waste organics. An anaerobic digester is the most difficult treatment unit to start up, since the methane-forming bacteria, essential to digestion, are not abundant in raw waste water. ②Furthermore, these anaerobes grow very slowly and require optimum environmental conditions. Start-up of an anaerobic digester can be hastened considerably by filling the tank with waste water and seeding with a substantial quantity of digesting sludge from a nearby treatment plant. Raw sludge is then fed at a reduced initial rate, and lime is supplied as necessary to hold pH. ③Even under these conditions, several months may be required to get the process fully operational.

[2]　The most important factors affecting biological growth are temperature, availability of nutrients, oxygen supply, pH, presence of toxins and, in the case of photosynthetic plants, sunlight. Bacteria are classified according to their optimum temperature range for growth. Mesophilic bacteria grow in a temperature range of 10 to 40℃, with an optimum of 37℃. Aeration tanks and trickling filters generally operate in the lower half of this range with waste-water temperatures of 20 to 25℃ in warm climates and 8 to 10℃ during the winter in northern regions. ④

[3]　Municipal waste waters commonly contain sufficient concentrations of carbon, nitrogen, phosphorus, and trace nutrients to support the growth of a microbial cul-

ture. Theoretically, a BOD to nitrogen to phosphorus ratio of 100/5/1 is adequate for aerobic treatment, with small variations depending on the type of system and mode of operation.⑤ Average domestic waste water exhibits a surplus of nitrogen and phosphorus with a BOD/N/P ratio of about 100/17/5. If a municipal waste contains a large volume of nutrient-deficient industrial waste, supplemental nitrogen is generally supplied by the addition of anhydrous ammonia (NH_3) or phosphoric acid (H_3PO_4) as is needed.

[4]　　Diffused and mechanical aeration basins must supply sufficient air to maintain dissolved oxygen for the biota to use in metabolizing the waste organics. Rate of microbial activity is independent of dissolved oxygen concentration above a minimum critical value, below which the rate is reduced by the limitation of oxygen required for respiration. The exact minimum depends on the type of activated sludge process and the characteristics of the waste water being treated. The most common design criterion for critical dissolved oxygen is 2.0 mg/l, but in actual operation values as low as 0.5 mg/l have proved satisfactory. Anaerobic systems must, of course, operate in the complete absence of dissolved oxygen; consequently, digesters are sealed with floating or fixed covers to exclude air.

[5]　　Hydrogen ion concentration has a direct influence on biological treatment systems which operate best in a neutral environment. The general range of operation of aeration systems is between pH 6.5 and 8.5. Above this range microbial activity is inhibited, and below pH 6.5 fungi are favored over bacteria in the competition for metabolizing the waste organics.⑥ Anaerobic digestion has a small pH tolerance range of 6.7 to 7.4 with optimum operation at pH 7.0 to 7.1. Domestic waste sludge permits operation in this narrow range except during start-up or periods of organic overloads. Limited success in digester pH control has been achieved by careful addition of lime with the raw sludge feed. Unfortunately, the buildup of acidity and reduction of pH may be a symptom of other digestion problems, for example, accumulation of toxic heavy metals which the addition of lime cannot cure.

[6]　　Biological treatment systems are inhibited by toxic substances. Industrial wastes from metal finishing industries often contain toxic ions, such as nickel and chromium; chemical manufacturing produces a wide variety of organic compounds that can adversely affect microorganisms. Since little can be done to remove or neutralize toxic compounds in municipal treatment, pretreatment should be provided by industries prior to discharging wastes to the city sewer.⑦

New Words and Expressions

decompose * [ˌdiːkəmˈpəuz]	v.	分解，溶解
activated [ˈæktiveitid]	a.	活化了的，激活后的
aerobic [ɛəˈrəubik]	a.	需氧[气]的
inoculum [iˈnɔkjuləm] (pl. inocula)	n.	细菌培养液
slime [slaim]	n.	（粘，软，矿，煤）泥

trickle	['trikl]	v.	（使）滴（下），一滴滴的流
trickling filter			生物（滴）滤池
diffuse *	[di'fju:z]	v.	（扩，分）散，传播，散布
clarifier	['klærifaiə]	n.	澄清［滤清］器，沉淀槽
digester	[di'dʒestə]	n.	消化池
anaerobe	[ə'neiərəub]	n.	厌氧［气］菌［微生物］
toxin	['tɔksin]	n.	毒素［质］
photosynthetic	[ˌfəutəusin'θetik]	a.	光合的
mesophilic	[ˌmesə'filik]	a.	中温的，嗜温的
anhydrous	[æn'haidrəs]	a.	无水的
phosphoric	[fɔs'fɔrik]	a.	磷的，含（五价）磷的
biota	['baiətə]	n.	生物群
metabolize	[me'tæbəlaiz]	vt.	使新陈代谢
critical	['kritikəl]	a.	临界的，极限的
respiration	[ˌrespə'reiʃən]	n.	呼吸
criterion *	[krai'tiəriən]	n.	标准，规范，依据；准数，指标
inhibit	[in'hibit]	vt.	防［阻，制］止，抑制
buildup *	['bildʌp]	n.	增加［强，大］
symptom	['simptəm]	n.	征兆，迹象，症状［侯］
finishing	[finiʃiŋ]	n.	精修［制］，精［最终］加工
nickel *	['nikl]	n.	镍
adversely	['ædvə:sli]	ad.	反向地，有害地，不利地
neutralize	['nju:trəlaiz]	vt.	使中和，平衡，抵［相］消

Notes

①The answer is…bacteria and protozoa present in domestic wastes seed….
　present…wastes 为形容词短语作后置定语。seed 用作动词，意为"给…接种"。

②An anaerobic digester…, since…bacteria, essential to digestion, are not….
　since 引导原因状语从句，其中，两逗号之间部分为形容词短语，作 bacteria 的定语。

③…and lime is supplied as necessary to hold pH.
　as 短语为主语 lime 的补足语。

④Aeration tanks…operate in…of this range with waste-water temperatures…in northern regions.
　this range 承上指 a temperature range of 10 to 40℃，with 短语作状语，修饰 operate，用来表示一种附带的情况。

⑤…a BOD to nitrogen to phosphorus ration…, with small variations depending on…
　ration 前为一名词短语作前置定语。逗号后为 with 结构，作状语，用以补充说明。

⑥…favored over…in the competition for….

这一结构意为"在与…较量中…比…更受喜爱（更占上风）"。

⑦Since little can be done…prior to discharging wastes to the city sewer, 句中，little 用作名词，意为"几乎没有什么"。prior to 为短语介词，第二个介词 to 为 discharging 所要求。

Exercises

Reading Comprehension

Ⅰ. Say whether the following statements are true (T) or false (F) according to the text.
1. Colloidal and dissolved organic substances are decomposed and removed from the solution in a biological treatment system. ( )
2. People who know little about the way wastewater is working often wonder where the desirable biological cultures are got from. ( )
3. Rate of microbial activity is independent of dissolved oxygen concentration. ( )
4. To keep the rate of microbial activity, it is advisable to make the criterion for dissolved oxygen a little higher than needed. ( )
5. Since industrial wastes often contain toxic ions, pretreatment by industries is necessary. ( )

Ⅱ. Choose the best answer for each of the following.
1. What is mainly discussed in the first paragraph?
   A. The advantages of biological processing.
   B. The principle of a biological treatment system.
   C. The operational process of the biological treatment system.
   D. Both b and c.
2. What treatment unit is the most difficult to start up?
   A. A treatment chamber.   B. A trickling filter.
   C. An aerator.   D. An anaerobic digester.
3. The phrase "to get the process fully operational" (at the end of Para. 1) means ___ .
   A. getting the digestion process fully operational
   B) getting the biological treatment process fully operational
   C. getting the process of starting-up an anaerobic digester fully operational
   D. getting the process of removing pollutants fully operational
4. The growth of a microbial culture is supported by ___ .
   A. carbon.   B. nitrogen and phosphorus.
   C. trace nutrients   D. all of the above
5. According to the text, what would affect microbial activity?
   A. Dissolved oxygen concentration   B. Hydrogen ion concentration

C. pH   D. Dissolved oxygen

Vocabulary

Ⅰ. Fill in the blanks with the words given below, changing the form where necessary.

> metabolize   digester   decompose
> critical   diffuse

1. Bacteria _____ the waste solids, producing new growth while taking in dissolved oxygen and releasing carbon dioxide.
2. Aerobic biological activity is independent of dissolved oxygen above a minimum _____ value.
3. Most treatment plants have two kinds of _____; primary and secondary.
4. By _____ carbon dioxide gas through water, we can restore the carbon dioxide removed by the reaction with lime.
5. Raw sludge must be both stabilized to retard further _____ and dewatered for ease of disposal.

Ⅱ. Match the words in Column A with their Corresponding definitions or descriptions in Column B.

Column A	Column B
1. inhibit	a. the act or action of increasing
2. buildup	b. (in chemistry) to destroy the distinctive or active properties of
3. toxic	c. to hold back (from something)
4. neutralize	d. an established rule, standard, or principle, on which a judgment is based
5. criterion	e. of, related to, or caused by poisonous substances

Translation   综合练习

在翻译实践中，所需的翻译技能往往并不单纯，经常要涉及到多种技能的运用。

Translate the following sentences into Chinese, paying attention to the underlined words.

1. This remedy is simple and cheap, if it <u>works</u>.
2. The clarified liquid <u>escapes</u> over a V-notch weir.
3. Ozonisation is a more powerful source of oxygen than chlorine and has no after-taste <u>trouble</u>.
4. Catch basins under street inlets are connected to <u>the main storm sewer</u> located in the street right-of-way, often along the center line, by short pipelines.
5. Dewatering is <u>seldom</u> used as an intermediate process, <u>unless</u> the sludge is to be inciner-

ated.
6. Every sewer does not serve as the gravity conduit.
7. The third treatment step involves the removal of grit or sand.
8. The 'activated' carbon is a very finely divided carbon which presents a high surface area for adsorption.
9. A major difference in design philosophy between sanitary and storm sewers is that the latter are assumed to surcharge and overflow periodically.
10. Many people consider that the sparkling clear hard waters obtained from the chalk are second to none for drinking.

Reading Material A

Biological Towers

In recent years, several forms of manufactured media have been marketed for trickling filters. ① The main advantage, relative to crushed rock, is the high specific surface (m^2/m^3) with a corresponding high percentage of void volume that permits substantial biological slime growth without inhibiting passage of air supplying oxygen. Other advantages include: a uniform media for better liquid distribution, light weight facilitating construction of deeper beds, chemical resistance, and the ability to handle high-strength and unsettled waste waters.

Introduction of synthetic media has broadened the application of biological filtration in treating both industrial and domestic waste waters. High-strength soluble food-processing wastes, while generally not suited to rock-filled filters, can be handled by multiple-stage biological towers. Rock or slag in existing filters may be replaced to improve operation or degree of treatment. However, this type of installation with a rotary distributor and bed depth of only 1.5 to 2 m does not provide optimum use of the media. Better results are achieved, and greater organic loadings can be applied, when the beds are 6 m or more in depth. These towers allow a greater contact time and the liquid can be applied continuously by fixed distributors, instead of by rotating arms. In special cases, existing treatment plants may install a biological tower preceding primary settling. This type of unit, referred to as a roughing filter, improves overall plant efficiency by: reducing influent BOD, enhancing settleability by preaeration, and leveling out (absorbing) shock loads of high-strength industrial wastes discharged to the municipal system. ②

Normal high-rate filtration plants use flow patterns similar to rock-filled filter systems. Direct recirculation is preferred for increased BOD removal, and gravity flow from the final clarifier returns settled solids to the head of the plant for removal in the primary. For strong municipal waste waters, two towers may be set in series with or without an intermediate clarifier. Increased BOD removal is possible by returning settled solids from the final clarifier to the tower influent. If the waste is sufficiently strong, this recirculation results in a buildup of activated sludge in the flow passing through the tower. Thus the system responds as both a filter, with fixed biological growth, and a mechanical aeration system with suspended microbial floc. ③There is another alternative for processing strong municipal wastes. The tower serves as a roughing filter, with direct recirculation to absorb shock loads, prior to activated sludge treatment in a second-stage aeration basin.

Allowable organic loadings on deep beds range from 400 to 2,400 g/m^3 d BOD with hydraulic loadings up to 10 m^3/m^2 d. BOD removal efficiencies rely on volumetric organic loading, and are generally independent of bed depth if it is greater than about 3 m; normally towers are constructed with 6 m depth of media. The exact design loading for a biological tower is based on: placement of the unit within the treatment scheme; waste-water recirculation pattern and ratio; type of synthetic media employed; and strength, biodegradability, and temperature of the waste water. Design parameters for a particular synthetic media and application are available from the manufacturer.

Notes

①近几年来，用于滴滤池的几种介质已大批生产并在市场上销售。
②referred to as a roughing filter 被称为粗滤池。
③这样，这一系统既起到带有固定生物生长的滤池的作用，又能起到具有悬浮微生物絮体的机械曝气系统的作用。

Reading Material B

Biological Aeration

Raw waste water flowing into the aeration basin contains organic matter (BOD) as a food supply. Bacteria metabolize the waste solids, producing new growth while taking in dissolved oxygen and releasing carbon dioxide. Protozoa graze on bacteria for energy to reproduce. Some of the new microbial growth dies releasing cell contents to solution for resynthesis.① After the addition of a large population of microorganisms aerating raw waste water for a few hours removes organic matter from solution by synthesis into microbial cells.② Mixed liquor is continuously transferred to a clarifier for gravity separation of the biological floc and discharge of the clarified effluent. Settled floc is returned continuously to the aeration basin for mixing with entering raw waste.

The liquid suspension of microorganisms in an aeration basin is generally referred to as a mixed liquor, and the biological growths are called mixed liquor suspended solids

(MLSS). The name activated sludge was originated in referring to the return biological suspension,③ since these masses of microorganisms were observed to be very "active" in removing soluble organic matter from solution. This extraction process is a metabolic response of bacteria in a state of endogenous respiration, or starvation.

Activated sludge systems are truly aerobic, since the microbial floc is suspended in mixed liquor containing oxygen. Even though the dissolved oxygen may reduce to zero in the final clarifier, this rarely produces offensive odors since the organic matter has been thoroughly oxidized during aeration. Transfer to the waste water is a two-step process. Air bubbles are created by compressed air forced through a submerged diffuser, or by mechanical aeration where turbulent mixing entrains air in the liquid. The rate of dissolved oxygen utilization is essentially a function of the food-to-microorganism ratio (BOD loading and aeration period) and temperature. This biological uptake is generally less than 10 mg/l · h for extended aeration processes, about 30 mg/l · h for conventional, and as great as 100 mg/l · h for high rate aeration. Aerobic biological activity is independent of dissolved oxygen above a minimum critical value. Below this concentration, the metabolism of microorganisms is limited by reduced oxygen supply. Critical concentrations reported for various systems range from 0.2 to 2.0 mg/l, the most common being 0.5 mg/l.

Knowledge of basic concepts of oxygen transfer and uptake is helpful in understanding operational problems generally associated with aeration processes. It is possible to have a deficiency in an aerating basin if the rate of biological utilization exceeds the capability of the equipment. For example, organic overloading of an extended aeration system that is equipped with coarse bubble diffusers set at a shallow depth can result in a dissolved oxygen level less than 0.5 mg/l even though the tank contents are being vigorously mixed by air bubbles emitting from diffusers. Perhaps a situation that occurs more frequently in practice is uneconomical operation from overaeration producing a dissolved oxygen level greater than is necessary in the mixed liquor. Since biological activity is just as great at low levels and the transfer rate from air to dissolved oxygen increases with decreasing concentration, it is logical to operate a system as close to critical minimum dissolved oxygen as possible. It may be feasible to operate the air compressors at reduced capacity, or even turn off one blower on weekends, to conserve electrical energy with no adverse effects to the biological process. The best method for determining suitable operation is to make oxygen measurements at various times, particularly during periods of maximum loading, and then to adjust the air supply accordingly.

Notes

①新生长的微生物一部分死亡，向溶液中释放细胞原生质，以求再合成。
②在添加了大量的微生物以后，向原污水充气几个小时，即可通过合成微生物细胞，从溶液中除去有机物。
③活性污泥这一名称的由来与回流生物悬浮体有关。

UNIT EIGHT

Text   Characteristics of the Sludges

[1]   The characteristics of sludges of interest depend entirely on what is to be done with a sludge. For example, if the sludge is to be thickened by gravity, its settling and compaction characteristics are important. On the other hand, if the sludge is to be digested anaerobically, the concentrations of volatile solids, heavy metals, etc., are important.

[2]   Another fact of immense importance in the design of sludge handling and disposal operations is the variability of the sludges. In fact this variability can be stated in terms of three "laws":

1. No two wastewater sludges are alike in all respects.
2. Sludge characteristics change with time.
3. There is no "average sludge".

[3]   The first statement reflects the fact that no two wastewaters are alike, and that if the variable of treatment is added, the sludges produced will have significantly different characteristics.[①]

[4]   The second statement is often overlooked by designers. For example, the settling characteristics of chemical sludges from the treatment of plating wastes [e.g., $Pb(OH)_2$, $Zn(OH)_2$ or $Cr(OH)_3$] vary with time simply because of uncontrolled pH changes. Biological sludges are of course continually changing, with the greatest change occurring when the sludge changes from aerobic to anaerobic (or vice versa).[②] It is thus quite difficult to design sludge handling equipment, since the sludge may change in some significant characteristic in only a few hours.

[5]   The third "law" is constantly violated. Tables showing "average values" for "average sludges" are useful for illustrative and comparative purposes only, and should not be used for design.

[6]   With that caveat, we now proceed to discuss some characteristics of "average sludges".

[7]   The first characteristic, solids concentration, is perhaps the most important variable, defining the volume of sludge to be handled, and determining whether the sludge behaves as a liquid or a solid. The importance of volatile solids is, of course, in the disposability of the sludge. With high volatiles, a sludge would be difficult to dispose of into the environment.[③] As the volatiles are degraded, gases and odors are produced, and thus a high volatile solids concentration would restrict the methods of disposal.

[8]   The rheological characteristics of sludge are of interest in that this is one of only a few truly basic parameters describing the physical nature of a sludge.[④] Two-phase mixtures like sludges, however, are almost without exception non-Newtonian and thixotrop-

ic. Sludges tend to act like pseudoplastics, with an apparent yield stress and a plastic viscosity. The rheological behavior of a pseudoplastic fluid is defined by a rheogram. The term thixotropic relates to the time dependence of the rheological properties.

[9] Sludges tend to act more like plastic fluids as the solids concentration increases. True plastic fluids can be described by the equation

$$\tau = \tau_y + \eta(du/dy)$$

where τ=shear stress

τ_y=yield stress

η=plastic viscosity

du/dy=rate of shear, or the slope of the velocity (u)-depth (y) profile

[10] The yield stress can vary from above 40 dyn/cm^2 for 6% raw sludge, to only 0.07 dyn/cm^2 for a thickened activated sludge. The large differences suggest that rheological parameters could well be used for scale-up purposes. Unfortunately, few researchers have bothered to measure the rheological characteristics (such analyses are not even included in Standard Methods) and many gaps exist in the available data.

[11] The chemical composition is important for several reasons. First, the fertilizer value of the sludge is dependent on the availability of N, P and K, as well as trace elements. A more important measurement, however, is the concentration of heavy metals and other toxins which would make the sludge toxic to the environment. The ranges of heavy metal concentrations are verylarge (e.g. cadmium can range from almost zero to over 1000 mg/kg). Since a major source of such toxins is in industrial discharges, a single poorly operated industrial firm may contribute enough toxins to make the sludge worthless as a fertilizer. Most engineers agree that although it would be most practical to treat the sludge at the plant in order to achieve the removal of toxic components, there are no effective methods available for removing heavy metals, pesticides and other potential toxins from the sludge, and that the control must be over the influent (that is, tight sewer ordinances).[5]

[12] In addition to the physical and chemical characteristics, the biological parameters of sludge can also be important. The volatile solids parameter is in fact often interpreted as a biological characteristic, the assumption being the VSS is a gross measure of viable biomass.[6] Another important parameter, especially in regard to ultimate disposal, is the concentration of pathogens, both bacteriological and viral. The primary clarifier seems to act like a viral and bacteriological concentrator, with a substantial fraction of these microorganisms existing in the sludge instead of the liquid effluent.

New Words and Expressions

of interest   值的注意的，重要的
thicken * ['θikən]   v.   （使）变厚［粗，浓，密，稠］
variability [ˌvɛəriə'biliti]   n.   易［可，能］变性，变化［异］性

plating ['pleitiŋ]		n.	（电，喷）镀
vice versa ['vaisi'və:sə]		ad.	反之亦然
violate * ['vaiəleit]		vt.	违犯［背，反，章］
illustrative ['iləstreitiv]		a.	说明［解说］性的
caveat ['keiviæt]		n.	防止误解的说明
disposability [dis‚pəuzə'biliti]		n.	任意处理［处置］性
rheological [ri:ə'lɔdʒikəl]		a.	流变的
thixotropic [θiksə'trɔpik]		a./n.	触变性液体；触变（性）的
pseudoplastic ['psju:dəu'plæstik]		n.	假塑性体
viscosity * [vis'kɔsiti]		n.	粘性，粘度
rheogram ['ri:əgræm]		n.	流变图
profile * ['prəufail]		n.	断［剖，切］面（图），侧［立］面图
approximation * [ə‚prɔksi'meiʃən]		n.	近似（值，法）
dyn=dyne [dain]		n.	达因
scale-up		n.	按比例放大［扩大，升高］
cadmium ['kædmiəm]		n.	镉
pesticide ['pestisaid]		n.	杀虫剂，农药
influent ['influənt]		n.	进水，流入液体
ordinance ['ɔ:dinəns]		n.	条例，条令
assumption * [ə'sʌmpʃən]		n.	假设，设想，前提
VSS=volatile suspended solid			挥发性悬浮固体
viable * ['vaiəbl]		a.	活的，有活力的
biomass ['baiəumæs]		n.	生物量

Notes

①The first statement reflects the fact that…, and that if…is added, the sludges….
the fact 后跟 that 引导的并列同位语从句，用逗号和 and 连接。第二个 that 以后又套有 if 引导的条件从句。

②Biological sludges…with the greatest change occurring….
with 结构在句中作状语，用以补充说明。

③With high volatiles, …difficult to dispose of….
with 引导的介词短语作原因状语。to dispose of… 为不定式短语作 difficult 的状语。

④The rheological characteristics…in that…a sludge.
in that 引导原因状语从句。

⑤Most engineers agree that although it would be…there are, and that the control must be
… (that is, tight sewer ordinances).
动词 agree 后跟两个并列的宾语从句，用逗号和 and 连接。第一个宾语从句又含有 although 引导的让步状语从句，第二个宾语从句中的括号内部分为其同位语。

⑥The volatile solids parameter…, the assumption being…

逗号后为一分词独立结构，表示一个伴随情况。being 和后面的从句构成系表关系。

Exercises

Reading Comprehension

Ⅰ. Say whether the following statements are true (T) or false (F) according to the text.
1. The variability of the sludges is a very important fact in the design of sludge treating and disposal operations. ( )
2. The sludge handling equipment must be designed according to the sludge characteristics. ( )
3. In the expression, "average values" for "average sludges", the word average suggests the same meaning. ( )
4. "a high volatile solids concentration"(Para. 7)means that the concentration of volatile solids is high. ( )
5. Rheological properties and rheological characteristics are the same thing. ( )

Ⅱ. Find out the best answer for each of the following.
1. The expression "of interest" that appears in the text means _____ .
   A. worth mentioning　　　　　　B. of importance
   C. arousing interest　　　　　　D. having an interest
2. The sludge handling equipment is difficult to design mainly because the sludge may vary in some significant characteristic with _____ .
   A. time　　　　　　　　　　　B. pH
   C. solid concentration　　　　　D. the volume of sludge
3. Which of the following statements is the closest in meaning to the sentence "With high volatiles, a sludge would be difficult to dispose of into the environment."?
   A. It would be difficult to dispose of a sludge and make it fulfill the environment requirements.
   B. It would be not allowed to put a sludge with high volatiles into the environment.
   C. As the volatiles are degraded to gases and odors, a large proportion of a sludge with high volatiles has gone without any disposal into the environment.
   D. Because of gases and odors, a sludge with high volatiles would be difficult to dispose of.
4. What characteristics of the sludges does the author think ought to have been paid much attention to by the researchers?
   A. Solids concentration　　　　　B. The variability of the sludges
   C. The rheological characteristics　D. The biological characteristics

5. Which of the following statements is NOT true?
   A. With sufficient available N.P.K and trace elements, the sludge can be used as a fertilizer.
   B. The engineers agree that there will probably be no problem in treating the sludge at the plant to remove toxic components.
   C. The engineers put forward tight sewer ordinances, because they believe heavy metals, pesticides and other potential toxins go into the sewer with the influent.
   D. After the primary clarifying, most of the viral and bacteriological microorganisms are kept in the sludge instead of the clarified effluent.

Vocabulary

I. Fill in the blanks with the words given below, changing the form where necessary.

biomass	viscosity	pathogen
compact	thicken	

1. Aerobic digestion at ambient temperatures is not very effective in the destruction of _____.
2. The populations of organisms responsible for the transfer of nutrients to _____ are large and varied.
3. The wastes from treatment plants can be _____ to serve as fuel.
4. Mechanical gravity dewatering units operate in two steps, _____ followed by compression or cake-formation.
5. The fluid properties that affect the flow are _____ and specific weight.

II. Match the words in Column A with their corresponding definitions or descriptions in Column B.

Column A   Column B
1. viable   a. able to exist; capable of surviving
2. profile   b. the quality of being changeable
3. variability   c. to break (a law, rule, promise, etc.)
4. influent   d. (in engineering) a vertical section through a work
5. violate   e. anything flowing in

Translation　　　　　　　　被动语态（I）

　　被动语态在科技英语中使用广泛，翻译起来也比较灵活。一般可译为汉语被动句，汉语主动句两种。本单元只针对前一种译法设置练习。译成汉语被动句可采用"由"、"被"、"靠"、"受"、"加以"等词译出。

例1. The superstructure should be preferably designed by architect.

上部结构<u>由</u>建筑师来设计更好。

例2. The second statement is often overlooked by designers.

这第二条<u>被</u>设计者们忽略。

例3. Lime stabilization is achieved by adding lime to the sludge.

石灰稳定处理可以<u>靠</u>向污泥中添加石灰来完成。

Translate the following sentences into Chinese, paying attention to the underlined words.

1. If a digester goes "sour", the mathane formers <u>have been inhibited</u> in some way.
2. The sludge to be dewatered <u>is poured</u> on the sand beds about 15cm deep.
3. If dewatering by sand beds <u>is considered</u> impractical, mechanical dewatering technique must be employed.
4. The organic acids <u>are</u> in turn degraded further by a group of strict anaerobes called mathane formers.
5. Pumps <u>are</u> conveniently <u>compared</u> by reference to their 'specific speeds'.

Reading Material A

Sludge Stabilization

There are three primary means of sludge stabilization
- lime
- aerobic digestion
- anaerobic digestion

Lime stabilization is achieved by adding lime (either as hydrated lime, $Ca(OH)_2$ or as quicklime, CaO) to the sludge and thus raising the pH to about 11 or above. This significantly reduces the odor and helps in the destruction of pathogens. The major disadvantage of lime stabilization is that it is temporary. With time (days) the pH drops and the sludge once again becomes putrescible.

Aerobic stabilization is merely a logical extension of the activated sludge system. Waste activated sludge is placed in dedicated aeration tanks for a very long time, and the concentrated solids allowed to progress well into the endogenous respiration phase, in which food is obtained only by the destruction of other viable organisms. This results in a net reduction in total and volatile solids. Aerobically digested sludges are, however, more difficult to dewater than anaerobic sludges.

The third commonly employed method of sludge stabilization is anaerobic digestion. The biochemistry of anaerobic decomposition of organics is a staged process, with the solution of organics by extracellular enzymes being followed by the production of organic acids by a large and hearty group of anaerobic microorganisms known, appropriately enough, as the *acid formers*. ①The organic acids are in turn degraded further by a group of strict anaerobes called *methane formers*. These microorganisms are the prima donnas of wastewater treatment, getting upset at the least change in their environment②. The success of anaerobic treatment thus boils down to the creation of a suitable condition for the methane formers. ③Since they are strict anaerobes, they are unable to function in the presence of oxygen and very sensitive to environmental conditions such as temperature, pH and toxins. If a digester goes "sour", the methane formers have been inhibited in some way. The acid formers, however, keep chugging away, making more organic acids. This has the effect of further lowering the pH and making conditions even worse for the methane formers. A sick digester is therefore difficult to cure without massive doses of lime or other antacids.

Most treatment plants have two kinds of digesters-primary and secondary. The primary digester is covered, heated and mixed to increase the reaction rate. The temperature of the sludge is usually about 35℃ (95℉). Secondary digesters are not mixed or heated and are used for storage of gas and for concentrating the sludge by settling. As the solids settle, the liquid supernatant is pumped back to the main plant for further treatment. The cover of the secondary digester often floats up and down, depending on the amount of gas stored. The gas is high enough in methane to be used as fuel, and is in fact usually used to heat the primary digester.

The production of gas from digestion varies with the temperature, solids loading, solids volatility and other factors. Typically, about 0.6 m^3 of gas per kg volatile solids added (10 ft^3/lb) has been observed. This gas is about 60% methane and burns readily, usually being used to heat the digester and answer additional energy needs within a plant. It has been found that an active group of methane formers operates at 35℃ (95℉) in common practice, and this process has become known as *mesophilic digestion*. As the temperature is increased, to about 45℃ (115℉), another group of methane formers predominates, and this process is tagged *thermophilic digestion*. Although the latter process is faster and produces more gas, it is also more difficult and expensive to maintain such elevated temperatures.

All three stabilization processes reduce the concentration of pathogenic organisms, but to varying degrees. Lime stabilization achieves a high degree of sterilization, due to the high pH. Further, if quicklime (CaO) is used, the reaction is exothermic and the elevated temperatures assist in the destruction of pathogens. Aerobic digestion at ambient temperatures is not very effective in the destruction of pathogens.

Notes

①…, with the solution of organics by extracellular enzymes being followed by the production of organic acids by a large and hearty group of anaerobic microorganisms known, appropriately enough, as the acid formers. ……有机物被细胞外酶溶解后,紧接着大量的厌氧微生物产生有机酸,这些微生物叫做产酸菌非常合适。

②the prima donnas of wastewater treatment 废水处理中极为敏感的成分。

③boils down to 归结起来是……。

Reading Material B

Sludge Dewatering

Dewatering is seldom used as an intermediate process, unless the sludge is to be incinerated. Most wastewater plants use dewatering as a final method of volume reduction prior to ultimate disposal.

In the United States five dewatering techniques have been most popular: sand beds, vacuum filters, pressure filters, belt filters and centrifuges. Each of these is discussed below.

Sand beds have been in use for a great many years and are still the most cost-effective means of dewatering when land is available and labor is not exorbitant. The beds consists of tile drains in gravel, covered by about 26 cm (10 in.) of sand. The sludge to be dewatered is poured on the beds at about 15 cm (6 in.) deep. Two mechanisms combine to separate the water from the solids: seepage and evaporation. Seepage into the sand and through the tile drains, although important in the total volume of water extracted, lasts for only a few days. ①The sand pores are quickly clogged, and all drainage into the sand ceases. The mechanism of evaporation takes over, and this process is actually responsible for the conversion of liquid sludge to solid. In some northern areas sand beds are enclosed under greenhouses to promote evaporation as well as prevent rain from falling into the beds.

For mixed digested sludge, the usual design is to allow for 3 months drying time. Some engineers suggest that this period be extended to allow a sand bed to rest for a month after the sludge has been removed. This seems to be an effective means of increasing the drainage efficiency once the sand beds are again flooded.

Raw sludge will not drain well on sand beds and will usually have an obnoxious odor. Hence raw sludges are seldom dried on beds. Raw secondary sludges have a habit of either seeping through the sand or clogging the pores so quickly that no effective drainage takes place. Aerobically digested sludge can be dried on sand, but usually with some difficulty.

If dewatering by sand beds is considered impractical, mechanical dewatering techniques must be employed. The first successful mechanical dewatering device employed in sludge treatment was the *vacuum filter*. The vacuum filter consists of a perforated drum covered with a fabric. A vacuum is drawn in the drum and the covered drum dipped into sludge. The water moves through the filter cloth, leaving the solids behind eventually to be scraped off.

The pressure filter uses positive pressure to force the water through a filter cloth. Typically, the pressure filters are built as plate-and-frame filters, where the sludge solids are captured in the spaces between the plates and frames, which are then pulled apart to allow for sludge cleanout.

The *belt filter* operates as both a pressure filter and by a gravity drainage.② As the sludge is introduced onto the moving belt, the free water drips through the belt but the solids are retained. The belt then moves into the dewatering zone where the sludge is squeezed between two belts. These machines are quite effective in dewatering many different kinds of sludges and are being widely installed in small wastewater treatment plants.

Centrifugation became popular in wastewater treatment only after organic polymers were available for sludge conditioning. Although the centrifuge will work on any sludge (unlike the vacuum filter which will not pick up some sludges, resulting in zero filter yield③ without good conditioning, most sludges can not be centrifuged with greater than 60% or 70% solids recovery.

The centrifuge most widely used is the solid bowl decanter, which consists of a bullet-shaped body rotating on its long axis. The sludge is placed into the bowl, the solids settle out under about 500 to 1000 gravities (centrifugally applied) and are scraped out of the bowl by a screw conveyor.

Notes

①虽然渗流量在被排出的总水量中数量可观，但渗流进入砂中并通过瓦管排出管道只持续几天的时间。

②带式过滤器既能起到压力过滤器的作用，又能起到通过重力排水进行过滤的作用。

③unlike the vacuum filter which will not pick up some sludges, resulting in zero filter yield
与真空过滤器不同，它对某些污泥无法选择处理，造成零过滤。

UNIT NINE

Text   Pumps and Pumping Stations

[1]   Pumps and pumping machinery serve the following purposes in water systems: (1) lifting water from its source (surface or ground), either immediately to the community through high-lift installations, or by low lift to purification works; (2) boosting water from low-service to high-service areas, to separate fire supplies, and to the upper floors of many-storied buildings; and (3) transporting water through treatment works, backwashing filters, draining component settling tanks, and other treatment units, withdrawing deposited solids and supplying water (especially pressure water) to operating equipment.①

[2]   Today most water and wastewater pumping is done by either centrifugal pumps or propeller pumps. How the water is directed through the impeller determines the type of pump. There is (1) *radial flow* in open-or closed-*impeller pumps*, with volute or turbine casings, and single or double suction through the eye of the impeller, (2) *axial flow* in *propeller pumps*, and (3) *diagonal flow* in *mixed-flow*, *open-impeller pumps*. Propeller pumps are not centrifugal pumps. Both can be referred to as *rotodynamic* pumps.

[3]   Open-impeller pumps are less efficient than closed-impeller pumps, but they can pass relatively large debris without being clogged. Accordingly, they are useful in pumping wastewaters and sludges. *Single-stage pumps* have but *one impeller*, and *multistage pumps* have *two or more*, each feeding into the next higher stage. ②Multistage turbine well pumps may have their motors submerged, or they may be driven by a shaft from the prime mover situated on the floor of the pumping station.

[4]   In addition to centrifugal and propeller pumps, water and wastewater systems may include (1) displacement pumps, ranging in size from hand-operated pitcher pumps to the huge pumping engines of the last century built as steam-driven units; (2) rotary pumps equipped with two or more rotors (varying in shape from meshing lobes to gears and often used as small fire pumps); (3) hydraulic rams utilizing the impulse of large masses of low-pressure water to drive much smaller masses of water (one half to one sixth of the driving water) through the delivery pipe to higher elevations, in synchronism with the pressure waves and sequences induced by water hammer; (4) jet pumps or jet ejectors, used in wells and dewatering operations, introducing a high-speed jet of air or water through a nozzle into a constricted section of pipe; (5) air lifts in which air bubbles, released from upward-directed air pipe, lift water from a well or sump through an eductor pipe; and (6) displacement ejectors housed in a pressure vessel in which water (especially wastewater) accumulates and from which it is displaced through an eductor pipe when a float-operated valve is tripped by the rising water and admits compressed air to the vessel.③

[5]   Pumping units are chosen in accordance with *system heads* and *pump characteris-*

tics. The system head is the sum of the static and dynamic heads against the pump. As such, it varies with required flows and with changes in storage and suction levels. When a distribution system lies between pump and distribution reservoir, the system head responds also to fluctuations in demand. Pump characteristics depend on pump size, speed, and design. For a given speed N in revolutions per minute, they are determined by the relationships between the rate of discharge, Q, usually in gallons per minute, and the head H in feet, the efficiency E in percent, and the power input P in horsepower. For purposes of comparison, pumps of given geometrical design are characterized also by their specific speed N_s, the hypothetical speed of a homologous (geometrically similar) pump with an impeller diameter D such that it will discharge 1 gpm against a 1-ft head. ④Because discharge varies as the product of area and velocity, and velocity varies as $H^{1/2}$, Q varies as $D^2 H^{1/2}$. But velocity varies also as $\pi DN/60$. Hence $H^{1/2}$ varies as DN, or N varies as $H^{3/4}Q^{1/2}$.

[6] Generally speaking, pump efficiencies increase with pump size and capacity. Below specific speeds of 1000 units, efficiencies drop off rapidly. Radial-flow pumps perform well between specific speeds of 1000 and 3500 units; mixed-flow pumps in the range of 3500 to 7500 units; and axial-flow pumps after that up to 12,000 units. For a given N, high-capacity, low-head pumps have the highest specific speeds. For double-suction pumps, the specific speed is computed for half the capacity. For multistage pumps, the head is distributed between the stages. This keeps the specific speed high and with it, also, the efficiency.

[7] Specific speed is an important criterion, too, of safety against cavitation, a phenomenon accompanied by vibration, noise, and rapid destruction of pump impellers. Cavitation occurs when enough potential energy is converted to kinetic energy to reduce the absolute pressure at the impeller surface below the vapor pressure of water at the ambient temperature. ⑤Water then vaporizes and forms pockets of vapor that collapse suddenly as they are swept into regions of high pressure. Cavitation occurs when inlet pressures are too low or pump capacity or speed of rotation is increased without a compensating rise in inlet pressure. Lowering a pump in relation to its water source, therefore, reduces cavitation.

New Words and Expressions

fire supply		消防给水
propeller [prə'pelə]	*n.*	螺旋桨
propeller pump		轴流泵,螺旋泵
impeller [im'pelə]	*n.*	叶轮,涡轮
radial * ['reidiəl]	*a.*	径向的
radial flow		辐向流,径向流
volute [və'lju:t]	*n./a.*	螺旋形(的),涡旋形的
casing ['keisiŋ]	*n.*	壳(体),外壳

diagonal *	[daiˈægənl]	a.	对角（线）的
rotodynamic	[ˌrəutədaiˈnæmik]	a.	旋转动力的
debris	[ˈdebriː]	n.	碎片；粗砂，垃圾
shaft *	[ʃɑːft]	n.	（传动，旋转）轴
mover	[ˈmuːvə]	n.	发动机，马达
prime mover			原动机
pitcher	[ˈpitʃə]	n.	水罐
meshing	[ˈmeʃiŋ]	n.	啮［咬］合
lobe	[ləub]	n.	突齿，凸起；瓣［叶形］轮
ram	[ræm]	n.	夯（锤），锤头，锤体
synchronism	[ˈsiŋkrənizm]	n.	同步
induce *	[inˈdjuːs]	vt.	引起，招致，导致
ejector	[iˈdʒektə]	n.	喷射器，喷射泵
dewater	[diːˈwɔːtə]	v.	排［去，脱，抽］水
nozzle *	[ˈnɔzl]	n.	喷管［嘴，头］
constricted	[kənˈstriktid]	a.	狭窄的
sump	[sʌmp]	n.	（集水，污水，排水）坑
eductor	[iˈdʌktə]	n.	喷射器，排放管
trip	[trip]	v.	（使）脱扣［开］；切断，关闭
fluctuation	[ˌflʌktjuˈeiʃən]	n.	波［振，变］动，升降，振幅
specific speed			比速
hypothetical	[ˌhaipəuˈθetikəl]	a.	假定［设，想］的
homologous	[hɔˈmɔləgəs]	a.	相应的，相［类］似的，同调［系，族］的
cavitation	[ˌkæviˈteiʃən]	n.	空蚀［气蚀，空穴］作用
vibration	[vaiˈbreiʃən]	n.	振［摆］动
kinetic *	[kaiˈnetik]	a.	（运）动的，动力（学）的
ambient *	[ˈæmbiənt]	a.	周围的，环境的

Notes

① … (2) boosting water…to high-service areas, to separate fire supplies, and to the upper floors of…

三个 to 引导的介词短语在句中作并列状语，说明 boosting 的终点。

② Single-stage pumps have but one impeller, …, each feeding…stage

句中 but 为副词，意为"仅仅"，修饰 have。each feeding…stage 为分词独立结构，用以补充说明。

③ … (3) hydraulic rams utilizing … to drive …, in synchronism with … water hammer. utilizing…water hammer 为分词短语修饰 rams，其中的不定式短语 to drive…表目的，in synchronism with 引导的介词短语为分词短语的状语。

…(6) displacement ejectors housed…vessel in which water…and from which it is…an eductor pipe when…

housed 引导的分词短语修饰 ejectors，短语中的 vessel 又被 in which… 和 from which…两个定语从句修饰。第二个定语从句中 it 指 water 并含有 when 引导的时间状语从句。

④…pumps of…specific speed Ns, the hypothetical speed…such that…a 1-ft head. the hypothetical speed…a 1-ft head 为同位语，解释 specific speed Ns：其中，such that 作连词用，引导一个结果状语从句。

⑤Cavitation occurs…is converted to kinetic energy to reduce…

converted 后，介词 to 为其所要求。to reduce…为不定式短语，作结果状语。

Exercises

Reading Comprehension

I. Say whether the following statements are true (T) or false (F) according to the text.

1. Both a centrifugal pump and a propeller pump can be called rotodynamic pumps. ( )

2. Open-impeller pumps are not so good as closed impeller pumps. ( )

3. Water and wastewater systems include displacement pumps, rotary pumps, hydraulic rams, etc., but not centrifugal pumps or propeller pumps. ( )

4. The pumping system head varies with flows in demand and changes in storage and suction levels. ( )

5. Pump characteristics vary with pump size, speed, and design. ( )

II. Choose the best answer for each of the following.

1. When used in the well or dewatering operations, _____.

    A. a jet pump makes a high-speed jet of air or water through a nozzle which is inserted into a narrowed part of a pipe

    B. a jet pump makes a high-speed jet of air or water pass through a nozzle and into a narrowed part of a pipe

    C. a jet pump forces a high-speed jet of air or water through a nozzle and out of a pipe

    D. a jet pump can only introduce the water through a nozzle into a pipe

2. For a pump with a given speed N in revolutions per minute, its characteristics are determined _____.

    A. by the relationship between the rate of discharge Q and the head H, and the relationship between the efficiency E and the power input P

    B. by the three relationships between the rate of discharge Q and the head H, Q and the efficiency E, and Q and the power input P

    C. by the relationship between the rate of discharge Q, the head H and the efficiency

E, the power input P

   D. by the two relationships between the rate of discharge Q, the head H and the efficiency E, and the power input P

3. The word "against" in "…it will discharge 1 gpm against a 1-ft head." (Para. 5) means _____ .

   A. in an opposite direction B. having as a background
   C. touching for support D. in opposition to

4. Generally speaking, pump efficiency increases with _____ .

   A. specific speed B. pump size
   C. pump size and capacity D. pump speed

5. Cavitation can be reduced by _____ .

   A. lowering a pump in relation to its water source
   B. converting enough potential energy to kinetic energy
   C. sweeping pockets of vapour into regions of high pressure
   D. reducing the absolute pressure at the impeller surface

Vocabulary

I. Fill in the blanks with the words or expressions given below, changing the form where necessary.

   | dewater | radial | impeller |
   | fire supply | specific speed | |

1. Mixed-flow pumps are those in which the flow through the impeller is partly axial and partly _____ .
2. Pumps are conveniently compared by reference to their _____ .
3. Centrifugal pumps, preferably the open _____ types, are commonly used.
4. Aerobically digested sludges are more difficult to _____ than anaerobic sludges.
5. Large industrial establishments are generally equipped with high-pressure _____ and distribution networks of their own.

II. Match the words in Column A with their corresponding definitions or descriptions in Column B.

   Column A   Column B
   1. propeller   a. to bring about, cause to produce
   2. induce   b. of or about movement
   3. displace   c. to force out of the usual place
   4. kinetic   d. to provide (sb. or sth.) with a balancing effect for someloss or sth. lacking
   5. compensate   e. revolving shaft with blades for driving a ship or aircraft

Translation 被动语态（Ⅱ）

本单元翻译练习是将英语被动句译成汉语主动句，或汉语无主句，或将英语被动句中的"by"等词引出的动作发出者译成汉语句的主语。

例 1. The storage reservoir <u>was completed</u> three weeks ahead.
   这个蓄水库比原计划提前三周<u>竣工</u>。
例 2. <u>It has been found</u> that an active group of mathane formers operates 35℃ in common practice, and this process has become known as mesophilic digestion.
   <u>已经发现</u>，一组活性产甲烷菌一般情况下可使温度达到35℃。这个过程叫做中温消化。
例 3. Solids may <u>be separated</u> from liquids <u>by filtration</u>.
   用过滤法可将固体与液体分离开来。

Translate the following sentences into Chinese, paying attention to the underlined words.

1. Little water <u>is found</u> at depths greater than 600m.
2. The primary digester <u>is covered</u>, heated and mixed to increase the reaction rate.
3. It <u>has been found</u> <u>by experience</u> that, if sufficient chlorine <u>is added</u> to a water to give an excess of free chlorine over and above that <u>absorbed</u> <u>by organic and vegetable matter</u> in the water, tastes and odors <u>are reduced</u>.
4. It <u>is suggested</u> that a pumping station <u>should be built</u> between the water source and the city.
5. In America, though air scour is but little used, it <u>has been found</u> necessary <u>in some plants</u> to add to the effectiveness of water backwashing by directing water jets on to the surface of the sand bed so as to agitate and clean those layers which are usually the dirtest.

Reading Material A

Choice of Pumps

Among the many varieties of pumps manufactured, those used for sewage are centrifugal, mixed-flow and axial-flow. For smaller flows, the compressed air ejector is very suitable, and for certain more specialized duties (particularly at sewage treatment works) use is made of reciprocating pumps, air lifts, and the more recently developed screw-type pumps.

Centrifugal pumps (radial flow pumps), are generally suitable for outputs of up to 1000 m^3/h for heads up to about 40m. They are not self-priming, and as foot valves are only suitable for relatively clean liquids, if these pumps are to operate automatically they must be installed below the level of the sewage to be pumped. This normally entails the construction below ground of a 'dry well' to house the pumps, adjacent to the 'wet well' containing the sewage. ①Some submersible pumps are, however, available for use in the wet well itself, but in general pumps installed in a separate dry well are easier to maintain.

It is usually convenient to choose vertical spindle pumps and to install the motors at a higher level. In this way all electrical equipment can be kept above flood level. Pumps with built-in priming devices are available in the smaller ranges for automatic-operation, thereby allowing the use of horizontal spindle pumps installed at ground level, but their use is limited. ②Fully submersible pumps are also available, where both pump and motor operate in the wet well.

Axial-flow pumps are more useful for lifting large quantities through a limited head (capacities over about 2500 m^3/h at heads of 6.0 to 18.0 m). They are unsuitable for use with liquids containing solids, and they therefore find more favour for pumping surface water and for recirculation of final effluent rather than for foul sewage duties. ③Axial-flow type pumps are used extensively for fen drainage work. They are of comparatively simple construction, and generally operate at higher speeds than centrifugal pumps.

Mixed-flow pumps are those in which the flow through the impeller is partly axial and partly radial. They are useful for storm sewage duties and are generally available for outputs up to 1400 or 1500 m^3/h, and for heads up to approximately 15m.

Ejectors are normally self-contained, with their own automatically controlled compressors and 'air bottle'. Maintenance is fairly straightforward and, being very reliable, they are suitable for isolated houses or small groups of houses, and for low-level installations, such as basements and public conveniences.

The choice between a centrifugal, a mixed-flow, or an axial-flow pump is basically a matter of comparison of speed, output and head conditions. With the three types, the flow increases as the head decreases. The decrease in head is more rapid with axial-flow pumps than with centrifugal or mixed-flow pumps.

Pumps are conveniently compared by reference to their 'specific speeds'. Specific speed can be defined as that speed, in revolutions per minute, at which an impeller generally similar to the one under consideration, and reduced in size, will develop unit head at unit output. ④Although the specific speed is essentially a matter for the pump manufacturer, it is useful for the design engineer to have a general understanding of the subject, as it will give him an indication of the type of pump which will be required for a particular duty.

Notes

①通常要求将水泵间建在'干井'基础以下，靠近容纳污水的'吸水井'。

②Pumps with built-in priming devices are available in the smaller ranges for automatic-operation 内部带有启动装置的水泵适用于较小范围以利于自动启动。

③they therefore find more favour for pumping surface water and for recirculation of final effluent rather than for foul sewage duties 这些泵更适用于抽吸地表水和最终出水的再循环，而不适用于抽排污浊的废水。

④比转速可定义为一种速度（即每分钟的转数），在此转速下，通常一个尺寸缩小、与设计叶轮相似的叶轮会以单位输水量提高单位水头。

Reading Material B

Pump Station Buildings

A pumping station will generally consist of two parts, the substructure and the superstructure. While the substructure is basically a matter for engineering design, the superstructure should preferably be designed by an architect. If the substructure is divided into wet and dry wells, it is usual for the dry well to be directly under the superstructure and to have access from inside the building. Access to the wet well should be from the open air.

The substructure will normally be constructed of either mass or reinforced concrete. As with the design of manholes, it is usually necessary to check that the structure will not float when empty. ①If this is possible this may entail thickening up the floor slab or walls, or extending the floor slab beyond the walls to utilize the weight of the surrounding earth.

The wet well should preferably be divided into two compartments either of which can be isolated from the incoming flow for cleaning. The incoming sewer should then discharge through an inlet chamber to either or both compartments. The floor of the wet well should slope at 1 in 1, or steeper, to a sump at the pump suctions. Many engineers prefer a slope of about 1.75 vertical to 1 horizontal, but on the other hand these steeper slopes are inconvenient for maintenance. It may be preferable to construct a long, deep channel at the suction pipes, with a benching sloping at about 1 in 6; if this form of construction is used the lowest pump cut-off level should then be in the channel itself (i.e. below the level of the benching).

The suctions should preferably be not more than $2D$ apart (where D is the diameter of the suction) and, to avoid the deposition of solids between the suctions when turned down, the distance of the suction above the floor should be between $D/2$ and $D/3$. ②

The superstructure will normally be of brickwork, with either a pitched tiled roof or a flat roof. The roof must be high enough to accommodate any lifting beam together with the lifting tackle. Sufficient space must be allowed for the vertical lift required; this may be quite considerable with extended spindle pumps. For very small stations, factory-made 'cubicles' are available, while for some installations no superstructure is required beyond perhaps a small cabinet to house the electrical switchgear.

Unfortunately, it is usually necessary to take precautions against vandalism at isolated buildings. Windows can be set high in the walls, while doors and locks should be more solid than required for normal industrial or domestic usage.

Fencing should always be provided around a pumping station to protect the equipment. Except at very small stations, a pair of double gates and an access road (minimum, 3.5m wide) should be provided to facilitate the installation and maintenance of the machinery. The site within the fence should be landscaped as necessary to blend with the surrounding area. This should generally be as simple as possible to reduce maintenance costs.

Washing and toilet facilities should be provided at all stations which are to be regularly attended. A small electrically operated water heater should be included. Drainage of these facilities can, of course, be taken to the wet well in a foul sewage pumping station. Roof and access road drainage can often also be taken to the wet well, or it may be preferable to discharge this to a neighbouring ditch or stream. The provision of a tap and hosepipe will ensure that the well can be hosed down regularly; this will not only improve working conditions in the well, but will also remove accumulations of solids which might cause septicity and subsequent odours.

Heating is necessary in the motor room to prevent condensation in electrical motors and switchgear. This may take the form of special anti-condensation heaters in the equipment itself, but in addition it is usual to provide wall heaters, as these will prevent the freezing of the plumbing in cold weather and also maintain a comfortable temperature for any attendants. These heaters should be thermostatically controlled.

Notes

①同设计检查井一样，验证一下该结构放空时不致浮动通常是很有必要的。
②to avoid the deposition of solids between the suctions when turned down, the distance of the suction above the floor should be between $D/2$ and $D/3$ 吸水管下调时，为避免固体物质沉降于各吸水管之间，吸水管距槽底的距离应在 $D/2$ 和 $D/3$ 之间。

UNIT TEN

Text   Classification of Water Pollutants

[1]   To understand the effects of water pollution and the technology applied in its control, it is useful to classify pollutants into various groups or categories. First, a pollutant can be classified according to the nature of its origin as either a point source or a dispersed source pollutant.

[2]   A point source pollutant is one that reaches the water from a pipe, channel, or any other confined and localized source.① The most common example of a point source of pollutants is a pipe that discharges sewage into a stream or river. Most of these discharges are treatment plant effluents, that is, treated sewage from a water pollution control facility; they still contain pollutants to some degree. But in a few isolated instances, untreated or raw sewage is discharged.

[3]   A dispersed or nonpoint source is a broad, unconfined area from which pollutants enter a body of water. Surface runoff from agricultural areas, for example, carries silt, fertilizers, pesticides, and animal wastes into streams, but not at one particular point. These materials can enter the water all along a stream as it flows through the area. Acidic runoff from mining areas is a dispersed pollutant. Stormwater drainage systems in towns and cities are also considered to be dispersed sources of many pollutants. Even though they are often conveyed into streams or lakes in drainage pipes or storm sewers, there are usually many of these discharges scattered over a large area.②

[4]   Point source pollutants are easier to deal with than are dispersed source pollutants;③ those from a point source have been collected and conveyed to a single point where they can be removed from the water in a treatment plant.④ The point discharges from treatment plants can easily be monitored by regulatory agencies.

[5]   Pollutants from dispersed sources are much more difficult to control. Many people think that sewage is the primary culprit in water pollution problems, but dispersed sources cause a significant fraction of the water pollution in the United States. Perhaps the most effective way to control the dispersed sources is to set appropriate restrictions in land use.⑤

[6]   In addition to being classified by their origin, water pollutants can be classified into groups of substances, based primarily on their environmental or health effects. For example, the following list identifies nine specific types of pollutants:

  1. Pathogenic organisms
  2. Oxygen-demanding substances
  3. Plant nutrients
  4. Toxic organics

    5. Inorganic chemicals
    6. Sediment
    7. Radioactive substances
    8. Heat
    9. Oil

[7]　　Domestic sewage is the primary source of the first three types of pollutants. Pathogens, or disease-causing microorganisms, are excreted in the feces of infected persons and may be carried into waters receiving sewage discharges. Sewage from communities with large populations is very likely to contain pathogens of some type.

[8]　　Sewage also carries oxygen-demanding substances——the organic wastes that exert a biochemical oxygen demand as they are decomposed by microbes. This is BOD. BOD changes the ecological balance in a body of water by depleting the dissolved oxygen content. Nitrogen and phosphorus, the major plant nutrients, are in sewage too, as well as in runoff from farms and suburban lawns.

[9]　　Conventional sewage treatment processes significantly reduce the amount of pathogens and BOD in sewage, but do not eliminate them completely. Certain viruses, in particular, may be somewhat resistant to the sewage disinfection process. (A virus is an extremely small pathogenic organism that can only be seen with an electron microscope.) In order to decrease the amounts of nitrogen and phosphorus in sewage, usually some form of advanced sewage treatment must be applied.

[10]　　Toxic organic chemicals, primarily pesticides, may be carried into water in the surface runoff from agricultural areas. Perhaps the most dangerous type is the family of chemicals called chlorinated hydrocarbons such as chlordane, dieldrin, heptachlor, and the infamous DDT. They are very effective poisons against insects that damage agricultural crops. But unfortunately they can also kill fish, birds, and mammals, including humans. And they are not very biodegradable, taking more than 30 years in some cases to dissipate from the environment.

[11]　　Toxic organic chemicals, of course, can also get into water directly from industrial activity. This would be from improper handling of chemicals in the industrial plant, or, as has been more common, from improper and illegal disposal of chemical wastes.⑥ Proper management of toxic and other hazardous wastes is one of the key environmental issues of the 1980s, particularly with respect to the protection of groundwater quality. Poisonous inorganic chemicals, specifically the "heavy metal" group such as lead and mercury, also usually originate from industrial activity and are considered hazardous wastes.

[12]　　Oil is washed into surface waters in runoff from roads and parking lots. Accidental oil spills from large transport tankers at sea occasionally occur, causing significant environmental damage. And blowout accidents at offshore oil wells can release many thousands of tons of oil in a short period of time. Oil spills at sea may eventually move toward shore, affecting aquatic life and damaging recreation areas.

New Words and Expressions

disperse * [disˈpəːs]	vi.	分散
facility [fəˈsiliti]	n.	工厂
runoff [ˈrʌnɔf]	n.	径流
acidic [əˈsidik]	a.	酸性的
convey [kənˈvei]	vt.	传送；排放
monitor [ˈmɔnitə]	vt.	监测；管理
regulatory * [ˈregjuleitəri]	a.	管理的
culprit [ˈkʌlprit]	n.	罪魁祸首
identify [aiˈdentifai]	n.	确定
pathogenic organism		病原有机体
sediment [ˈsedimənt]	n.	沉积
excrete [ekˈskriːt]	vt.	排泄
feces [ˈfiːsiːz]	n.	（复数）粪便
deplete * [diːˈpliːt]	vt.	耗尽
chlorinated hydrocarbon		氯化烃
chlordane [klɔːdein]	n.	氯丹
dieldrin [diːldrin]	n.	狄氏剂（一种杀虫剂）
heptachlor [ˈheptəklɔː]	n.	七氯（一种杀虫剂）
biodegradable [baiəudiˈgreidəbl]	a.	能进行生物降解的
dissipate * [ˈdisipeit]	vt.	清除
with respect to		关于；就……而论
exert [ikˈzəːt]	vt.	施加；产生
spill [spil]	n./vt.	泄油
blowout [ˈbləuaut]	n.	油田喷井
recreation area		游览胜地

Notes

①句中的"one"是代词，代替前的不定冠词加名词，即"a pollutant"。
②there are many … scattered …这是一个"there be"结构，句中的分词短语 scattered 为定语，修饰前面的 discharges，相当于 which are scat-tered …。
③than 后是一个省略倒装句。完整的、正常的句子应为 than dispersed source pollutants are easy to deal with。
④句中的 those 指 pollutants；where 引出的从句为定语从句，修饰前面表示地点的名词

"point"。

⑤不定式短语 "to control the dispersed sources" 作定语，修饰 "way"。

⑥This would be from improper handling of the chemicals in the industrial plant, or, as has been more common, from …. 本句中的 this 指代前面的句子。This would be from … 意为 This would be the result from。would be 为虚拟语气，表示不肯定性。as has been more common 中的 as 为代词，意为 "这一情况"。本句起补充说明作用。

Exercises

Reading Comprehension

I. Say whether the following statements are True (T) or False (F) according to the text.

1. A dispersed source is a narrow, confined area from which pollutants enter a body of water. ( )
2. As stormwater often flow into streams or lakes in drainage pipes or storm-sewers, it is considered to be a point source pollutant. ( )
3. Pollutants from dispersed sources are much more difficult to deal with than are point source pollutants. ( )
4. According to the text, the most effective way to control nonpoint source pollutants is to set appropriate restrictions in land use. ( )
5. By oxygen-demanding substances we mean the organic wastes that exert a biochemical oxygen demand as they are decomposed by microbes. ( )
6. Nitrogen and phosphorus, which exist only in sewage, are the two major plant nutrients. ( )
7. Traditional sewage treatment processes greatly decrease the amount of pathogen and BOD in sewage, but do not remove them completely. ( )
8. Toxic organic chemicals such as chlordane, dieldrin, heptachlor, and the DDT are not only effective to kill the insects that damage agricultural crops, but also apt to dissipate from the environment. ( )
9. Toxic organic chemicals are primarily pesticides while poisonous inorganic ones are especially the "heavy metal" groups such as lead and mercury. ( )
10. Oil spills at sea and blowout accidents of oil wells will cause significant environmental damage. ( )

II. Supply the missing words or expressions for the following sentences from the text.

1. According to the nature of its origin, a pollutant can be classified as either _____ or _____ pollutant.
2. Based primarily on their environmental or health effects, water pollutants can be classified into nine groups. They are _____, _____, _____, _____, _____, _____, _____, _____ and _____.

3. Domestic _____ is the primary source of the following pollutants——pathogenic organisms, oxygen-demanding substances and plant nutrients.
4. The most dangerous type of organic chemicals is the family of chemicals called _____ _____.

Vocabulary

I. Fill in the blanks with words given below, changing the form where necessary.

> culprit　deplete　dissipate　identify
> regulatory

1. It will take many years to _____ pesticides from the environment.
2. EPA is a _____ establishment which monitors environmental conditions.
3. By _____ the dissolved oxygen content, ecological balance in a body of water can be changed.
4. Sewage from factories is considered to be the _____ of water pollution.
5. Many types of pollutants have now been _____.

II. Match the words in Column A with their definitions or descriptions in Column B.

Column A	Column B
1. disperse	a. check or regulate the volume or quality of sth in recording
2. monitor	b. separate waste matter from the blood or tissue and eliminate from the body
3. sediment	c. cause to spread widely or scatter in different directions
4. acidic	d. of the nature of or having the properties of an acid
5. excrete	e. solid material that settles to the bottom of a liquid

Translation　　　　　　　　　倍数的翻译

（一）增加量的翻译

倍数增加量的翻译，因其英语表达方式不同，译时要加以适当区别。由于数字规律性较强，译文也较规律。英语倍数增加量的表达主要有以下三种：

倍数+as…as… 可译为"是（为）…的几倍"或"比…大几倍"。译成"是…的几倍"时，只要把原倍数照搬；如译成"比…大几倍"时，应把倍数减去一；数字+倍数+其他成分，译成"为…的几倍"，或"几倍于…"；带有增大意思的动词+by+倍数，译成"增加了…"，by后的倍数照搬。

例1. Since the sun is 400 times as large and as far as the moon, to us they look the same size.

由于太阳大小和距我们的距离都是月亮的大小与距我们的距离的 400 倍,看上去它们是一般大的。

例 2. This substance reacts three times as fast as that one.

这种物质的反应速度比那种物质快两倍。

例 3. The bandwidth between transmitter and receiver is at least twice that with digital carrier modulation.

发射机和接收机之间的带宽至少两倍于数字载波调制的带宽。

例 4. The output has increased by two times.

产量已增加了两倍。

Translate the following sentences into Chinese, paying attention to the underlined words.

1) On average we speak 150 words per minute <u>twice as fast as</u> most typists type.
2) Since the 1960's the speed of operation of the computer <u>has increased by about one million times</u>.
3) The population of Shanghai is <u>ten times that of Wuxi</u>.
4) The discharges from that factory is <u>5 times as many as that from this factory</u>.
5) The production of machine tools <u>has been increased by six times</u>.

Reading Material A

Regulations Concerning Water Pollution

At the core of the "Clean Water Act" of 1977 is the Refuse Act Permit Program.① It required some 40,000 industrial plants which discharged wastes into navigable waterways to specify the type and quantity of their effluents.② In order to continue this waste water discharge, they had to apply for and obtain a waste discharge permit from the U.S. Army Corps of Engineers.③ All new industries must similarly obtain this permit. In evaluating the applications, the Corps of Engineers supposedly analyzes the impact of the proposed activity on the public interest, including water quality. A permit will be issued only when the benefits outweigh the foreseeable detriments.

As a result of this law, guidelines have been set for many industries, listing the permissible amounts of various effluents. These guidelines are useful in considering the advisability of various discharge permit requests. Some of the industries for which guidelines are set include cement, lime, flat, glass, gypsum, asbestos, leather tanning, beverages, grain milling, pulp and paper, canned and preserved fruits and vegetables, aluminum refining, and meat products. Various substances are restricted, depending upon the industry.

In addition, the Water Pollution Control Act allows individuals or organizations to sue the EPA, if they feel the EPA is not doing its duty in pollution enforcement.

The Clean Water Act of 1977 became effective on December 27, 1977 and extended many of the provisions of the Water Pollution Control Act. The municipal waste water treatment construction grant program, previously in effect, has been continued, but emphasis is now being put on alternate waste water technology—recycling of waste water and sludge, land treatment, and methods to decrease waste water volumes. ④

In June of 1978, there was a court settlement between the EPA and several environmental groups. ⑤ These groups brought suit against the EPA for failing to implement portions of the Water Pollution Control Act. The settlement includes the provision that the EPA publish a list of toxic pollutants for which emission guidelines and limitations be set.

The settlement requires, additionally, new performance and pretreatment standards for 21 industrial categories. The 21 industrial categories include timber products, steam electric power plants, leather tanning and finishing, iron and steel production, petroleum refining, organic and inorganic chemicals manufacture, nonferrous metal production, paint and ink production, pulp and paperboard mills, foundries, electroplating, ore and coal mining.

The settlement did omit a listing of minimum detection levels. In addition, standard methods for collecting and preserving organic samples are not available, nor are standard methods for analyzing organics in complex waste waters. These must be developed.

Certain priorities were required when attempting to determine effluent limits and test methods. Classed as "priority" pollutants were 129 chemicals, including all the toxic substances plus many of the common pollutants. ⑥ These priority pollutants can be divided into nine groups: metals asbestos, total cyanide, pesticides, total phenols, purgeable compounds, compounds extracted under acidic conditions, and neutral extractable compounds. Methods for the monitoring and testing of each of these categories are now being developed.

In addition, a third category of "nonconventional pollutants" has been added to the two previous categories (the toxic and the conventional pollutans). This category of nonconventional pollutants includes nontoxic, thermal, or chemical pollution. The control deadline for this third category is July 1, 1987, unless the industry gets a waiver by being able to prove its discharges pose no danger to fish or to water quality. ⑦

Notes

①Clean Water Act 未污染水法案　Refuse Act Permit Program 废物排放许可法
②该计划要求大约四万家把废物排入水路航道中的工厂,精确测定其排放物的类型和数量。
③the U.S. Army Corps of Engineers　美国陆军工程队。
④… but emphasis is now being put on alternate waste water technology——recycling of waste water and sludge, ….　破折号以后的部分,是 alternate waste water technology 的同位语,起补充说明的作用。
⑤a court settlement 意为经法院达成的和解。

⑥Classified as "priority" pollutants were 129 chemicals, including … 为了上下文衔接更紧，本句使用了倒装语序，正常语序应为 129 chemicals were classified as "priority" pollutants, including …。

⑦… unless the industry get a waiver by … 句中 waiver 原意是"弃权声明书"，在本文中意为"排放许可证"。

Reading Material B

Sources of Water Pollution

The United States has more than 40,000 factories that use water, and their industrial wastes are probably the greatest single water pollution problem.

Organic wastes from industrial plants, at present-day treatment levels are equal in polluting potential to the untreated raw sewage of the entire population of the United States.① In most cases the organic wastes are at least treatable, in or out of the plant. Inorganic industrial wastes are much trickier to control, and potentially more hazardous. Chromium from metal-plating plants is an old source of trouble, but mercury discharges have only recently received their due attention.

As important as these and other well-known "heavy metal" might be, many scientists are much more concerned with the unknown chemicals.② Industry is creating a fantastic array of new chemicals each year, all of which eventually find their way to the water. For most of these, not even the chemical formulas are known, much less their acute, chronic genetic toxicity.③

Another industrial waste is heat. Heated discharges can drastically alter the ecology of a stream or lake. This alteration is sometimes called beneficial, perhaps because of better fishing or an ice-free docking area. The deleterious effects of heat, in addition to promoting modifications of ecological systems, include a lessening of dissolved oxygen solubility and increases in metabolic activity. Dissolved oxygen is vital to healthy aquatic communities, and the warmer the water, the more difficult it is to get oxygen into solution. Simultaneously, the metabolic activity of aerobic (oxygen-using) aquatic species increases, thus demanding more oxygen. It is a small wonder, therefore, that the vast majority of fish kills due to oxygen depletion occur in the summer.④

Municipal waste is a source of water pollution second in importance only to industrial wastes. Around the turn of the century, most discharges from municipalities received no treatment whatsoever. In the United States, sewage from 24 million people was flowing directly into our watercourses. Since that time, the population has increased, and so has the contribution from municipal discharges. It is estimated that presently the population equivalent of municipal discharges to watercourses is about 100 million.⑤ Even with the billions of dollars spent on building wastewater treatment plants, the contribution from municipal pollution sources has not been significantly reduced.

One problem, especially in older cities on the east coast of the United States, is the sewerage systems. When the cities were first built, the engineers realized that sewers were necessary for both stormwater and sanitary wastes, and they saw no reason why both stormwater and sanitary wastes should not flow in same pipelines. After all, they both ended up in the same river or lake. Such sewers are now known as combined sewers.

As years passed and populations increased, the need for treatment of sanitary wastes became obvious, and two-sewer systems were built, one to carry stormwater and the other, sanitary waste. Such systems are known as separate sewers.

Almost all of the cities with combined sewers have built treatment plants which can treat the dry weather flow, or in other words, sanitary wastes. As long as it doesn't rain, they can provide sufficient treatment. When the rains come, however, the flows swell to many times the dry weather flow and most of it must be bypassed directly into a river or lake. This overflow contains sewage as well as stormwater, and has a high polluting capacity. All attempts to capture this excess flow for subsequent treatment, such as storage in underground caverns and rubber balloons, are expensive. However, the alternative solution, separating the sewers, is estimated at a staggering $60 billion for the major cities in the United States.

In addition to industrial and municipal wastes, water pollution emanates from many other sources, such as agricultural wastes, sediment from land erosion, pollution from petroleum compounds, etc.

Notes

①就目前的处理水平而言，工厂的有机废物，与美国全体居民所排放出的未经处理的污水相比，在污染潜力方面是不相上下的。

②As important as these and other well-known "heavy metal" might be, …
本句相当于 Even though these and other well-known "heavy metal" might be important …

③… not even the chemical formulas are known, much less their acute, chronic or genetic toxicity. not even 放在句首，以加强语气，是为了和后面的 much less 相呼应，意为"甚至连…都不…，就更不用说…"。

④因此，夏天因氧的耗尽而导致鱼的大量死亡就不足为奇了。

⑤population equivalent 人口等效规模。

UNIT ELEVEN

Text   **Potential Impact of Air Contaminants on Water Quality**

[1]   Both natural and anthropogenic sources of contaminants contribute to water pollution. The major man-made sources are well known, and although the contributions of natural sources are recognized, the extent of their contributions is not accurately known. The potential contributions of air contaminants to water quality have received only cursory attention, and a controversy over the extent and magnitude of it still exists.

[2]   Apart from an intrinsic interest in environmental chemical cycles, the recent need for a methodology to assess the atmospheric contribution to water pollution is prompted by the need to develop regional water quality management plans.① Other types of planning and engineering also require that the various sources of water pollution be identified and quantified.②

[3]   Several investigators have concluded that the effect of atmospheric contributions to water quality is small. However, a number of studies support the thesis that atmospheric contributions have a significant impact on water quality.③ They show that in some instances, atmospheric contributions of certain substances to a body of water can be larger than the stream contributions of these substances.④

[4]   The general linkages between air and water environments can be thought of in the following terms. First, the impact of atmospheric contaminants on water quality can be divided into several components. The major components are the flux, or rate of deposition, of a contaminant on a land surface, the fraction of the deposited material that ends up in stream of a body of water, and the rate at which the deposited material reaches the body of water. Thus, the atmosphere is a potentially large source of water pollutants, but its impact on water quality depends on the fraction and rate of deposition of the material that reaches the water. An estimate of these various components is needed to provide an overall evaluation of the relative importance of each air contaminant to the deterioration of water quality. In addition, one must also consider all the significant reactions and interactions of a specific air contaminant in and with the air, land and water environments.⑤

[5]   An air contaminant can be transferred directly or indirectly onto the surface of a body of water. In direct air-water transfer, exchanges at the air-water interface for gases, liquids, and solids are possible during both dry and wet weather periods. They are referred to as dry or wet deposition. Dry deposition includes the fallout of atmospheric particulates owing to gravity and the turbulent deposition of both particulates and gases during dry weather periods.⑥ Wet deposition includes rainout, washout, snowout, and sweepout. Rainout and snowout refer to processes occurring within clouds, which respectively

condense. Washout and sweepout refer to the removal of material below the cloud level by falling rain or ice, respectively. (In the case of an ice cover over a body of water, the various exchanges are still possible, but the cover acts as a reservoir and a time delay is introduced in the contribution).

[6] The indirect transfer of contaminants from air to water is modified by the transport, transformation, and storage of contaminant on land. Storage can introduce a substantial time delay between the time when a contaminant reaches the land and the time when the contaminant shows up in the water.⑦ For example, contamination of groundwater takes up to 20 years to manifest itself, if there is not a direct connection between the runoff waters and the groundwater aquifer. The presence of snow can also introduce a time delay. In this case the contributions of precipitation to stream flow are delayed as well.

[7] Transformations (biological, chemical, and physical) are ever present in the air, water, and land environments. When, for example, hydrogen sulfide is introduced into the air, it generally ends up in the water environment in the form of sulfates. Once in the water, the sulfate ions can be converted back to hydrogen sulfide under anaerobic conditions and be released to the atmosphere. Ammonia in the air can reach the water as NH_4 or as the nitrite or nitrate ions. In the water the nitrogen species are incorporated into the fauna and flora and eventually released to the atmosphere in the forms of ammonia or nitrogen gas.

[8] The storage of air contaminants deposited on land provides ample opportunities for the contaminants to be transformed into other chemical form prior to their reaching waterways. Materials deposited on different vegetative surfaces or solids can also undergo chemical transformations, and the rates of deposition differ depending on the type of surface. In many instances the transformations and their rates are important to the amelioration or aggravation of water quality problems.

New Words and Expressions

impact [impækt]		n.	影响
anthropogenic [ˌænθrəupəu'dʒenik]		a.	由人类活动引起的
cursory ['kəːsəri]		a.	粗略的
intrinsic * ['intrinsik]		a.	内在的
controversy ['kɔntrəvəːsi]		n.	争论
methodology * [ˌmeθə'dɔlədʒi]		n.	方法（学）
quantify * ['kwɔntifai]		vt.	定量测定
flux * [flʌks]		n.	通量
deposition * [ˌdipə'ziʃən]		n.	沉积
respectively [ris'pektivl]		adv.	分别地；依次地
condense [kən'dens]		v.	浓缩

modify ['mɔdifai]	vt.	缓和
aquifer ['ækwifə]	n.	含水层
precipitation [pri,sipi'teiʃən]	n.	沉降
sulfate * ['sʌlfeit]	n.	硫酸盐
incorporate * [in'kɔːpəreit]	vt.	结合
nitrite ['naitrait]	n.	亚硝酸盐
nitrate ['naitreit]	n.	硝酸盐
vegetative ['vedʒitətiv]	a.	植物的
amelioration [ə,miːljə'reiʃən]	n.	改善，改良
aggravation [,ægrə'veiʃən]	n.	恶化
fauna ['fɔːnə]	n.	动物

Notes

① …, the recent need for … to assess … is prompted by the need …. 这是一个长句，句中第一个 need 为主语，for 引出的介词短语为定语修饰这个 need；不定式短语 to assess 可作 methodology 的定语。第二个 need 为 by 的宾语。句子的谓语部分是 is prompted。

② require that … be identify …. require 后的从句中用了虚拟语气，其构成为 should＋V. 或直接用 V。

③ …thesis that atmospheric contributions have a …. "that" 引出的是一个同位语从句。

④ …can be larger than the stream contributions of these substances. 句中 "of these substances" 后省略与前半句相同的成份，即 to a body of water。

⑤ … air contaminant in and with air, land and water environment. 介词 "in" 和 with 后分别接 air, land and water environment，即 in land, air and water environment 及 with air land and environment。

⑥ Dry deposition includes the fallout … and the turbulent deposition …. the fallout 和 the turbulent deposition 都是 includes 的宾语。

⑦ 句中两个 "when" 引导的从句均为定语从句，分别修饰两个表示时间的名词 "time"。

Exercises

Reading Comprehension

Ⅰ. Say whether the following statements are True (T) or False (F) according to the text.

1. Water pollution results both from natural and anthropogenic sources of contaminants. ( )

2. People have recognized not only the contributions of natural sources to water pollution, but also the extent of their contributions. ( )

3. Some researchers have come to a conclusion that atmospheric contributions have much effect on water quality. ( )
4. The impact of atmospheric contaminants on water quality depends on the fraction and rate of the deposited material that reaches the body of water. ( )
5. Direct air-water transfer refers to exchanges at the air-water interface for gases, liquids, and solids during both dry and wet weather periods. ( )
6. Provided that there is no direct connection between the runoff waters and the groundwater aquifer, it can take up to 20 years for contaminants to show up in the groundwater. ( )
7. Nitrogen in the air can reach the water as NH_4 or as the nitrite or nitrate ions. ( )
8. In the water the nitrogen species are included in the fauna and flora and finally released to the atmosphere only in the form of nitrogen gas. ( )
9. The storage of air contaminants deposited on land introduces a time delay before they end up in the water, thus air contaminants have plenty of opportunities to be transformed into other chemical form. ( )
10. The transformations of contaminants and their rates have a significant impact on water quality. ( )

II. Supply the missing words or expressions for the following sentences from the text.
1. Dry deposition includes the _____ of atmospheric particulates and the turbulent _____ of both particulates and gases.
2. Wet deposition includes _____, _____, _____, _____.
3. An air contaminant can be transferred _____ or _____ onto the surface of a body of water. The indirect transfer is modified by the _____, _____ and _____ of contaminant on land.
4. Transformations are ever present in the _____, _____ and _____ environments.

Vocabulary

I. Fill in the blanks with words given below, changing the form where necessary.

> controversy   cursory   impact   respectively
> intrinsic

1. It is the _____ interest and the need to develop regional water quality management plans that prompt the methodology to assess the atmospheric contribution to water pollution
2. It is still almost impossible to predict the _____ of discharges of certain contaminants.
3. We have only a _____ knowledge of the extent of the contributions of natural sources to the environment.
4. The contaminants condense _____ within the clouds.

5. There is still a _____ about what is the culprit of environmental pollution.

Ⅱ. Match the words in Column A with their definitions or descriptions in Column B.

Column A Column B
1. quantify   a. water bearing stratum of permeable rock, sand or gravel
2. flux   b. determine, express or measure the quantity or amount of sth
3. aquifer   c. showing irregular eddying motion of particles in a fluid
4. turbulent   d. depositing
5. deposition   e. rate of flow of fluid, heat or force across a certain surface area

Translation　　　　　　　　　倍数的翻译

（二）减少量的翻译

英语中表示倍数的减少和增加类似，也有许多不同的方式，主要有下列二种译法：

成几倍地减少，即减少前的数量为减少后的数量的几倍，译时须算成分数，译成"减少到1/倍数"，或"减少了多少倍"这时句中常有表示"少、减、缩"等的动词；倍数＋表示少、短、轻等形容词的比较级，表示减少了几倍，即减少前的数量比减少后的数量大几倍。译时须换成分数，译为"减少了倍数/（倍数＋1）"或"为…的1/（倍数＋1）"。

例1　The operating cost decreased three times.
　　　操作费用减少到三分之一（或减少了三分之二）

例2　The equipment under development will reduce the error probability 7 times.
　　　正在研制的设备将使误差概率减小到七分之一。（或减少七分之六）

例3　This rope is 4 times shorter than that one.
　　　这根绳比那根绳短了4/5（是那根绳的1/5）

例4　This kind of film is twice thinner than ordinary paper.
　　　这种薄膜的厚度只有普通纸的三分之一。（或比普通纸薄三分之二）

Translate the following sentences into Chinese, paying attention to the underlined words.

1) Switching time of the new type transistor is shortened 2 times.
2) The total enthalpy(热函) of the gas to be cooled would also be three to four times smaller.
3) The steel output last year was twice less than that of this year.
4) When the signal has increased by 10 times, the gain may have been reduced by 8 times.
5) The mass of an electron is 1850 times lighter than that of a hydrogen atom.

Reading Material A

The Need for Water Quality Studies

Understanding the water quality of natural aqueous systems requires knowledge of the disciplines of chemistry, microbiology, ecology, and engineering, and how they interact. Although the areas of water and wastewater treatment require the application of biological and chemical phenomena, neither of these areas is as heavily dependent on it as is the study of water quality. A great deal of literature has appeared in the past 30 years that shows how natural processes can be applied to treat wastes of various types, and the sophistication of treatment techniques has increased only with an understanding of these natural processes.

The quantification of similar processes in natural systems, however, has remained relatively unexplored. The complexity of most natural systems, for example, streams and lakes, has precluded the rigorous quantification of many common natural processes. In addition, so many parameters affect natural systems that it is difficult to isolate the individual units of the process. Therefore, a scientific engineering approach to problems of water quality is still unrefined. As an example, it is still almost impossible to predict the environmental impact of discharges of certain contaminants into aqueous systems. This is owing in part to the fact that we do not fully understand the natural processes responsible for the movement of the various contaminants. ① It is imperative that the specifics of these processes be understood, for they determine the degree of wastewater treatment required before release. ② Because each level of waste treatment costs increasingly larger amounts of money, a quantification of the resultant environmental damage caused by contaminants is important. Indeed, many environmental contaminants have very low threshold levels and should never be discharged into aqueous systems. ③

Perhaps the most important reason for studying water quality is the increasing worldwide demand for potable water. Many civilizations in the past failed because of a lack of fresh water. Recent evidence indicates that certain parts of the United States will run short of fresh water in the very near future. It is apparent that we should protect water supplies by preventing discharges of materials that can render a supply inusable for drinking even after treatment. ④ Statistics shows the uses and sources of water in the United States from 1955 to 1975. It can be seen that total use increases from approximately 240 billions to 420 billions of gallons per day in just 20 years. This increase in consumption is still continuing, and it is expected to increase at an even faster rate in the future. It should also be noted that most serere environmeneal problem. That is determination of the toxicity of many of the water currently used comes from surface water supplies. Surface water is the source most easily contaminated by human activity. It is the surface water systems, then, that must be carefully protected from contamination.

Water quality studies should determine which contaminant poses the most severe emironmental problem. That is, determination of the tonicity of many of the contaminants, or at least of model contaminants for specific groups, should be made. Heavy metals, organic pollutants, pathogenic organisms, etc., should all be understood with respect to their viability in natural systems and ability to cause environmental damage. With this information the threshold levels of the various contaminants can be determined and they can be regulated by imposing standards.

Notes

①这部分地是由于我们没有充分理解由于各种污染物的流动而产生的自然过程。
②迫切需要理解这些过程的细节，因为它们决定着废水在排放前所需处理的程度。
③ threshold level 临阈级。
④很显然，我们应该通过阻止各种物质的排放来保护水供应，因为这些物质的排放能致使水即便是经过处理，但仍不适合饮用。

Reading Material B

Water Quality Standards

When water quality is to be managed by controlling waste inputs, some bases for the degree of treatment required must be developed. Sound engineering practice dictates that the treatment of waste water be both as economic as possible and effective for protecting the quality of receiving waters.① For this to be a reality, the limits for pollutants in receiving waters must be carefully defined and given a sound scientific basis. The basis of these limits should be, first, the public health of the community, and second, the environmental health of biological systems within the receiving water.

The limits that are set on water contaminants may have different names. McKee and Wolfe, in their classic work "Water Quality Criteria", differentiate between water quality standards and water quality criteria as parameters for limiting pollutants in water.② They noted that criteria refer to limits of pollutants that are not established by legal authority. They contend that "standards" should be the legal term for defining such limits. In any case, it is a "water quality standard" that defines the level of pollutants allowed in a water system.

As mentioned previously, standards are important for deciding on the degree of treatment of polluted inputs required in a particular drainage system.③ One goal of setting standards is to ensure that water supplies can be effectively treated by common engineering procedures to attain desired use levels. This basic assumption is fundamental to all water quality standards.

The value of standards was evaluated by McGauhey, who lists certain recognizable virtues of water quality standards:

(1) they encourage the measurement of quality factors;
(2) they permit self-control by discharges;
(3) they preserve fairness in the application of police power;
(4) they furnish a historical documented story of an event and therefore assist in controlling the future;
(5) they make possible the definition of a problem;
(6) they establish goals for system designs;
(7) they force people to face their own ignorance or, when facing arbitrary standards, to define why they are inappropriate;
(8) they assess the benefits we receive from a system.

These properties of water quality standards help to satisfy social demands for pure water. Originally, only public health concerns, that is, the prevention of specific illness, were important for determining water quality. However, in recent years there have been demands for clean or pure water for all uses of a water resource. There is therefore a strong social pressure to establish standards to maintain clean water throughout water systems.

There are four classes of standards used to achieve the goal of overall water purity:

(1) standards directly on the disease-causing agents;
(2) index standards, for cases in which some associated factor is easier to measure than the agent itself (e.g., coliform);
(3) standards on precursors or elements that enter into reactions that affect water quality (e.g., BOD and nutrients);
(4) standards on major environmental factors that produce effects worthy of concern (e.g., solar energy).

Perhaps the most important concern is the attainability of the standard. Although a given level of a pollutant in water can be estimated using medical evidence, the actual safe level cannot always be precisely defined. Therefore, appropriate safety factors are generally added to prevent public health problems. However, the final value used as a standard must be reasonable, and any discharger should be able to achieve the standard through common engineering practices.

If extremely stringent standards are established that cannot be obtained by a discharger, their validity will inevitably be challenged. Therefore, unless standards are established using sound scientific and/or medical evidence, they will not withstand legal challenges. We will see that standards for certain water uses, for example, drinking water can be more easily documented using medical studies than can standards set for recreation.④

Notes

①正确的工程处理方法要求对废水的处理要做到既尽量经济又行之有效，以达到保护受水水域的水质。句中 receiving water 是指"接纳污水的水域"。

②…differentiate between water quality standards and water quality criteria as parameters for limiting pollutants in water. ……把水质标准和水质规范区分开，以此作为限制水中污染物的参数。句中"standards"是法律术语，指"标准"，而"criteria"是指"规范"。

③正如前面所提到的那样，水质标准之所以重要，是因为它们决定着特定的水系要求对所排放污水加以处理的程度。

④我们会意识到，对水的某些用途订立标准，比方说，通过医学研究规定饮用水的标准，要比给娱乐用水规定标准要来得容易。句中"than"引导一个比较状语从句，为了保持句子的平衡，使用了倒装句。

UNIT TWELVE

Text   Hazardous Waste

[1]　　Ordinarily, municipal solid waste that is generated in the average household or commercial establishment is not considered dangerous. But in our modern society, large quantities of dangerous materials are generated by chemical manufacturing companies and related industries. These dangerous or hazardous wastes can cause serious illness, injury, or death; they also pose a serious threat to environmental quality if improperly transported or "dumped."[①]

[2]　　There are hundreds of recent incidents on record in which illegal or improper disposal of hazardous waste caused harm to the public and to the environment. Many of these cases involve contamination of groundwater that was used for public water supply.[②] Indiscriminate handling of hazardous waste can also lead to contamination of rivers and lakes. One such incident, called "Valley of the Drums" by the news media, occurred in Kentucky in the late 1970s. About 6000 damaged and leaky metal drums holding hazardous substances spilled their contents on the ground where they were dumped. Consequently, the soil and surface waters in the area were polluted with about 230 different organic chemicals and metals.

[3]　　Another infamous hazardous waste incident in the United States occurred near Niagara Falls, New York, also in the late 1970s. Chemical wastes, buried more than 25 years previously, gradually leaked out of the metal assessed in order to determine the appropriate response at contaminated sites.[③] Presently, sites that have more than 1 μg/L (one part per billion) of dioxin in the soil would be subject to remedial action in order to protect public health.

[4]　　Reactive wastes are those that are unstable and tend to react vigorously with air, water, or other substances. The reactions either cause explosions or form toxic vapors and fumes. Ignitable wastes, including organic solvents such as benzene or toluene, burn at relatively low temperatures and present an immediate fire hazard. Corrosive wastes, including strong alkaline or acidic substances, destroy materials and living tissue by chemical reaction. Reactive, ignitable, and corrosive wastes all can cause immediate harmful effects on living organisms or on the physical environment. They present particularly difficult problems related to transport, storage, and disposal, and they must be managed with special care.

[5]　　Infectious or biological waste material includes human tissue from surgery, used bandages and hypodermic needles, microbiological material, and other substances generated by hospitals and biological research centers. This type of hazardous waste must be handled and disposed of properly to avoid infection and the spread of disease among the general

public.

[6]   Radioactive waste, particularly from nuclear power plants, is also of special concern. Excessive exposure to ionizing radiation can harm living organisms. And radioactive material may persist in the environment for thousands of years before it decays appreciably. But because of the scope and technical complexity of this problem, radioactive waste disposal is generally considered separately from other forms of hazardous waste.

[7]   It has been estimated by the EPA that about 10 percent of all nonradioactive industrial waste in the United States is hazardous. ④ This amounts to roughly 60 million tons per year. Until the mid-1980s, only about 10 percent of this material was disposed of in an environmentally sound manner. Most of it has been "swept under the rug," so to speak, and poses a continuous threat to public health and environmental quality. ⑤ It is estimated that there are as many as 40,000 hazarddrum containers and percolated through the soil into the yards and basements of homes built on the site. Hundreds of families were evacuated after an excessive number of unusual health problems were observed among the residents. Many of the approximately 80 different chemicals identified at the site are suspected of causing cancer in humans.

[8]   Hazardous wastes differ from other solid wastes in form as well as in behavior. They often are generated in liquid form, but they may also occur as solids, sludges, or gases. Usually they are contained and confined in metal drums or cylinders. There are four primary classifications or groups of hazardous wastes, based on the properties of toxicity, reactivity, ignitability, and corrosivity. Two additional types include infectious and radioactive waste material.

[9]   Toxic wastes are poisons, even in very small or trace amounts. Some may have an acute or immediate effect on humans or animals, causing death or violent illness. Others may have a chronic or long-term effect, slowly causing irreparable harm to exposed persons. Some toxic wastes are considered to be carcinogenic, causing cancer many years after initial exposure. Others may be mutagenic, causing biological changes in the children or offspring of exposed people and animals.

[10]   Most toxic wastes are generated by industrial activities, including the manufacture of chemicals, pesticides, paints, petroleum by-products, metals, textiles, and many other products. There are hundreds of different chemicals specifically identified and listed as toxic by the Environmental Protection Agency, and the list is growing.

[11]   The pesticide dioxin has been categorized by the EPA as "one of the most perplexing and potentially dangerous chemicals ever to pollute the environment. " A special control strategy has been adopted for this particular substance, including a systematic investigation to identify the location and extent of dioxin contamination. Health risks will be dangerous waste "dumps" in the United States, many of which pose serious health and environmental problems. The cost of cleanup is expected to reach billions of dollars.

New Words and Expressions

indiscriminate [ˌindisˈkrimineit]		a.	不加区别的
drum [drʌm]		n.	桶
dioxin [daiˈɔksin]		n.	二噁英
be subject to			必须得到
remedial [riˈmi:djəl]		a.	补救的
reactive * [riˈækfiv]		a.	反应的
ignitable [igˈnaitəbl]		a.	可燃的
benzene [ˈbenzj:n]		n.	苯
toluene [ˈtɔljui:n]		n.	甲苯
living tissue			活性组织
excessive [ikˈsesiv]		a.	过多的
hypodermic [haipəˈdə:mik]		a.	皮下的；皮下组织的
ionizing radiation			电离辐射
persist in			坚持；留在……上
so to speak			打个比方
percolate [ˈpə:kəleit]		vt.	渗漏
evacuate * [iˈvækjueit]		vt.	转移、撤出
cylinder * [ˈsilində]		n.	钢瓶
toxicity [tɔkˈsisiti]		n.	毒性
reactivity [riækˈtiviti]		n.	反应性
ignitability [ignitəˈbiliti]		n.	可燃性
corrosivity [kərəuˈsiviti]		n.	腐蚀性
acute * [əˈkju:t]		a.	急性的
chronic [ˈkrɔnik]		a.	长期的；慢性的
carcinogenic [kɑ:ˈsinədʒenik]		a.	致癌的
mutagenic [ˌmju:təˈdʒenik]		a.	诱变的
perplexing [pəˈpleksiŋ]		a.	使人困惑的
strategy [ˈstrætidʒi]		n.	计策；政策

Notes

①…if improperly transported or dumped. 本句为一个省略从句，句中省去了主语和谓语部分的助动词 they are。

②Many of these cases involve contamination of groundwater that… 句中 these cases 指上句中的 incidents on record；involve 意为 have as a result. 本句的意思是"许多这些非法

或不恰当地处理事件的结果必会污染地下水……。"

③…assessed in order to …。assessed 为过去分词，在句中作定语，修饰前面的名词metal，相当于 which was assessed……。

④EPA＝Environmental Protection Agency 美国环境保护局

⑤sweep under the rug 本意为"扫到地毯下"，文中的意思为把问题掩盖起，没有得到彻底解决。

Exercises

Reading Comprehension

Ⅰ. Say whether the following statement are True (T) or False (F) according to the text.
1. Usually, domestic or commercial solid waste is considered dangerous.   (   )
2. Improper handling of hazardous waste will cause harm to the public and to the environment as well.   (   )
3. Those that are unstable and tend to react vigorously with air, water or other substances are called reactive wastes.   (   )
4. As reactive, ignitable, and corrosive wastes pose a serious threat to living organisms or to the environment they must be transported, stored and disposed with special care.   (   )
5. Radioactive waste may exist in the environment for a thousand years before it delays considerably.   (   )
6. It has been estimated by the EPA that about 10 percent of all radioactive industrial waste in the U.S. is not hazardous.   (   )

Ⅱ. Skim through the text and complete the following table:

	Hazardous	waste	
	Type		Example
1	toxic waste	1)	
2	reactive waste	2)	
3		3)	organic solvents
4	corrosive waste	4)	
5		5)	human tissue from surgery, used bandages, microbiological material, etc.
6	radioactive waste	6)	

Vocabulary

Ⅰ. Fill in the blanks with words given below, changing the form where necessary.

> acute ignitable evacuate remedial
> indiscriminate

1. Only dry wood is _____ and can be used to make fire.
2. Some pollution has _____ effects on our environment and some pollution has chronic effects.
3. Contamination of rivers and lakes can be caused by _____ handling of hazardous wastes.
4. Many people had to _____ because the areas where they lived were heavily polluted.
5. We must take _____ action to control the environmental conditions of certain areas.

II. Match the words in Column A with their definitions or descriptions in Column B.

Column A   Column B
1. dump   a. cancer causing
2. carcinogenic   b. pertaining to or characterized by reaction
3. percolate   c. live mass of cells and cell-products in an animal body
4. reactive   d. place where rubbish may be unloaded and left; place for dumping waste material
5. living tissue   e. drip or filter through small holes or spaces

Translation   定语从句的翻译

（一）限定性定语从句的翻译

翻译限定性定语从句的方法是多变的，在不同的文章中，不同的语境中，都可有所不同，这里介绍最常用的二种方法：前置法：把英语的限定性定语从句译成带"的"的定语词组，放在被修饰词之前，从而将复合句译成汉语单句；后置法：如果从句结构复杂，译成汉语前置定语显得太长，而不符合汉语表达习惯，往往可以译成后置的并列分句。

例1   Presently, sites that have more than 1μg/L of dioxin in the soil would be subject to remedial action.
      目前，土壤里只要有超过一μg/L 的二噁英的地区就要采取补救措施。

例2   A point source pollutant is one that reaches the water from a pipe, channel or any other confined and localized source.
      点污染是指从管道、沟渠或其他任何限制的或局部的地点来的污染物。

例3   A dispersed or nonpoint source is a broad, unconfined area from which pollutants enter a body of water.
      分散源或非点源是指广阔的、无限制的区域，污染物从这一区域进入到水体中。

例4   He managed to raise a crop of 200 miracle tomatoes that weighed up to two pounds each.
      他居然种出了二百个奇迹般的西红柿，每个重达两磅。

Translate the following sentences into Chinese, paying attention to the underlined words.

1. The limits that are set on water contaminants may have different names.
2. There are, of course, the sludges which result from water treatment.
3. A great deal of literature has appeared in the past 30 years that shows how natural processes can be applied to treat wastes of various types.
4. Almost all cities have built treatment plants which can treat sanitary wastes.
5. Land treatment which is not the same as landfilling may be used.

Reading Material A

Treatment of Hazardous Waste

Some types of hazardous waste can be detoxified or made less dangerous by either chemical, biological, or physical treatment methods. Treatment of hazardous waste may be costly, but it can serve to prepare the material for recycling or for ultimate disposal in a manner safer than disposal without treatment. ①

Some common chemical treatment processes include ion exchange, neutralization, oxidation/reduction, and precipitation. ② The process of incineration is a high temperature or thermal-chemical process which not only can detoxify certain organic wastes, but can essentially destroy them as well. These processes are discussed briefly in the following paragraphs.

In the ion exchange process, industrial wastewater is passed through a bed of resin that selectively absorbs charged metal ions. An example of its use in the metal finishing industry is for removal of waste chromic acid from the production rinse water. Neutralization refers to pH adjustment, for reducing the strength and reactivity of acidic or alkaline wastes. Limestone, for example, can be used to neutralize acids, and compressed carbon dioxide may be used to neutralize strong bases.

Oxidation and reduction are complementary chemical reactions that involve the transfer of electrons among ions. Oxidation of waste cyanide by chlorine renders it less hazardous. Precipitation refers to a type of reaction in which certain chemicals are made to settle out of solution as a solid. An example of its application is in the battery industry. In this industry, the addition of lime and sodium hydroxide to acidic battery waste causes lead and nickel (toxic heavy metals) to precipitate out of solution.

Incineration, or burning of organic hazardous waste at very high temperatures, can convert the waste to an ash residue and gaseous emissions. The combustion detoxifies the waste material by altering its molecular structure and breaking it down into simpler chemical substances. Although the ash may be treated as a hazardous material, a much smaller volume of waste is left for ultimate disposal.

Not all hazardous waste can be incinerated. Heavy metals, for example, would not be destroyed, but would enter the atmosphere in vapor form. However, incineration has been successfully applied to such potent hazardous waste as chlorinated hydrocarbon pesticides, PCBs, and other organic substances. ③

Biological treatment uses living microorganisms. The microbes utilize the waste material as food and convert it by their natural metabolic processes into simpler substances. It is most commonly used for stabilizing the organic waste in sewage, but certain types of industrial waste can also be treated by this method. Organic waste material from the petrochemical industry, for example, can be treated biologically. It is necessary, though, to utilize bacteria that are acclimated to the waste. In some cases, genetically engineered species of bacteria may be used.

In addition to the traditional biological treatment systems, such as activated sludge and the tricking filter, land-farming or land treatment (which is not the same as landfilling) may be used. The waste is carefully applied to and mixed with the surface soil; micro-organisms and nutrients may also be added to the mixture, as needed. ④ The toxic organic material is degraded biologically, whereas inorganics are absorbed and retained in the soil.

Landfarming can provide a relatively inexpensive method for treatment as well as being a way to ultimately dispose of certain types of hazardous waste. But food or forage crops should not be grown on the same site because they could take up toxic material. A disadvantage of land treatment as a hazardous waste management option, then, is that relatively large tracts of land must be withdrawn from productive agricultural use. ⑤

Notes

①…but it can serve to prepare the material for recycling or for ultimate disposal in a manner safer than disposal without treatment. ……但是有害废物的处理可以使废物回收或者对其进行最终的处理，而这种处理方式要比未经处理就加以处置更安全。
②几种常见的化学处理方式包括离子交换、中和、氧化/还原和沉淀。
③PCB =polychlorinated biphenyl 多氯联苯
④… as needed. 本句是省略句，相当于 as micro-organisms and nutrients are needed.
⑤因而，作为处理有害废物的一种方案——土壤处理法的弊病在于：大片土地不得进行农业生产。

Reading Material B

Radioactive Waste Management

The objective of the environmental engineer is to prevent radiation from being introduced into the biosphere over the lifeline of the radioactive waste. Control of the potential direct impact on humans is necessary, but, as we have seen, it is not sufficient because water, air and land pathways transmit radioactivity to current and future generations. A "lifetime" is defined by the half-life of the radioisotopes, but also by current and future reprocessing technologies which can and will retrieve all or part of the waste as a recycled resource.① Recycling is an option now and will be in the future, but massive amounts of waste are produced today that are destined not for reprocessing but for long-term storage.

Engineers charged with radioactive waste control must, because of current technical, economic and political factors outside their control, focus on long-term storage technologies, i. e., disposal. With the given half-lives of many radioisotopes, it is difficult to imagine any technology which truly offers ultimate disposal for these wastes; thus, we will think in terms of long-term storage: 10,100 or 10, 000 years or longer. Many options have been suggested for the long-term storage of radioactive waste. These options can be grouped into four major categories:

1. land disposal
   - liquid injection into geological formations
   - burial in deep caverns
   - burial in deep holes
2. ocean disposal
   - direct ocean dumping
   - disposal in trenches
   - sea bed disposal
3. polar ice disposal
4. spaceship technology

Alternatives have been proposed with varying degrees of forethought. Each option must be ranked by a list of criteria which includes: retrievability of the waste, length of time available for undisturbed storage, probable storage capacity, and cost of disposal.

Several types of geological formations exist under land masses which could be used as storage facilities: bedded salt, granite deposits, shales, metamorphic rock.② The ideal formation is one in which rock units are homogeneous, thick, and deep, with adequate hydraulic and mechanical stability to maintain isolation of radioactive material. For many years, bedded salt has been favored. Granite crystalline rocks have been considered as alternative formations for radioactive waste disposal. Such rocks tend to have greater mechanical strength than salt, but also have little if any plasticity and are often scarred with cracks and fissures.③

Ocean disposal is not attractive for several reasons. Direct dumping would immediately endanger public health, and the integrity of any container system located along the ocean floor could not be guaranteed because of the corrosiveness of seawater. In addition, the residence time of deep seawater is only in the range of 100 to 1000 years, so isotopes with long half-lives would escape and be transported upward to ocean layers where the human food chain could be impacted. Little is understood about the transport of sediment along the ocean floor; thus the risks associated with burial in the sediment or in trenches are open to speculation.④

Polar ice disposal is not a good alternative for several reasons. Most of the ice in the Antarctic, for example, was deposited less than 100,000 years ago and is not particularly stable. If a radioactive mass were placed on the surface of the ice and allowed to melt down to the bedrock, the hole could seal itself (temperatures in many regions of Antarctica have remained below freezing for more than 1 million years). However, the continued heating after the mass reached bedrock might result in a pool of water under the ice pack that eventually could find its way to the open sea and the human food chain.⑤

Spaceship disposal of solidified waste is very expensive. The expense could be justified, particularly in the era of the space shuttle, but probably only smaller volumes of long-lived elements like iodine 129 could be separated from other waste.⑥ In addition, the risks associated with suborbital and orbital flight prior to the space-dump are not negligible.

Notes

①"生存期"被放射性同位素的半衰期所定义，同样也可被当前和未来的回收技术所确定，而这些技术终将能够回收所有的或部分的废料用作再生资源。句中"half-life"是（放射性同位素的）半衰期。

②存在于地块之下的几种地质结构可作存放（放射性废物的）场所，它们是层状盐、花岗岩、沉积岩、页岩、变质岩。

③…but also have little if any plasticity… 此句是省略句，相等于but also have little plasticity if there is any plasticity。

④对于海底沉积物的迁移，人们知之甚微。因而，封置于沉积物中或埋置在深沟中有关的冒险活动还有待于探索。

⑤但是，如果放射性物质到达基岩继续升温的话，会在流冰群下产生大量的融化水，这些水最终会流入大海，进入人类的食物链。

⑥特别是进入航天飞机的时代，或许是只有到了较小量的存留期长的元素，比如碘129能与其他废物分开的时代，这种费用也许会证明是合理的。

UNIT THIRTEEN

Text   Air Pollution

[1]   Quantitative discussions of air pollution are hampered by the lack of a clear definition for "clean air". Most scientists assume "air" to be a mixture of the gases listed in Table 1. If this is clean air, then any constituent of air can be called a pollutant. However, one never finds such "clean air" in nature. It may thus be more appropriate to define air pollutants as those substances which exist in such concentrations as to cause an unwanted effect. ① These pollutants can be natural (such as smoke from forest fires) or man-made (such as automobile exhaust) and can be in the form of gases or particulates (liquid or solid particles larger than 1 micron).

Table 1   **Components of Normal Dry Air**

Nitrogen	780, 900	ppm
Oxygen	209, 400	ppm
Argon	9, 300	ppm
Carbon dioxide	315	ppm
Neon	18	ppm
Helium	5, 2	ppm
Methane	1.0 to 1.2	ppm
Krypton	1.0	ppm
Nitrous oxide	0.5	ppm
Hydrogen	0.5	ppm
Xenon	0.08	ppm
Nitrogen dioxide	0.02	ppm
Ozone	0.01 to 0.04	ppm

[2]   In the context of air pollution control, gaseous pollutants include substances that are gasses at normal temperature and pressure as well as vapors of substances that are liquid or solid at normal temperature and pressure. Among the gaseous pollutants of great importance in terms of present knowledge are carbon monoxide, hydrocarbons, hydrogen sulfide, nitrogen oxides, ozone and other oxidants and sulfur oxides. ② Carbon dioxide should be added to this list because of its potential effect on climate.

[3]   Particulate pollutants are classified as follows: dust, fume, mist, smoke and spray. Particulate pollutants found in the atmosphere or emitted from a source can be chemically complex, consisting of a variety of metallic and nonmetallic constituents.

[4]   Many of the pollutants of concern are formed and emitted through natural processes. For example, naturally-occurring particulates include pollen grains, fungus spores, salt spray, smoke particles from forest fires, and dust from volcanic eruptions. Gaseous pollutants from natural sources include carbon monoxide as a breakdown product in the degradation of hemoglobin, hydrocarbons in the form of terpenes from pine trees, hydrogen sulfide resulting from the breakdown of cysteine and other sulfur-containing amino acids by

bacterial action, nitrogen oxides, and methane.

[5]　　Man-made sources of pollutants can be conveniently classified as stationary combustion, transportation, industrial process, and solid waste disposal sources. The principal pollutant emissions from stationary combustion processes are particulate pollutants, as fly ash and smoke, and sulfur and nitrogen oxides. Sulfur oxide emissions are, of course, a function of the amount of sulfur present in the fuel. Thus, combustion of coal and oil, both of which contain appreciable amounts of sulfur, yields significant quantities of sulfur oxide. Nitrogen oxides are formed by the thermal fixation of atmospheric nitrogen in high-temperature processes. Accordingly, almost any combustion operation will produce nitric oxide (NO) which subsequently undergoes oxidation to nitrogen dioxide (NO_2). Other pollutants of interest from combustion processes are organic acids, aldehydes, ammonia and carbon monoxide. The amount of carbon monoxide emitted relates to the efficiency of the combustion operation, i.e., a more efficient combustion operation will oxidize more of the carbon present to carbon dioxide, reducing the amount of carbon monoxide emitted. Of the fuels used in stationary combustion, natural gas is perhaps the most desirable from the view of air pollution. ③ Natural gas contains practically no sulfur, and particulate emissions are almost nil.

[6]　　Transportation sources, particularly automobiles using the internal combustion engine, constitute a major source of air pollution. Particulate emissions from the automobile include smoke and lead particles, the latter usually as halogenated compounds. ④ Smoke emissions, as in any other combustion operation, are due to the incomplete combustion of carbonaceous material. On the other hand, lead emissions relate directly to the addition of tetraethyl lead to the fuel as an antiknock compound. Gaseous pollutants from transportation sources include carbon monoxide, nitrogen oxides, and hydrocarbons. Hydrocarbon emissions result from incomplete combustion and evaporation from the crankcase, carburetor, and gasoline tank.

[7]　　Significant progress has been made in controlling pollution from automobiles. Exhaust has been cleaned by better than 90% over 1963 models, and further improvement will be evident over the next 5 years.

[8]　　Pollution emissions from industrial processes reflect the ingenuity of modern industrial technology. Thus, nearly every imaginable form of pollutant is emitted in some quantity by some industrial operation.

[9]　　Solid waste disposal is often a major source of urban air pollution. Although solid waste disposal operations need not be a major source of air pollutants, many communities still permit backyard burning and/or disposal of solid waste by open burning dumps. ⑤ These techniques, which attempt to reduce the volume of waste, produce instead a variety of difficult-to-control pollutants. Among these are undesirable odors, carbon monoxide, small amounts of nitrogen oxides, organic acids, hydrocarbons, aldehydes, and great quantities of smoke. ⑥ (Both backyard burning and open burning dumps are prime examples of

inefficient combustion.)

New Words and Expressions

concentration [ˌkɔnsenˈtreiʃən]		n.	浓度；密度
carbon monoxide			一氧化碳
hydrocarbon * [ˌhaidrəuˈkɑːbən]		n.	碳氢化合物
nitrogen oxide			氧化氮
oxidant [ˈɔksidənt]		n.	氧化剂
dioxide * [daiˈɔksaid]		n.	二氧化物
metallic * [miˈtælik]		a.	金属的
spray [sprei]		n.	雾状物
spore [spɔː]		n.	孢子
degradation * [ˌdigreiˈdeiʃən]		n.	降解
hemoglobin [ˌhiːməuˈgləubin]		n.	血红蛋白
terpene [ˈtəːpiːn]		n.	萜烯
cysteine [ˈsistiːn]		n.	半胱氨盐
amino acid			氨基酸
bacterial [bækˈtiəriəl]		a.	细菌的
appreciable [əˈpriːʃəbl]		a.	可观的
thermal fixation			热固
nitric oxide			一氧化氮
aldehyde [ˈældihaid]		n.	乙醛
nil [nil]		n.	无；零
halogenate [ˈhælədʒineit]		vt.	使卤化
halogenated compound			卤化合物
carbonaceous [ˌkɑːbəuˈneiʃəs]		a.	含碳的
tetraethyl [ˌtetrəˈiːeail]		a.	四乙基的
antiknock [ˈæntiˈnɔk]		a.	抗爆的
crankcase [ˈkræŋkkeis]		n.	曲轴箱
carburetor [ˌkɑːbjuˈretə]		n.	汽化器
better than			超过
ingenuity [ˌindʒiˈnjuːəti]		n.	善于创新

Notes

①…which exist in such…as to cause an unwanted effect. 句中的 such…as to 意为"如此的…以致于"，as 引出的不定式短语表示结果。

②…of great importance in terms of present knowledge… of great importance 相当于 which are very important in terms of 意为 "就…而言"，"根据"；knowledge 在本句中的意思为 "了解" "知道"。

③，…natural gas is perhaps the most desirable from… the most desirable 相当于 the most desirable fuel…

④…, the latter usually as halogenated compounds，句中的 latter 指 lead particles。这部分的意思相当于 lead particles are emitted from automobile as halogenated compounds.

⑤… operation need not be a major source of …，句中的 "need" 为情态动词，意为 "需要"、"要"；need not 译为 "无需"、"不论"。

⑥Among these are undesirable … 句中 "these" 指代前句中的 difficult-to-control pollutants。本句为倒装句，其正常句序应为 "undesirable odors … are among these。

Exercises

Reading Comprehension

I. Say whether the following statement are True (T) or False (F) according to the text.

1. According to the text, an air pollutant can be classified as either a natural source or a man-made source pollutant. ( )
2. Natural sources of pollutants can be in the form of particulates such as carbon monoxide, hydrocarbons, hydrogen sulfide, nitrogen oxides and methane. ( )
3. Because of the amount of sulfur present in the fuel as coal and oil, combustion of them produces significant quantities of sulfur oxide. ( )
4. The amount of carbon dioxide emitted is connected with the efficiency of the combustion operation, that is, the more efficient combustion operation, the less amount of carbon dioxide emitted. ( )
5. Particulate pollutants from transportation sources include smoke emission, which result from the incomplete combustion of carbonaceous material, and lead emissions. ( )
6. Both backyard burning and open burning dumps constitute a major source of urban air pollution. ( )

II. Skim through the text and complete the following table:

	Air pollutants		
	Type		Example
1		1)	pollen grains, fungus spores, salt spray, nitrogen oxides, methane, etc
2	man-made pollutants	2)	
3	gaseous pollutants	3)	
4		4)	dust, fume, mist, smoke, spray etc.

Vocabulary

Ⅰ. Fill in the blanks with words given below, changing the form where necessary.

> concentration nil ingenuity metallic
> better than

1. Pollution emissions are the by-products of the _____ of modern industrial technology.
2. The output of this year has increased by _____ 50%.
3. The substances existed in such _____ that they caused some unwanted effects.
4. The air in this area is so clean that pollutants in the air are almost _____.
5. The pollutants in the air in certain areas consist of _____ components.

Ⅱ. Match the words in Column A with their definitions or descriptions in Column B.

Column A	Column B
1. oxidant	a. of or related to bacteria
2. hydrocarbon	b. liquid to be sprayed out under pressure
3. bacterial	c. chemical compound containing 2 atoms of oxygen to every one of another simple substance
4. dioxide	d. any one of a class of chemical compound containing only hydrogen and carbon
5. spray	e. an oxidizer, such as liquid oxygen, used for burning the fuel of missiles and rockets.

Translation　　　　　　　定语从句

（二）非限定性定语从句的翻译

英语的非限定性定语从句对先行不起限定作用。翻译这类定语从句常用下列方法：前置法：一些较短而具有描写性的非限定性定语从句，也可译成带"的"前置定语，放在被修饰词之前；译成并列句；译成独立句。

例1　The sun, which had hidden all day, now came out in all its splendor.

那个整天躲在云层里的太阳，现在又光芒四射地露面了。

例2　These oscillations are measured as number of pressure changes per second or, more scientifically in hertz, which means the same thing.

这些振荡是以每秒钟压力变化的数值来测定的，或者更科学地说，用赫兹表示，意义一样。

例3　The program is voluntary, which is one of the biggest difficulties in pollution solutions.

这个计划是靠捐助维持的。这是解决污染问题最大的困难之一。

Translate the following sentences into Chinese, paying attention to the underlined words.

1) An inversion is a layer of warm air aloft, <u>which prevents the pollulants from escaping</u>.
2) Industry is creating a fantastic array of new chemicals each year, <u>all of which eventually find their way to the water</u>.
3) The simplest physical process is evaporation, <u>which may be facilitated by using mechanical sprayers</u>.
4) Salt has a high thermal conductivity, <u>which helps dissipate heat that builds in waste containers</u>.
5) Prolonged exposure to noise can cause either temporary hearing loss, <u>which disappears in a few days</u>, or permanent loss.

Reading Material A

Meteorological Effects and Changes

Air pollution can have a major effect on the climate, both regionally and globally. Regionally, rainfall can be seriously changed by the presence of air pollution. For example, La Porte, Indiana, located 30 miles southeast of the major steel center of Gary, Indiana, and also southeast of Chicago, averaged 47% more rainfall than the localities upwind of Chicago.① In addition, as Chicago's haze and smog varies with the area's fuel use, so does La Porte's rainfall.

The reason for this behavior can be seen if we consider how and why rain forms. The moisture in the air collects in the tiny droplets, using a particulate as the nucleus. These tiny droplets collect and form clouds. If a sufficient concentration of moisture is present, the droplets can attract more water vapor to themselves and grow in size and eventually form rain. The presence of the particulate thus speeds up the initial moisture condensation and droplet formation.

Because of this behavior, air pollution can also have the opposite influence on rainfall. Too many particulates can encourage the formation of too many small, nuclear particles compared to the available moisture. Each particle cannot attract enough water vapor to itself, so it cannot grow enough to form rain droplets. The net effect is a decrease in rainfall.

The global climatic effects relate to the earth's heat balance. There are two proposed but opposing theories to predict the net effect of air pollution on the temperature:

1. The greenhouse effect. The increased burning of fossil fuels increases the amount of

atmospheric CO_2. This CO_2 is important in that it is nearly transparent to visible radiation, but is a strong absorber and back radiator of infrared (heat) radiation.② In this way, the atmospheric CO_2 acts as does the glass in a greenhouse.③ The visible light penetrates the CO_2 layer and is degraded on the earth's surface, and the heat formed cannot radiate back outward. Many large cities and metropolitan areas have become several degrees warmer, on the average, in recent years, and tend to be warmer than the surrounding rural areas.

2. The descrease in sunlight penetrating the air pollution layer. The presence of, especially, particulates in the atmosphere prevents as much sun from reaching the surface on the earth. Not only can the particulates themselves shield some of our cities, but also, more importantly, the presence of more particulates tends to increase the cloud cover at high altitudes, also preventing some sunlight from reaching the earth's surface.

Which of these two possibilities take the lead? Only time can tell. But an average change in either direction of only a few degrees could indicate either a new ice age or major flooding due to melting of the polar icecaps.④

Another possible global effect (not truly a climatic effect, however) is related to the earth's O_3 layer. The presence of the O_3 layer is very important to life on our planet, for it helps protect us from potentially damaging ultraviolet (UV) radiation. The nitrogen oxides can react with O_3 as such: $NO + O_3 \longrightarrow O_2 + NO_2$. Normally, the nitrogen oxides do not reach the stratospheric O_3, for they react before diffusing all round to that high, so this is not a major problem. NO_2 has a typical residence time of only three days, and NO, four days. However, the new supersonic transport planes (SST's) emit nitrogen oxides directly into the stratosphere, right at the O_3 layer, so it is possible that the effects could be serious.

The fluorochlorocarbon propellants used in many aerosol cans can also have possible harmful effects on the O_3 layer. Their relative nonreactivity, while making them good propellants, allows them to move into the stratosphere before reacting. Though their actual chemical effect is still being debated, some states have banned their use.

Notes

① 例如，印第安纳州的拉波特，位于该州主要的钢铁中心——加里东南处30英里；同样，也位于芝加哥的东南部，它比位于芝加哥的那些迎风地区平均多出47%的降水。

② in that 相当于 because。

③ …, the atmospheric CO_2 acts as does the glass in a greenhouse 句中 as 后接倒装句，does 代替 acts，以避免重复。

④ 但是，两者间任何一方只要温度发生几度的升降变化就意味着要么是一个新的冰河时代的到来，要么是由于覆盖极地的冰帽融化造成的洪水泛滥。

Reading Material B

Causes of Air Pollution

Air pollution may arise from acts of nature. There have been many times when people have been forced to seek shelter indoors during a severe sandstorm, when strong winds filled the air with swirling sand and grit. There have been instances when the wind-borne ash from erupting volcanoes encompassed large portions of the surface of the earth. Early in the 1950's, forest fires in some of the southeastern states blanketed an area of about 300,000 square mile. The smoke from the forest fires was so intense that air flights had to be canceled in many cities. Eighteen states from Maine to North Carolina were affected by the smoke. On the occasion the sun in New York city was blotted out at midday.

But acts of nature are often beyond the control of man. Of chief concern is the second and more pressing source of air pollution——the man-made pollutants.①

Cities must meet the inhabitants' need for heat, hot water, light, power, and transportation. The coal and fuel oil that are burned to produce these essential commodities create a major part of the pollution from which cities suffer. City dwellers leave in the wake a trail of waste paper and other refuse materials, which are disposed of in incinerators. Here again air pollution is produced. The exhausts from the vehicles in city traffic fill the air with still more pollutants. There is the pollution from certain factories where work results in creating waste chemicals that are permitted to escape into the air.②

The grinding of all kinds of surfaces against each other, and the ordinary wear and tear on shoes and the tires of automobiles also send tiny dust particles into the air, as do sanding, grinding, drilling, spraying, and demolishing operations.

Some of these pollutants, such as automobile gases, are discharged into the air at street level. Others, such as smoke from chimneys of apartment houses or power plants where electricity is generated, enter the atmosphere at higher levels.

The amount of pollution in the cities is affected by atmospheric conditions. Some conditions reduce the pollution and others increase it. If winds are strong enough, they blow pollutants up and away, and rain and snow wash the air. But these natural forces can be slow and also infrequent. Pollution is also lessened by the action of the currents in the air. Because the surface of the earth is normally warmer than the air above the surface, air currents are set up that rise into the higher atmosphere, carrying the pollutants with them. In this way the amount of pollution on the surface where people live is reduced. But sometimes, due to natural causes, the air above the earth's surface is warmer than the air at the surface. When this happens, the warm air remains in a layer above the cold air at the surface, and stops the normal flow of rising warm air. This is known as a temperature inversion.③ The air pollution and smog-forming substances become trapped between the two layers and hang over the city, often with serious effects on people's comfort, health and even life.

Two new words have been introduced into the English language in connection with the polluted air: smog, a combination of smoke and fog; and smaze, a combination of smoke and haze.

The development of the atom bomb and the later testing of other nuclear devices have added another source of air pollutants, commonly called fallout.④ The limitation of nuclear testing has diminished much of the hazard from fallout, but the matter requires careful attention and control.

Scientists are also concerned about the possibility that the increased smoke and dust discharged into the air may, in time, reduce the heat from the sun received on the earth's surface and affect clouds and rainfall.

Notes

①Of chief concern is the second and … 本句是倒装句，系动词 is 之后的部分是主语。
②有来自某些工厂的污染，这些工厂在生产过程中产生出准许进入空气中的废化学物质。
③temperature inversion 温度逆增；逆温。
④fallout 放射性尘埃。

UNIT FOURTEEN

Text   Health Effects of Noise

[1]   The most immediate and acute health effect of excessive noise is impairment of hearing. This is caused by damage to some part of the auditory system.

[2]   Sound pressure waves caused by vibrations set the ear drum (tympanic membrane) in motion. This activates the three bones in the middle ear. The hammer, anvil and stirrup physically amplify the motion received from the ear drum and transmit it to the inner ear. This fluid-filled cavity contains the cochlea, a snail-like structure in which the physical motion is transmitted to tiny hair cells. ① These hair cells deflect, much like seaweed swaying in the current, and certain cells are responsive only to certain frequencies. The mechanical motion of these hair cells is transformed to bioelectrical signals and transmitted to the brain by the auditory nerves.

[3]   Acute damage can occur to the ear drum, but this occurs only with very loud sudden noises. ② More serious is the chronic damage to the tiny hair cells in the inner ear. Prolonged exposure to noise of a certain frequency pattern can cause either temporary hearing loss, which disappears in a few days, or permanent loss. Much of the hearing loss in industry occurs in the middle range of frequencies. Unfortunately, speech frequencies are in the same area, and speech perception is thus hindered. Many older people, while still able to hear jet planes and rumbling trains quite well, complain that "everyone is whispering." They have experienced damage to certain hair cells which hinder the reception of sounds of a specific (speech) frequency.

[4]   Hearing loss occurs with advancing age even without environmental damage. It is difficult, therefore, to develop epidemiological data to show the loss due to excessive noise. Research has, however, shown that hearing loss due to noise is real and not imagined.

[5]   Another problem with noise is its effect on other bodily functions such as the cardiovascular system. It has been discovered that noise alters the rhythm of the heartbeat, makes the blood thicker, dilates blood vessels and makes focusing difficult. It is no wonder that excessive noise has been blamed for headaches and irritability. Noise is especially annoying to people who do close work, like watchmakers.

[6]   All of the above reactions are those which our ancestral caveman also experienced. Noise to him meant danger and his senses and nerves were "up," ready to repel the danger. In the modern noisefilled world, we are always "up," and it is questionable how much of our physical ills are due to this. ③

[7]   We also know that man cannot adapt to noise, in the sense that his body functions no longer react a certain way to excessive noise. People do not, therefore, get "used-to"

noise in the physiological sense.④

[8]　　In addition to the noise problem, it might be appropriate to mention the potential problems of very high or very low frequency sound, out of our usual 20-20,000 Hz hearing range. The health effects of these, if any, remain to be studied.⑤

[9]　　Numerous case histories comparing patients in noisy and quiet hospital point to increased convalescent time when the hospital was noisy (either from within or due to external noise). This can be translated directly to a dollar figure.⑥

[10]　　Recent court cases have been won by workers seeking damages for hearing loss suffered on the job. The Veterans Administration spends many, many millions of dollars every year for care of patients with hearing disorders.

[11]　　Other costs, such as sleeping pills, lost time in industry, and apartment soundproofing are difficult to quantify. The John F. Kennedy Cultural Center in Washington recently spent $5 million for soundproofing, necessitated by the jets using the nearby National Airport.

[12]　　It is even more difficult to measure the effect noise has had on the quality of life. How much is noise to blame for irate husbands and grumpy wives, for grouchy taxi drivers and surly clerks?

[13]　　Children reared in a noisy neighborhood must be taught to listen. They cannot focus their auditory senses on one sound, such as the voice of a teacher.

[14]　　Within the 80 to 90 dB circle around the Kennedy airport in New York are 22 schools. Every time a plane passes the teacher must stop talking and try to reestablish attention.

[15]　　Noise is a real and dangerous form of environmental pollution. Since people cannot adapt to it physiologically, we are perhaps adapting psychologically instead. Noise can keep our senses "on edge" and prevent us from relaxing. Our mental powers must therefore control this insult to our bodies. Since noise, in the context of human evolution, is a very recent development, we have not yet adapted to it, and must thus be living on our buffer capacity. One wonders how plentiful this is.⑦

New Words and Expressions

impairment [imˈpɛəmənt]	n.	降低
auditory [ˈɔːditəri]	a.	耳的；听觉的
tympanic [timˈpænik]	a.	鼓的
tympanic membrane		鼓膜
hammer [ˈhæmə]	n.	锤骨
anvil [ˈænvil]	n.	砧骨
stirrup [ˈstirəp]	n.	镫骨
cavity [ˈkæviti]	n.	空腔

cochlea ['kɔkliə]	n.	耳蜗
deflect * [di'flekt]	v.	转向
bioelectrical ['baiəuilek'trikəl]	a.	生物电的
rumble ['rʌmbl]	vi.	发生隆隆声
epidemiological [,epi,di:miə'lɔdʒikəl]	a.	流行病的
cardiovascula [,kɑ:diəu'væskjulə]	a.	心血管的
dilate [dai'leit]	vt.	扩大，扩张
irritability [iritəbiliti]	n.	烦燥
ancestral [æn'sestrəl]	a.	祖先的
convalescent [kɔnvə'lesent]	a.	恢复期的
irate [ai'reit]	a.	发怒的
necessitate * [ni'sesiteit]	vt.	使…成为必要
grumpy ['grʌmpi]	a.	暴燥的
grouchy ['grautʃi]	a.	愠怒的
surly ['sə:li]	a.	乖戾的
buffer ['bʌfə]	n.	缓冲

Notes

①…, a snail-like structure in which… 这是一个名词短语，在整个句子中起补充说明作用。短语中有一从句，由介词 in＋which 引出，修饰 structure。

②句中 this 指代前面的 acute damage；with 短语相当于从句 when there are very loud…。

③句中 it 为形式主语，真正的主语是 how much of …。

④介词短语 in the sense that …在句中起补充说明作用，说明什么叫人类不能适应噪声。

⑤The health effects of these, if any, remain…。
　　if any 等于 if there are any of the health effects of these。

⑥This can be …to a dollar figure 句子中的"this"指 increased convalescent time；dollar figure 意为用美元表示的数字，即经济上的影响。

⑦…how plentiful this is…this 指 buffer capacity；plentiful 修饰 buffer capacity 本句意为：we have plentiful buffer capacity。

Exercises

Reading Comprehension

Ⅰ. Say whether the following statement are True (T) or False (F) according to the text.

1. Very loud sudden noises will cause an acute damage to the ear drum.　　　　( )

2. If certain tiny hair cells are damaged, the reception of sounds of a certain frequency is

hindered. ( )
3. The tiny hair cells in the inner ear are responsive to any kinds of frequencies. ( )
4. Much of hearing loss is caused by prolonged exposure to noise of a certain frequency. ( )
5. It has been discovered that much of our physical ills are due to noise. ( )
6. According to the text, people cannot adapt to noise physiologically or psychologically ( )

II. Supply the missing words or expressions for the following sentences from the text.
1. Do you know how the human auditory system functions? Sound pressure waves caused by vibrations set the _____ in motion. _____ and _____ are the three bones in the middle ear. They amplify the motion received from the ear drum and transmit it to _____. This fluid-filled cavity contains _____, in which the physical motion is transmitted to tiny _____. Certain cells are responsive to certain _____. The mechanical motion of these hair cells is transformed to _____ and transmitted to the _____ by the auditory nerves.
2. Besides impairment of hearing, excessive noise has effect on other bodily functions. It changes the rhythm of the _____, makes the _____ thicker, dilates _____ and makes _____ difficult.

Vocabulary

I. Fill in the blanks with words given below, changing the form where necessary.

| necessitate deflect irate convalescent ancestral |

1. Noises around the hospital increased the _____ time of the patients there.
2. The increase of production _____ a greater supply of raw materials.
3. A gust of wind _____ the arrow's flight.
4. There was no such concept as environmental pollution for our-caveman.
5. Noise pollution in urban areas is serious and it tends to make people _____.

II. Match the words in Column A with their definitions or descriptions in Column B.

Column A   Column B
1. cavity   a. cause to expand or swell
2. dilate   b. make or cause to make deep heavy, continuous sound
3. rumble   c. diminishing or lessening in strength, value, quantity or quality
4. auditory   d. relating to the sense or organs of hearing
5. impairment   e. any empty space within a body

Translation   长难句（一）

在翻长难句时，首先要通读全句，根据主语和谓语动词的数目，及有无连词和连词类别，确定句子的种类。找出每个句子形式的主要成分，并进一步判明句子各次要成分和主要成分之间的关系。此外，还要判明每个句子的时态、语气和语态，以及是否强调句和否定句。

在进行句子分析，弄清语法关系，理解原文含义之后，可采用下列三种方法来进行翻译：顺译法，倒译法和分译法。

对科技英语而言，只要不太违反汉语习惯，一般尽可能采用顺译法。顺译法又可分为两种情况，一种是单纯顺译，即不在译文中采取任何修辞手段来改变原文的顺序或结构。另一种情况是添加总括性词语，即在句中表示原因、条件的状语或状语从句过于复杂或从句太长而难以直接表达时可适当改变句子结构，并添加总括性词语来统率下文然后依次译出。

例1 At equilibrium these two rates are equal, cupric ion is still reacting with ammonia molecules to form the complex and the complex is still decomposing, but just as much cupric ammonia complex is being decomposed in unit time as is being formed.
在平衡时，这两个速率相等；铜离子仍与氨分子发生反应以生成络离子，同时络离子仍在分解，但在单位时间内分解的氨铜铬离子正好与生成的一样多。

例2 Chemical requirements can play a large part in the economics of the solvent process, as is demonstrated in Figures 5 and 6, which show the relationship between feed metal concentration and the processing costs for systems covering both acidic and basic range of extraction.
化学药剂需要量在溶剂卒取法的经济方面起着很大的作用，从图5及6中就可以看出这一点；这两个图对下列体系即酸性或碱性的体系示出了给料中金属浓度和处理费用之间的关系。

Translate the following sentences into Chinese.

1. For example, a system initially containing a gaseous mixture of hydrogen, chlorine and liquid water would very soon closely approach equilibrium with respect to water vapour and liquid water until the partial pressure of water vapour in the gaseous phase (相) becomes essentially equal to the vapour pressure of liquid water at the temperature of the system.
2. When ordinary roll sulphur is dissolved in a small quantity of inflammable liquid known as carbon bisulphide and the solution is poured into a crystallizing dish, we find that the solvent slowly evaporates leaving the sulphur in the shape of small crystals.
3. There are many cases where older processes have been discontinued prematuredly because of pollution control; an example is the Fairfield Works of U.S. Steel where the open hearth (平炉法) was replaced by the Q-BOP (底吹氧气转炉法) process as a direct

consequence of action by local authorities objecting to the extensive pollution.
4. The general trend towards decreasing recovery of total product with increasing specific energy input is caused by increased removal of oxygen for more severe reaction conditions as well as the generally higher gas velocities throughout the collection system.

Reading Material A

Measurement and Control of Noise

Noise is commonly defined as unwanted sound. Modern treatment plants are equipped with a number of mechanical devices. These machines as well as the turbulence of treated sewage generate noise. Typical noise levels are given in Table 1.

The physical measure for noise is the sound pressure level, L.[①] It is defined as a logarithmic ratio of the sound intensity I of the given noise and the sound intensity I_0 of the lowest audible noise.[②] The unit expressing the noise level is decibel (to commemorate the inventor of the telephone Alexander G. Bell). A decibel (dB) is generally used in inventor practical measurements. As the noise intensity is proportional to the square of the noise pressure, the following equation can be used for converting sound pressure to decibels:[③]

$$L \text{ in dB} = 10\log\left(\frac{I}{I_0}\right) = 10\log\left(\frac{P^2}{P_0^2}\right) = 20\log\left(\frac{P}{P_0}\right)$$

Table 1 Noise Levels from Mechanical Sources

source	Noise Level in dB (A) 1 m from the Machine
Electric motors	75~90
Gear boxes	75~85
Compressors	85~95
Blowers	100~105
Combustion engines	95~100
Conveyor belts	95~100
Pumps	80~85
Aerators	80~90

where P_0 is the reference noise pressure at the lowest audible pressure of a sound with a frequency of 1,000 Hz.[④] The value of P_0 is commonly chosen as 0.0002μ bars (1 μ bar equals approximately 10^{-6} atm)[⑤].

The difference between the noise scale in dB and actual noise levels must be noted. Doubling the intensity by two identical sources of noise will increase the noise level by approximately 3 dB. In terms of hearing, about a 10 dB increase is necessary to make a sound seem twice as loud to a listener. It should be also noted that the human ear is more sensitive to softer sounds and less sensitive to louder sounds. Also the sensitivity of the ear varies with the frequency of the noise. The ear is more sensitive to rapid than to slow oscillations in air pressure. These oscillations are measured as the number of pressure changes per second or, more scientifically, in hertz (Hz), which means the same thing. To adjust for these differences in the sensitivity of the ear, a scale known as dB (A) has been defined that reduces the noise level values at higher frequencies. Most noise ordinances express the standards in terms of dB (A).

In the United States, the noise levels are controlled by the Noise Pollution and Abatement Act of 1970. The standards for noise were issued by the Environmental Protection Agency. An outdoor noise level criterion of dB (A) has been recommended. A corresponding interior noise level criterion is 55 dB (A). In Germany, a nighttime interior level of 40 dB (A) is recommended.

If the noise level is too high when compared with a standard or criterion, noise abatement measures must be implemented. Such measures work best if they are aimed at the source of the noise. This can be accomplished by good maintenance of the machinery or, in some cases, by replacement.

There are basically four different ways in which noise levels can be controlled or reduced:

1. Protect the person exposed to the noise
2. Intercept the noise by blocking its path
3. Increase the distance from the source
4. Reduce the sound intensity at the source.

If the reduction of the source noise emissions is not enough, interception or diversion of the noise may be feasible. Simple walls and sound barriers and/or thick hedges can reduce the noise levels by approximately 7 dB. Now noise is considered just another annoyance in a polluted world and much attention has given to it. We now have enough data to show that noise is a definite health hazard, and should be numbered among our more serious pollutants, It is possible, using available technology, to lesson this form of pollution. However, the solution costs money and private enterprises cannot afford to give noise a great deal of consideration until forced to by either the government or the consuming public.⑥

Notes

①噪声的物理测定标准为声压级,用 L 表示。
②其定义是:已知噪声声强(I)与最低可听噪声声强(I_0)的对数比率。
③由于噪声强度与噪声压的平方成正比,那么可用下面的公式把声压转换成分贝数来表示。
④Hz＝hertz 赫(兹)(频率单位)。
⑤p_0 的常值为 0.0002 微巴。句中 bar 是声压单位"巴"。atm＝atmospheric pressure(标准)大气压。

⑥ ···private enterprises cannot afford to give noise a great deal of consideration until forced to··· 本句是省略句相当于···until they are forced to give noise a great deal of consideration···。

Reading Material B

Noise Control

The control of noise is possible at three levels:

1. reducing the sound produced
2. interrupting the path of the sound
3. protecting the recipient

When we consider noise control in industry, in the community or in our home, we should keep in mind that all problems have these three possible solutions.

Industrial Noise Control

Industrial noise control generally involves the replacement of noise producing machinery or equipment with quiet alternatives. For example, the noise from an air fan can be reduced by increasing the number of blades or the pitch of the blades and decreasing the rotational speed.

The second method of decreasing industrial noise is to interrupt the path, for example, by covering a noisy motor with insulating material.

The third method of noise control is to protect the recipient by distributing earmuffs to the employees. But the problem is thus not really solved, and often the workers refuse to wear earmuffs, considering them sissy. There seems to be something masculine about being able to "take it."① Such misdirected masculinity will only end up in deafness.

Community Noise Control

The three major sources of community noise are aircraft, highway traffic and construction.

Construction noise must be controlled by local ordinances. Control usually involves the muffling of air compressors, jack hammers, hand compactors, etc. Since mufflers cost money, contractors will not take it upon themselves to control noise, and outside pressures must be exerted.

Aircraft noise in the United States is the province of the Federal Aviation Administration, which has instituted a two-pronged attack on this problem.② First, it has set limits on aircraft engine noise and will not allow aircraft exceeding these limits to use the airports. This has forced manufacturers to design for quiet as well as for thrust.

The second effort has been to divert flight paths away from populated areas; and whenever necessary to have pilots use less than maximum power when the takeoff carries them over a noise-sensitive area.③ Often this approach is not enough to prevent significant noise-induced damage or annoyance, and aircraft noise remains a real problem in urban areas.

Supersonic aircraft present a special problem. Not only are their engines noisy, but the sonic boom can create property damage and mental anguish. The magnitude of this problem will become known only when (and if) supersonic airlines begin regular service over land.④

The third major source of community noise is from highways. A modern passenger car is so well muffled that its most important contribution, at moderate and high speeds, is tire noise. Sports cars and motorcycles, on the other hand, contribute exhaust, intake and gear noise. The worst offender on the highways is the heavy truck. In most cases, the total noise generated by vehicles can be correlated directly to the truck volume.

A number of alternatives are available for reducing highway noise. First, the source can be controlled by making quieter vehicles; second, highways could be routed away from populated areas; and third, noise could be baffled with walls or other types of barriers. Other methods include lowering speed limits, designing for nonstop operation, and reducing all highways to less than 8% grade.

Noise in the Home

Private dwellings are getting noisier because of internally produced noise as well as external community noisier. The list of gadgets in a modern American home reads like a list of Halloween noisemakers.⑤

Otherwise similar products of different brands often will vary significantly in noise levels. When shopping for an appliance, it is just as important therefore to ask the clerk "How noisy is it?" as it is to ask him "How much does it cost?" And if he looks at you as if you had two heads, explain to him that he should know the dB(A) at the operator's position for all of his wares. He may actually bother to find out.

Notes

①能够忍受，似乎才具阳刚之气。句中"take it"是俚语，"忍受"的意思。
② a two-pronged attack 两面夹攻。
③…and whenever necessary to have pilots use less than maximum power when the takeoff

carries them over a noise-sensitive area. ……每当飞机起飞越过噪声敏感区的时候，让飞行员尽量不要开足马力。

④只有当超音速航空公司开始通航，这个问题的严重性才能为人知晓。

⑤Halloween（基督教）万圣节前夕（即10月31日之夜）。

UNIT FIFTEEN

Text Resource Recovery

[1] Recovery of resources from solid waste, commonly known as recycling, is theoretically very appealing. Unfortunately, our present economic system makes efficient (money-making) recycling difficult, although the picture is changing rapidly and resource recovery may in the near future become the most desirable means of solid waste management.

[2] In the heat of environmental concern, little attention has been paid to the total process necessary for resource recovery. ① "Recycling" has, in fact, been confused with "collection," but collection is only one step in the process. After the material has been collected from consumers, it must be cleaned, sold to an industry, transported, remanufactured and (most importantly) sold once again to consumers. This last step in fact controls the entire operation. If the remanufactured material cannot be sold, there is little sense in doing anything else. We must therefore not think of the collection of newspapers as "recycling," since the cycle is complete only when the paper is reused by consumers.

[3] The two basic reasons for recycling are (a) conservation of resources, and (b) reduction in volume of refuse to be disposed. ② Some of the common materials which have been suggested as recyclable are paper, metals, glass and organics.

[4] Paper is one product which is in plentiful supply and fairly clean. But only about 20% of our present supply is recycled since, unfortunately, virgin paper is much too cheap to make. The realization that each ton of paper recycled saves about 17 trees from the ax often prompts community paper drives. ③ This type of free labor is necessary in order to keep most repulping operations solvent.

[5] Unfortunately, the ton of waste paper so lovingly collected seldom saves the 17 trees. Only a small fraction of recycled paper ends up as paper, and most of that is shipped overseas. ④Recycling paper to paper is simply more expensive than making virgin paper.

[6] The only way paper can be recycled so as to truly save our forests is to create a market for recycled paper, and make virgin paper artificially expensive. This can be accomplished either through public support, legislation, or taxes.

[7] Metals can be easily recycled from industrial scrap, and this is the largest source of "secondary metals". The second largest source of waste metal is wrecked automobiles. Unfortunately, the present methods of making steel can tolerate only limited scrap input, and thus scrap steel has low market value.

[8] Some aluminum companies have conducted successful drives to collect aluminum cans. These cans are especially obnoxious as litter since they do not rust when discarded and remain as visible trash almost indefinitely.

[9] Glass is the perfect product for recycling. It is clean, plentiful, easy to reprocess,

and can be used in many ways. Unfortunately, it is also cheap. It is about as expensive to make a new glass bottle as to recycle or refill an old one.⑤ In addition, the raw materials for glass are in such plentiful supply that there does not seem to be anything gained through recycling.

[10]　　Organics can be converted into several useful products. The most common process, used extensively in many countries, is composting.

[11].　　Composting is, in contrast to the landfill, an aerobic method of decomposing solid waste. Typically, a composting operation involves (a) the segregation of refuse into organic and inorganic components (either by the household or at the plant); (b) grinding of the organic portion; and (c) stabilizing in either open piles or in mechanical "digesters".

[12]　　The segregation operation is the weak link in the process. Most communities have not had much luck in asking the citizens to separate paper and garbage from glass and tin cans; hand sorting at the compost plant, an expensive and often unreliable operation, has been necessary.

[13]　　Considerable research is directed toward finding better separation methods, because it is felt that if this problem were solved, composting would be a much more attractive method of resource recovery.⑥

[14]　　After grinding and usually after the separation of metals, the organic material is commonly placed in long piles called windrows, 8 to 10 feet wide and 4 to 6 feet high. Under these conditions, sufficient moisture and oxygen are available to support aerobic life. The piles must be turned periodically to allow sufficient oxygen to penetrate to all parts of the pile.

[15]　　Temperatures within a windrow approach 140°F, due entirely to biological activity. The pH will approach neutrality after an initial drop. With most wastes, additional nutrients are not needed. The composting of bark and other materials, however, is successful only with the addition of nitrogen and phosphorus nutrients.

[16]　　Moisture must usually be controlled. Excessive moisture makes it difficult to maintain aerobic conditions while a dearth inhibits biological life. A 40%~60% moisture content is considered desirable.

[17]　　There has been some controversy over the use of inoculants, freeze-dried cultures, used to speed up the process. Once the composting pile is established, which requires about two weeks, the inoculants have not proven to be of any significant value. Most municipal refuse contains all the organisms required for successful composting, and "mystery cultures" are thus not needed.

[18]　　The end point of a composting operation can be measured by noting a drop in temperature. The compost should have an earthy smell, similar to peat moss, and should have a dark brown color.

[19]　　Several composting plants are in operation in the U.S., most with some type of "automated windrows." These units, often referred to as "digesters", aerate the mixture

and help maintain an optimum moisture concentration. The detention time can thus be reduced to a few days instead of a few weeks.

[20]   Although compost is an excellent soil conditioner, it is not widely used by U.S. farmers. Inorganic fertilizers are cheap and easy to apply and most farms are located where soil conditions are good. The plentiful food supply in most developed countries does not dictate the use of marginal lands where compost would be of real value.

New Words and Expressions

conservation [kɔnsə'veiʃən]	n.	保护
in volume		在体积上；在数量上
virgin ['və:fdʒin]	a.	原始的；洁白的
drive [draiv]	n.	趋势；回收热
free labour		无偿劳动
repulp [ri'pʌlp]	v.	再生产；再浆化
obnoxious [ɔb'nɔkʃəs]	a.	讨厌的
discard [dis'kɑ:d]	vt.	丢弃
landfill ['lændfil]	v.	掩埋
segregation * [segri'geiʃən]	n.	分离
digester [di'dʒestə]	n.	消化池；蒸煮器；
sort [sɔ:t]	vt.	分类
grind [graind]	vt.	碾碎
windrow ['windrau]	n.	堆料
penetrate ['penitreit]	v.	渗入
neutrality [nju:'træliti]	n.	中性
bark [bɑ:k]	n.	树皮
inoculant [inə'kjulənt]	n.	接种剂
dearth [də:θ]	n.	缺乏
peat [pi:t]	a.	泥炭的
moss [mɔs]	n.	沼泽
automated windrow		自动调节堆料
optimum moisture concentration		合适的湿气浓度
dictate ['dikteit]	vt.	要求
marginal * ['mɑ:dʒinəl]	a.	页边的；边远的

Notes

①in the heat of environmental concern, …the total process necessary for….
necessary for… 相当于 which is necessary for….
②to be disposed 不定式的被动态常表示将来时，本句中的意思是"将要处理的"。
③句中的"recycled"为过去分词，作后置定语。单个的过去分词作定语常置于被修饰名词之后。
④…most of that is shipped… 句中的 that 指前面的 paper。
⑤as…as to recycle or refill an old one. 句中的 as…as 为同等比较。第二个 as 后省略了"it is expensive"。
⑥…because it is felt that this problem…. it is felt that 是一个无人称句。this problem 指 separate paper and garbage。

Exercises

Reading Comprehension

Ⅰ. Say whether the following statement are True (T) or False (F) according to the text.
1. Theoretically resource recovery from solid waste is very appealing, but practically recycling is not so easy.   (   )
2. When one thinks of collection, often it is regarded as "recycling".   (   )
3. Virgin paper is much cheaper than paper recycled, thus only about 30% of our present supply of paper is recycled.   (   )
4. Scrap steel can be easily recycled from industrial scrap and there is a good market for it.   (   )
5. The cost of recycling an old glass bottle is almost the same as making a new one.
                                                                                                    (   )
6. If we had better ways to segregate refuse, composting would be a much more attractive method of resource recovery.   (   )
7. A shortage of moisture with a windrow hinders biological life whereas too much moisture makes it hard to maintain aerobic conditions.   (   )
8. Inocculants have proven important in a composting operation.   (   )
9. A composting operation will come to an end when temperature within a windrow drops.   (   )
10. U.S farmers use compost because it is an excellent soil conditioner.   (   )

Ⅱ. Supply the missing words or expressions for the following sentences from the text.
1. Collection is different from _____ in that collection is only one step in the total pro-

cess of resource recovery.
2. Some common recyclable materials are paper, _____, _____ and _____.
3. The only way to recycle paper to paper is to create a market for _____ paper and make _____ paper artificially expensive by means of public support, _____ or ____.
4. _____ is the most common process to convert organics into useful products.
5. A typical composting operation consists of three steps. First, the _____ of refuse into organic and _____ components. Second, _____ of the ogranic portion. Third, _____ in either open piles or in mechanical "digesters".

Vocabulary

I. Fill in the blanks with words given below, changing the form where necessary.

| dearth obnoxious dictate discard |
| sort |

1. Cans _____ as litter can be collected and recycled.
2. Wastes are _____ by machine before they are to be reused.
3. A _____ of aerobic conditions inhibits biological life.
4. The lack of food supply in some countries _____ the use of marginal lands.
5. Ammonia gives off an _____ odor.

II. Match the words in Column A with their definitions or descriptions in Column B.

Column A	Column B
1. component	a. written or printed at the margin of a page or sheet
2. grind	b. one of the parts that make up a whole
3. segregation	c. put air or gas into sth
4. aerate	d. putting apart from the rest
5. marginal	e. crush into bits or powder

Translation　　　　　　　　　　　　长难句（二）

英语有些句子结构与汉语相反，在理解和翻译时，从后往前推便可一气哈成，层次分明，可用倒译法；所谓分译法是指把大句子化成小句子，把句中的某些成分单独译成独立的句子，而且顺序也可以调整。

例1　Second, closely related to the perception of energy transition has been the concept of an ultimate backstop technology, such as solar energy or nuclear fusion that can fill all of society's energy need.
　　第二，像太阳能及核裂变这种最后的"保底"技术，能满足全社会对能源的需要。这一概念一向与能源转移技术关系密切。

例2　First, a popular conception of future energy paths, reflected in many of the titles of well-known energy studies, portrays the transition from a steady-state system existing before 1973 to another steady-state system, often based/on solar energy, at some point in the next century.

首先，开发未来能源是流行概念，是从 1973 年以前的一个稳态方式，转入另一个稳态方法。这种新的稳态方式主要是依靠太阳能，有些人认为要到下一个世纪。这在许多著名能源研究课题中都有所反映。

Translate the following sentences into Chinese.

1) People were afraid to leave their house for although the police had keen ordered to stand by in case of emergency, they were just as confused and helpless as anybody else.
2) Aluminium remained unknown until the nineteenth century, because nowhere in nature is it found free, owing to its always being combined with other elements, most commonly with oxygen, for which it has a strong affinity（亲和力）
3) To a large extent he had made possible the enormous changes in communications that occurred during the 73 years of his life.
4) In the case of copper concentrates, the resultant calcine（焙砂）from a fluid bed reactor would be in the desired physical condition for chemical leaching to recover copper or for treatment to recover copper and precious metals by the solid state segregation process recently developed.

Reading Material A

Disposal of Solid Waste-Landfilling

The dump is the most inexpensive and thus most popular means of solid waste disposal. The dump does, however, have drawbacks, including rats, insects, odor, and fires. More acceptable means of solid waste disposal are not being used by most communities, usually at the insistence of federal or state governments.

Sanitary landfills differ markedly from open dumps. The latter are simply places to dump wastes, while sanitary landfills are engineered operations, designed and operated according to acceptable standards.①

The basic principle of a landfill operation is to deposit the refuse, compact it with bulldozers, and cover the material with at least 6 inches of dirt at the conclusion of each day's operation and a final cover of 2 feet when the area is full. The 2 feet is necessary to prevent rodents from burrowing into the refuse.

The selection of a landfill site is a sticky problem. The engineering aspects include (a) drainage——rapid runoff will lessen mosquito problems, but proximity to streams or well supplies might result in water pollution; (b) wind——it is preferable that the landfill be downwind from the community; (c) distance from collection; (d) size——a small site with limited capacity is generally not acceptable since the trouble of finding a new site is considerable; (e) ultimate use——can the area be utilized for public or private use after the operation is complete?

Perhaps even more important than the engineering problems are the social and psychological problems. No one in his right mind will be happy about having a sanitary landfill in his back yard. Right?

Surprisingly enough, however, there have been many cases where property values have actually been enhanced by a landfill or, more correctly, by what was done with the landfill site after the operation was complete. ② Golf courses, playgrounds and tennis courts can be rewards for tolerating a landfill operation for a few years. ③ If the operation is conducted according to accepted practice, there should be little adverse environmental impact from landfills. This is, as you might suspect, a difficult thing to explain to the community, especially since most "sanitary landfills" have in the past been glorified dumps. The landfill operation is actually a biological method of waste treatment. Municipal refuse deposited as a fill is anything but insert. ④ In the absence of oxygen, an aerobic decomposition steadily degrades the organic material to more stable forms. But this process is very slow. After 25 years the decomposition can still be going strong.

The end products of this decomposition are mostly gases: CO_2, CH_4, NH_3, and a little H_2S. These must obviously find some means of escape, and it is good practice to install vents in landfills to prevent the build-up of these gases. The decomposition reactions are self-sustaining, and temperatures often attain 135°F or higher.

The biological aspects of landfills as well as the structural properties of compacted refuse dictate the ultimate use of landfill sites. Uneven settling is often a problem, and it is generally suggested that nothing be constructed on a landfill for at least two years after completion. With poor initial compaction, it is not unreasonable to expect 50% settling within the first five years.

Landfills should never be disturbed. Not only will this cause additional structural problems, but trapped gases can be a hazard. Buildings constructed on landfill sites should have spread footings (large concrete slabs) as foundations, although some have been constructed on pilings which extend through the fill and onto rock or other adequately strong material. ⑤

The cost of operating a landfill varies from about \$1 to \$2 per ton of refuse and represents the least-cost method of acceptable disposal for many communities.

Ocean disposal is another alternative for getting rid of solid wastes. Fortunately, this uncivilized practice is strongly discouraged by the governments of many countries and hopefully will eventually cease to be an acceptable alternative.

Notes

① …while sanitary landfills are engineered operations, designed and operated according to acceptable standards. ……而垃圾填埋是经工程监督的工作,是按照认可的标准设计和操作的。

② …there have been many cases where property values have actually been enhenced by a landfill or, more correctly, by what was done with the landfill site after the operation was complete. ……通过垃圾填埋,或者更确切地说,垃圾填埋工作结束后,通过对垃圾填埋地所做的一切,有许多例子表明地产实际上得到了增值。

③ 经历了数年的垃圾填埋,其上建起高尔夫球场、运动场和网球场,以此作为补偿。

④ 句中 but 相当于 except。

⑤ 句中 spread footings 是指放宽的底脚; some 是指 some buildings。

Reading Material B

Solid Wastes

When one thinks of solid waste, often the problems and processes which immediately come to mind are those associated with municipal disposal.① These substances generally are, of course, the products of various industries, but their disposal is not directly the responsibility of the industry which created them. The industries have their own problems-their own types of solid wastes which must be disposed of.

The ideal solution, economically, energetically, and environmentally, would be to recover and reuse many of the solid wastes.② Many industries have been attempting to recover their wastes, with varying degrees of success. As with most industry-related issues, pollution control and economics can't be separated. The primary responsibility of an industry official is to protect his company's financial position; if he doesn't, the company will soon be out of business, and the shareholders will suffer. The financial incentive may be to avoid fines, court cases, or costly enforcement squabbles, or it may be byproduct recovery, but unless the incentive is there, little progress will be made.

There are several types of solid wastes an industry may have to handle. There are, of course, the sludges which result from water treatment. There are also the process solids, such as collected particulates and slags. Many of these are composed of various minerals, though their form and actual chemical composition may vary significantly, depending upon the source.

More than one billion tons of solid wastes are produced annually by the minerals processing industries alone. These ores usually contain only small percentages of the desired substances (such as copper, iron, gold, or silver); thus the spent ores, or tailings, accumulate very rapidly.③ Tailings are typically composed of silica (sand), and various silicates and carbonates of calcium, magnesium, and possibly aluminum. These tailings, often consisting of very fine particles, are piled near the processing plant, creating a nuisance because of their size and physical instability; plant growth often must be encouraged to stabilize the piles. Few recovery methods have been found to be economically feasible for many of these wastes.

Table 1 Composition of Typical Fly Ash

Compound	Percent
SiO_2	31.6～39.7
Al_2O_3	16.9～19.0
Fe_2O_3	10.6～18.8
TiO	0.5～ 0.7
CaO	15.3～18.8
MgO	3.0～ 3.6
K_2O	1.0～ 1.6
Na_2O	0.6～ 0.7
Carbon	～2

Many industries also generate fly ash, the coal ash which results from, among other things, power generation.④ Fly ash is one substance on which much research has been done, looking for more and better ways for its usage. The composition of a typical fly ash is given in Table 1. In 1968, about 18% of the fly ash was recovered for byproduct reuse. Hopes are that this percentage will increase (although, at the same time the amount generated is also increasing).

Fly ash has been used fairly widely as an additive for cement. The fine fly ash can be added to the ground cement clinker, increasing for some purposes the desirable cement characteristics. For example, the U. S. Corps of Engineers uses fly ash in much of its concrete. Unfortunately, this is not the solution for fly ash disposal. Many cement companies have found the cement not to be marketable, primarily due to its dark color.

Fly ash is also used as one of the raw materials for the production of sintered lightweight aggregate, such as used in concrete blocks and other precast forms.⑤ It can be used as a filler in asphalt pavings, as a soil stabilizer for embankments, as raw material for bricks, and in the bases for road beds. Recent studies have shown its feasibility as a plastics filler. Some of the fly ash generated by power companies is bought by companies such as American Admixtures of Chicago for reuse. The remainder of the fly ash must be landfilled or piled near the plant.

Notes

①当人们想起固体废物，常常立刻联想到与城市废物处理有关的问题和办法。

② The ideal solution, economically, energetically, and environmentally, would be to recover … 从经济、能源和环境的角度来看，理想的办法是回收……
③ spent ores 废矿石。
④ 许多种工业也产生飞尘，其中包括发电业产生出的煤尘。
⑤ sintered lightweight aggregate 多孔轻集料。

UNIT SIXTEEN

Text Removal of Organic Vapour from Effluent Gases

[1]   There are a number of industrial processes where large quantities of organic vapour are emitted into the atmosphere. Refinery operations, coated-fabric units, polymer-processing, synthetic-fibre industries, solvent extraction, leather processing, paper and plastic processing, combustion of fossil fuels in boilers, furnaces and internal-combustion operations, etc. add to atmospheric pollution. It may be noted that once the organic materials escape into the atmosphere, there is hardly any method by which they can be fixed. [1] They may even escape into the upper regions of the earth's atmosphere and deplete the ozone layer, a protection from unwanted radiations reaching the earth's surface. [2] Photochemical reactions with organic materials can lead to the formation of compounds which are directly harmful to living bodies, or bring about atmospheric changes affecting visibility, forming smog, etc. Pollution due to organic materials is not a local problem. It crosses national boundaries and has repercussions on all living beings.

[2]   It is very important to employ hoods which suck out organic vapour along with air from the processing area. With a proper collection system the gases containing organic vapour can be treated by the methods outlined below.

1. Absorption of vapour in suitable liquids
2. Condensation of vapour at low temperatures
3. Adsorption of vapour in suitable media
4. Destruction of vapour by combustion

[3]   As in the case of absorption of gases, the efficiency of the absorption equipment depends on factors such as the effective interfacial area of contact, time of contact of the phases, concentration of solute in the absorbing liquid and rate of reaction between the phases, if any. The liquid absorbent may be reactive or non-reactive where the pollutant is concerned. A reactive-type absorbent removes the pollutant through a chemical reaction, transforming the latter into a relatively less-toxic form. Very often the reactive or non-reactive type absorbents can be regenerated after processing and may be used again in the process.

[4]   The temperature of the gases containing vapour should normally bewell below 100°C for satisfactory operation of the absorption equipment. It is, therefore, necessary to cool the tail or stack gases. For absorption of other pollutants also, if present, it is necessary to cool the gases before they are sent into the adsorption unit. A direct-contact cooler can be used for this purpose. It can be a spray, packed or venturi type. The last named is efficient but there is a large pressure drop. Yet it is commonly used because of its compact size and simplicity of operation. It may, however, be necessary to make use of a demister

after a venturi scrubber. Spray and packed type units are used when the flow rate of gases is very high and less pressure loss is desired. During the absorption of vapour or other pollutants, there is always a carryover of finer absorbent droplets. The carryover is higher in high-efficiency contactors.

[5]　The vapour-gas mixture is cooled to its dewpoint temperature when the vapour condenses out and can be collected. The dew point of vapour-gas, however, keeps decreasing as the concentration of vapour in the gas decreases. It is necessary, therefore, to progressively reduce the temperature of the gas mixture so that more and more of the material is recovered. The extent of recovery of the material or the final concentration of vapour in the exit gas depend on the final temperature to which the gases are cooled. ③ If the cooling is done in a shell and tube condenser the material obtained by the condenser is pure. As the cost of cooling the gases is very high and the final concentration of the gases highly dependent on the temperature of the vapour-gas mixture, it may not be possible to recover the material totally by condensation alone. Condensation of vapour from the gases as a method of recovery is, therefore, applicable only in those cases where the vapour-gas mixture is rich in vapour or saturated with it. In fact, it is most desirable that as much of the material as possible is recovered by condensation by cooling the gases to a temperature which is economically viable. ④ Condensation of organic material, therefore, can at best serve as a preliminary-removal method prior to treatment by methods such as adsorption or combustion.

[6]　As discussed earlier, cooling and absorption of vapour-gas mixtures are economically feasible only when the concentration of vapour is high. One or both of these methods are used for the preliminary recovery or removal of a major quantity of the vapour. The quantity left may be still too great to be let out into the atmosphere. Further polishing of the gases for the residual vapour quantities in the exit stream is required. Adsorption is by far the best method when the quantity of organic vapour in the gas is small (500 ppm or less) and where absorption and condensation cannot be used due to economic considerations. ⑤

[7]　For adsorption, activated carbon of suitable pore size and surface area is used in fixed or fluidized beds. Fluidized beds are cheaper for higher gas-flow rates, have lower over-all operating costs, low steam consumption due to high solvent loading are less fire hazardous. ⑥

[8]　Destruction of organic vapour by combustion, called incineration, can be brought about by one of the following three methods depending upon the nature of the components in the vapour, their composition and concentration.
　1. Direct flame combustion
　2. Thermal incineration
　3. Catalytic incineration

New Words and Expressions

coated-fabric unit		胶布厂
polymer-processing		聚合物加工
photochemical [ˌfəutəu'kemikəl]	a.	光化学的
visibility [visi'biliti]	n.	能见度
repercussion [ˌriːpə'kʌʃən]	n.	影响
hood [hud]	n.	通风橱
suck out		吸出
interfacial [ˌintə'feiʃəl]	a.	界面的；面际的
solute ['sɔliju:t]	n.	溶质；溶解物
absorbent [əb'sɔːbənt]	n.	吸收剂；吸收质
stack [stæk]	n.	烟道
venturi scrubber		文丘里涤气器
demister [di'mistə]	n.	除雾器
carryover ['kæriəuvə]	n.	携带
dew point		露点
preliminary [pri'liminəri]	a.	初步的；预备的
adsorption [æd'sɔːpʃən]	n.	吸附作用
pore size		孔径大小
incineration [inˌsinə'reiʃən]	n.	焚化
catalytic [ˌkætə'litik]	a.	催化的

Notes

①It 是形式主语，真正的主语是 that 引导的从句，在主语从句中包含了一个由 once 引导的表示时间的状语从句。

②…, a protection from…. 这是名词短语，相当于从句 which is a protection…。

③句中的"to which"意思是"to the temperature"。介词 to 是"cool to"，即"冷却到"。

④句中的第一个 by 短语修饰 recovered；第二个 by 短语修饰 condensation，即通过冷却来达到冷凝。

⑤句中两个从句 when…和 where…均为状语从句，前一个表示什么时候这种方法最好；后一个表示在什么情况下使用最好。

⑥句中 have lower over-all operating costs 的主语是 Fluidizd beds. due to high solvent loading 在后一分句中作状语表示原因，说明主语的情况。

Exercises

Reading Comprehension

I. Say whether the following statements are True (T) or False (F) according to the text.

1. We note that once the organic materials go into the atmosphere, they can be fixed.
   (   )
2. There are four methods to treat organic vapour.   (   )
3. The efficiency of absorption equipment depends only on the time of contact.   (   )
4. The temperature of the gases containing vapour should be above 100 °C.   (   )
5. The venturi type is commonly used because it is easy to operate.   (   )
6. It is important to reduce the temperature of the gas mixture so as to recover more of the material.   (   )
7. It may not be possible to recover the material completely by condensation because the cost of cooling the gases is very high.   (   )
8. Cooling and absorption of vapour-gas mixtures are feasible only when the concentration of vapour is high.   (   )
9. Where absorption and concentration cannot be used due to economic consideration, it is best to use adsorption.   (   )
10. Cooling and absorption of vapour-gas mixtures are always economically feasible.
    (   )

II. Supply the missing words or expressions for the following sentences from the text.
1. _____, _____, _____, _____, _____, _____, _____, _____, _____ add to atmospheric pollution.
2. The four methods of treatment of gases containing organic vapour are _____, _____, _____, and _____.
3. The vapour-gas mixture is cooled to its _____ when the vapour condenses out and can be collected.
4. Destruction of organic vapour by combustion is called _____.
5. The three methods of destruction of organic vapour by combustion is _____, _____, and _____.

Vocabulary

I. Fill in the blanks with words given below, changing the form where necessary.

| residual   incineration   repercussion |
| suck out   preliminary |

1. It is sometimes difficult to remove the _____ poisons in polluted water.
2. We can dispose of the waste by _____ .
3. He confirmed in his belief after some _____ experiments.
4. Water pollution has serious _____ on fish in rivers or lakes.
5. The doctor tried to _____ the poison _____ of the wound.

Ⅱ. Match Column A with their definitions and descriptions in Column B.

    Column A   Column B
    1. solute   a. attraction and holding a gas or liquid to its surface
    2. absorbent   b. a liquid in which sth is dissolved
    3. demister   c. a device which removes the mist from…
    4. adsorption   d. a substance that is able to take in moisture
    5. stack   e. tall chimney or funnel for carrying away smoke.

Translation   综合翻译练习

Translate the following sentences into Chinese.

1. Although it is important to avoid conditions in natural streams and in treatment plans that are supposedly aerobic, there are circumstances under which anaerobic microorganism provide a useful part of treatment.
2. This method of solid-waste disposal has achieved more success in countries where synthetic fertilizers are not readily available.
3. Disposal of this waste, which is increasing at a rate faster than that of the expanding population, poses a particularly difficult problem.
4. In 1975, the output value of Shanghai's heavy industry multiplied 18 times as against 1949.
5. If two atoms of chlorine combine, we have a molecule of chlorine gas, which is how the free element chlorine exists in nature.
6. You might consider atoms as extremely small building blocks, each one of any single element being chemically the same, but no atoms of different elements being similar.
7. The filter material is cleaned from time to time, by reversing the flow of water so that the filter material is washed through with cleanwater and by using compressed air bubbles to agitate the material so that the accumulated dirt is separated, rises to the top and can be removed.
8. With the use of advanced treatment technology, sewage discharges in this city has been reduced by five times.

Reading Material A

Managing Climatic Change

The burning of fossil fuels and, to a lesser extent, the loss of vegetative cover, particularly forests, through urban-industrial growth increase the accumulation of CO_2 in the atmosphere. ① The pre-industrial concentration was about 280 parts of carbon dioxide per million parts of air by volume. ② This concentration reached 340 in 1980 and is expected to double to 560 between the middle and the end of the next century. Other gases also play an important role in this 'greenhouse effect', whereby solar radiation is trapped near the ground, warming the globe and changing the climate.

After reviewing the latest evidence on the greenhouse effect in October 1985 at a meeting in Villach, Austria, organized by the WMO, UNEP, and ICSU, scientists from 29 industrialized and developing countries concluded that climate change must be considered a 'plausible and serious probability'. ③ They further concluded that: 'Many important economic and social decisions are being made today on ⋯ major water resource management activities such as irrigation and hydropower; drought relief; agricultural land use; structural designs and coastal engineering projects; and energy planning-all based on the assumption that past climatic data, without modification, are a reliable guide to the future. This is no longer a good assumption'.

They estimated that if present trends continue, the combined concentration of CO_2 and other greenhouse gases in the atmosphere would be equivalent to a doubling of CO_2 from pre-industrial levels, possibly as early as the 2030s, and could lead to a rise in global mean temperatures 'greater than any in man's history. Current modelling studies and 'experiments' show a rise in globally averaged surface temperatures, for an effective CO_2 doubling, of somewhere between 1.5 ℃ and 4.5 ℃, with the warming becoming more pronounced at higher latitudes during winter than at the equator. ④

An important concern is that 2 global temperature rise of 1.5—4.5 ℃, with perhaps a two to three times greater warming at the poles, would lead to a sea level rise of 25—140 centimeters. A rise in the upper part of this range would flood low-lying coastal cities and agricultural areas, and many countries could expect their economic, social, and political structures to be severely disrupted. It would also slow the 'atmospheric heat-engine', which is driven by the differences between equatorial and polar temperatures, thus influencing rainfall regimes. Experts believe that crop and forest boundaries will move to higher latitudes; the effects of warmer oceans on marine ecosystems or fisheries and food chains are also virtually unknown.

A four-track strategy is needed, combining:

- improved monitoring and assessment of the evolving phenomena;
- increased research to improve knowledge about the origins, mechanisms, and effects of the phenomena;
- the development of internationally agreed policies for the reduction of the causative gases; and
- adoption of strategies needed to minimize damage and cope with the climate changes, and rising sea level.

While these strategies are being developed, more immediate policy measures can and should be adopted. The most urgent are those required to increase and extend the recent steady gains in energy efficiency and to shift the energy mix more towards renewables. Carbon dioxide output globally could be significantly reduced by energy efficiency measures without any reduction of the tempo of GDP growth. ⑤ These measures would also serve to abate other emissions and thus reduce acidification and urban-industrial air pollution. Gaseous fuels produce less carbon dioxide per unit of energy output than oil or coal and should be promoted, especially for cooking and other domestic uses.

Gases other than carbon dioxide are thought to be responsible for about one-third of present global warming, and it is estimated that they will cause about half the problem around 2030. Some of these, notably chlorofluorocarbons used as aerosols, refrigeration chemicals, and in the manufacture of plastics, may be more easily controlled than CO_2. These, although not strictly energy-related, will have a decisive influence on policies for managing carbon dioxide emissions.

Apart from their climatic effect, chlorofluorocarbons are responsible to a large extent for damage to the earth's stratospheric ozone. The chemical industry should make every effort to find replacements, and governments should require the use of such replacements when found (as some nations have outlawed the use of these chemicals as aerosols). Governments should ratify the existing ozone convention and develop protocols for the limitation of chlorofluorocarbon emissions, and systematically monitor and report implementation.

Notes

① fossil fuels 矿物燃料（如煤、石油和天然气）
② 按体积计算，工业化以前的浓度是每百万份空气中大约有二百八十份二氧化碳。
③ WMO＝World Meteorological Organization（联合国）世界气象组织，UNEP＝United Nations Environment Programme 联合国环境规划署，ICSU＝International Council of Scientific Unions 国际科学协会理事会。
④ 目前模拟研究以及实验表明，随着冬天高纬度地区的暖热趋势比赤道地区更趋明显，如果二氧化碳成倍增长成为现实的话，全球性的平均表面温度将上升，有些地方将增加1.5度至4.5度。

⑤GDP=gross domestic product 国内生产总值。

Reading Material B

Pollution Prevention or Cure

Pollution is an inevitable consequence of most human activity. The Commission of the European Communities (CEC, 1979) has put this concisely:

Almost all human activities make some impact on the natural environment, and almost all industrial processes which transform natural resources into products for man's use give rise to some pollution. Acceptance of the reality of this situation is now general, although there are still some who call for a removal of all pollution, not realising that this would signal the end of human activity, as well as of industrial civilisation as we know it.①

Despite the popular belief that pollution is getting worse, the available information indicates that trends vary greatly between individual pollutants. In general, acute local pollution has become very rare, whereas widespread low-level pollution has been increasingly recognised as a potential problem.② Localised elevated pollution levels associated with particular industrial and other stationary sources still cause serious (and sometimes avoidable) problems.

It is generally accepted that pollution prevention is better than cure and, in the phrase that Royston (1979) has popularised, that 'pollution prevention pays'.③ Royston gave many anecdotal examples of this maxim and the European Commission stated that 'several studies show that the cost of preventing pollution and nuisances is less than the cost of repairing the damage caused and introducing anti-pollution measures'.

The Commission (1979) found that:

Too much economic activity has taken place in the wrong place, using environmentally unsuitable technologies. The consequence has often been a choice between accepting pollution as a necessary evil or paying very large sums for its elimination.

The Commission's environmental policy is overtly directed towards prevention by anticipatory, or prospective, control: 'the best environmental policy consists in preventing the creation of pollution or nuisances at source rather than subsequently trying to counteract their effects'④ (CEC, 1977: 6). This theme of anticipatory action is now widely recognised and is being promoted by a number of international bodies, such as the International Union for Conservation of Nature and Natural Resources (1980). Planning pollution prevention i.e., incorporating pollution controls at the planning stage during the siting process for a pollution source, is one of the cornerstones of sustainable development.

Needless to say, the intention to prevent does not invariably preclude the necessity to cure. However carefully considered, prospective controls cannot always anticipate either changes in technology or future trends in production, which may result in unexpected pollution levels, or changes in public attitudes, which may lead to the decreasing acceptability of once-tolerated levels.⑤ Similarly, it must be remembered that achieving pollution control compliance in the first instance is no guarantee that it will continue indefinitely. Consequently most countries adopt a two-pronged, mutually reinforcing approach to pollution control. Holdgate (1979) has summarised this as being:

1. through a land use planning or development control process in which the distribution of sources of pollution is adjusted so as to be compatible with other priority land uses, and so that pollution from new development is constrained from the outset;⑥

2. through controls, operated by various official agencies or voluntarily within industries, limiting existing sources of pollution and ensuring that new sources comply with conditions imposed when they are built.⑦

Notes

①…although there are still some who call for a removal of all pollution, not realising that this would signal the end of human activity, as well as of industrial civilisation as we know it.…… 尽管还有一些人要求消灭一切污染,他们没有意识到这样做将会终止人类的活动,结束我们所共识的工业文明。

②一般来说,严重的局部污染已不再常见,但分布广的低程度污染已日益被视为一个潜在的问题。

③… in the phrase that Royston has popularised, that 'pollution prevention pays'. ……… 正如 Royston 所大肆宣传的那样"污染防止是值得的"。

④… 'the best environmental policy consists in preventing the creation of pollution or nuisances at source rather than subsequently trying to counteract their effects'. …… 最佳的环境保护政策在于:对污染或者诸如此类恼人的事情要防患于未然,而不是随之造成诸多影响后再加以抵制。

⑤不管经过多么审慎地考虑,这些防范措施未必能预测技术的变化,或者是生产方面的未来趋势,其结果可能是意想不到的污染程度;或者是会导致公众对一度还能容忍的污染程度变得越来越不可接受。

⑥through a land use planning or development control process in which the distribution of sources of pollution is adjusted so as to be compatible with other priority land use,…. 通过土地使用规划或者是控制发展的办法,用这种办法对污染源分布进行调整使之与其他优先考虑的土地使用相适应……。

⑦通过各官方机构或行业间自愿执行的抑制措施,限制现有的污染源,确保新污染源在建设的同时遵守必须执行的条件。

Appendix I   Vocabulary

absorbent n. 吸收剂，吸收质	16
acetone n. 丙酮	06
acidic a. 酸性的	10
acitivate * vt. 使活化	14
activated a. 活化了的，激活后的	07
acute * a. 急性的	12
adsorption n. 吸附作用	
advent * n. 到来，出现	01
adversely ad. 反向地，有害地，不利地	07
aerate vt. 充气	15
aerobic a. 需氧[气]的	07
easthetically ad. 从审美角度看	03
aggravation n. 恶化	11
agitation n. 搅动（作用），搅拌（作用）	04
aldehyde n. 乙醛	13
alleviate vt. （使）减轻，（使）缓和	04
all to 可惜太，过于	01
alternate v./a. （使）交替，（使）轮流；交替的，轮流的	03
ambient * a. 周围的，环境的	09
amelioration n. 改良，改善	11
amino a. 氨基的	06
amino acid 氨基酸	13
ammonia * n. 氨（水）	06
anaerobe n. 厌氧[气]菌[微生物]	07
anhydrous a. 无水的	07
anthracite n. 无烟煤	04
anthropogenic a. 由人类活动引起的	11
antiknock a. 抗爆的	13
anvil n. 砧骨	14
appreciable * a. 相当可观的	13
approximation * n. 近似（值法）	08
aquatic a. 水生[产，上，中]的	02
aquifer n. 含水层	11
asbestos * n. 石棉	05
assumption * n. 假设，设想，前提	08
auditory a. 耳的；听觉的	14
automated windrow 自动调节料堆	
backflow n. 回流，倒流	01
backyard n. 后天井，后院	
bacterial a. 细菌的	13
bacteriologically ad. 按细菌学的观点	03
bark n. 树皮	15
basin n. 流域，排水区域	03
benzene n. 苯	12
be subject to 必须得到	12
better than 超过	13
biodegradable a. 生物可降解的	06
bioelectrical a. 生物电的	14
biomass n. 生物量	08
biota n. 生物群	07
bloom n. 大量增值，旺发	04
blowout n. 油田喷井	10
bond n. 键，链	06
breakthrough * n. 渗漏，穿透	04
buffer n. 缓冲	14
buildup * n. 增加[强，大]	07
cadmium n. 镉	08
calibrate * vt. 校准[正]，标定	02
carbonaceous a. 含碳的	13
carbon monoxide 一氧化碳	13
carburetor n. 汽化器	13
carcinogenic a. 致癌的	12
cardiovascula a. 心血管的	14
caries n. 龋；骨疡	03
carryover n. 携带	16
casing n. 壳（体），外壳	09
catalytic a. 催化的	16

149

caveat　　n. 防止误解的说明		08
cavitation　　n. 空蚀[气蚀,空穴]作用		09
cavity *　　n. 空腔		14
challenge　　n.（提出的复杂）问题，		
（造成的）困难		03
chlordane　　n. 氯丹		10
chlorination　　n. 氯化处理，氯化灭菌		01
chlorindated hydrocarbon　　氯化烃		10
chlorine　　n. 氯（气）		01
cholera　　n. 霍乱		01
chronic　　a. 长期的，慢性的		12
cistern　　n. 蓄水池		01
clarifier　　n. 澄清[滤清]器，沉淀槽		07
clog　　v./n. 阻[堵，填]，障[妨]		
碍（物）		04
closet　　n. 洗室，厕所		05
coagulation　　n. 絮凝		01
coated-fabric unit　　胶布厂		16
collecting sewer　　污水支管		05
colloquially　　ad. 口语地，通俗地		05
cochlea　　n. 耳蜗		14
concentration　　n. 浓度，密度		13
conditioning　　n. 调理[节、整、解]		04
conduit　　n. 水[输送]管，水[沟]渠		05
conservation　　n. 保护		15
constricted　　a. 狭窄的		09
contamination *　　n. 污染		01
controversy　　n. 争论		11
convalescent　　a. 恢复期的		14
convey　　v. 排放		10
corrosivity　　n. 废蚀性		12
crankcase　　n. 曲轴箱		13
creek　　n. 小溪，小河		01
criterion *　　n. 标准，规范，依据		07
critical　　a. 临界的，极限的		07
culprit　　n. 罪魁祸首		10
culture　　n.（人工，细菌）培养，繁殖		07
cursory　　a. 粗略的		11
cylinder *　　n. 钢瓶		12
cysteine　　n. 半胱氨酸		13
deamination　　n. 脱氨基（作用）		06
dearth　　n. 缺乏		15
debris　　n. 碎片，粗砂，垃场		09
decompose *　　v. 分解，溶解		07
deflect *　　v. 转向		14
degradation *　　n. 降解		13
degrade *　　n. 降低，下降，褪化		03
demineralize　　vt. 脱[去]矿质，除盐，		
软化		03
demister　　n. 除雾器		16
deplete *　　vt. 耗尽		10
depletion　　n. 消耗，减少，降低		02
deposition *　　n. 沉积		11
detergent　　n./a. 洗涤[净]剂,去污剂,		
洗净的清洁的		06
detrimental *　　a. 有害的，不利的		05
dewater　　v. 排[去，脱，抽]水		09
dew point　　露点		16
diagonal *　　a. 对角（线）的		09
dictate　　vt. 要求		15
dieldrin　　n. 狄氏剂（一种杀虫剂）		10
digester　　n. 消化池；蒸煮器		07
dioxide *　　n. 二氧化物		13
dioxin　　n. 二噁英		12
discard　　vt. 丢弃		15
disinfect　　vt.（给…）消毒，杀菌，洗		
净		03
disinfection　　n. 消毒，灭菌		01
disperse *　　v. 分散		10
disposability　　n. 任意处理[处置]性		08
disposal　　n. 处理[置]，消[清]除		03
dissipate *　　vt. 清除		10
distribntion　　n. 传输		01
drive　　n. 趋向；回收热		15
drum　　n. 桶		12
dyn=dyne　　n. 达因		08)
dysentery　　n. 痢疾		01
easement　　n. 附属建筑物		05

英文	释义	页
eductor	n. 喷射器，排放管	09
ejector	n. 喷射器，喷射泵	09
electrode *	n. 电极；电焊条	02
electrolyte *	n. 电解（溶）液，电解（离）质	02
elevation *	n. 高程［度，地］；上升，提高	05
empirical *	a. 实验（上）的，以实验为根据［基础］的	06
enact	vt. 制［规］定，颁布	03
enhance *	vt. 增（加）强，提高，增加	04
enzyme	n. 酶，酵素	06
estrogen-mimicking	仿雌性的	16
ethanol	n. 乙醇，酒精	06
ether	n. 醚，乙醚	06
eutrophication	n. 富（营）养化水体加富过程	03
evacuate *	vt. 转移，撤出	12
even	vt. 使平均［平衡］	05
exposure	n. 暴露	12
facet	n. 方面	01
facility	n. 工厂	10
fauna	n. 动物	11
feces	n.（复数）粪便	10
filter run	过滤周期，过滤循环	04
finishing	n. 精修［制］，精［最终］加工	07
fire supply	消防给水	09
fluctuation	n. 波［振、变］动，升降，振幅	09
fluidize	vt. 使液体化，使变成流体	04
flume	n. 水［渡］槽	05
fluoridation	n. 氟化作用［反应］，加氟作用	03
fluoride	n. 氟化物	03
flush *	v./n.（强液体流）冲［清］洗；冲水［砂］	03
flux *	n. 通量	11
fraught (with)	a. 充满…的，伴随着…的	02
free labor	无偿劳动	15
galvanic	a.（流）电的，（电池）电流的	02
granular	n. 粒状［面］的，晶［颗］粒的	04
grease *	n. 油［动物］脂	06
grit	n. 勇气和耐力	01
grouchy	a. 愠怒的	14
grumpy	a. 暴燥的	14
halogenate	vt. 使卤化	13
halogenated compound	卤化物	13
hammer	n. 锤骨	14
hemoglobin	n. 血红蛋白	13
heptachlor	n. 七氯（一种杀虫剂）	10
heterogeneous *	a. 不均匀的；多相的；非均质的	06
hexane	n. 己烷	06
homologous *	a. 相应的，相［类］似的，同调［系，族］的	09
hood	n. 通风橱	16
hydrate	n./v. 水合［化］物，水合［化］作用；（使成）氢氧化物，（使）成水合物	06
hydrocarbon *	n. 碳氢化合化物	14
hypothetical	a. 假定［设，想］的	09
identify	vt. 确定	10
ignitability	n. 可燃性	12
ignitable	a. 可燃的	12
ignition	n. 点火，引燃起爆	08
illustrative	a. 说明［解说］性的	08
impact	n. 影响	11
impairment	n. 降低	14
impeller	n. 叶轮，涡轮	09
impotent	a. 不起作用的，软弱无能的	01
inactivation	n. 灭活，失活，纯化（作用）	04

incidence *	n. 发生（率，影响（范围，程度，方式）	03
incineration	n. 焚化	16
incorperate *	v. 结合	11
in-depth	a. 深层的，深入的，彻底的	04
indiscriminate	a. 不加区别的	12
induce *	vt. 引起，招致，导致	09
inflow	n. 流入物，流入（量），进水[气]	05
influent	n. 流入液体，进水；渗流	04
ingenuity	n. 善于创新	13
inhibit	vt. 防[阻，制]止，抑制	07
inoculum (pl. inocula)	n. 细菌培养液	07
inoculant	a./n. 接种的；接种剂	15
insulate *	vt. 使绝缘（热）	02
integral	a. 主要的，必备的	01
intercept *	vt. 截取[断，击]，拦截	05
interception	n. 截流，拦截，阻断	04
interceptor	n. 截流管，截水沟	05
interfacial	a. 界面的，面际的	16
interstitial	a. 间[缝、填]隙的，隙间的	04
in the context of	在…过程中	13
intrinsic *	a. 内在的	11
in volume	在体积上；在数量上	15
iodide	n. 碘化物	02
iodine	n. 碘	02
ion *	n. 离子	02
ionizing radiation	电离辐射	12
irate	a. 发怒的	14
irritability	n. 烦燥	14
keep clear of	避开，不接触	05
kinetic *	a. 运动的，动力（学）的	09
landfill	n. 掩埋	15
lay	v. 消除	01
lignin	n. 木质素，木质	06
lipid (e)	n. 类脂（化合）物	06
lipoprotein	n. 脂（肪）蛋白	06
living tissue	活性组织	12

lobe	n. 突齿，凸起；瓣[叶形]轮	09
mandatory	a. 必须遵循的，强制性的	05
manganese *	n. 锰	02
manganaous	a. （亚，二价，含）锰的	02
manhole	n. 人孔，检查[修]孔，探[检查]井	05
marginal *	a. 页边的	15
membrane *	n. （薄，隔）膜片[状物]	02
meshing	n. 啮[咬]合	09
mesophilic	a. 中温的，嗜温的	07
metabolize	vt. 使新陈代谢	07
metallic *	a. 金属的	13
methodology *	n. 方法（学）	11
microammeter	n. 微安计，微安表	02
modify	vt. 缓和	11
monitor	vt. 监测	10
moss	n. 沼泽	15
mover	n. 发动机，马达	09
multimedia	n. 多层滤料	04
mutagenic	a. 诱变的	12
necessitate *	vt. 使…成为必要	14
neutrality	n. 中性	15
neutralize	vt. 使中和，平衡，抵消	07
nickel *	n. 镍	07
nil	n. 无；零	13
nitrate	n. 硝酸盐	11
nitric oxide	一氧化氮	13
nitrite	n. 亚酸盐	11
nitrogen oxide	氧化氮	13
nozzle *	n. 喷管[嘴，头]	09
objectionable *	a. 不能采用的，不好的，有害的	03
obnoxious	a. 讨厌的	15
odor	n. 气味	03
of interest	值得注意的，重要的	08
optimum *	a./n. 最佳的（值点，状态）	04
ordinance	n. 条例，条令	08

outhouse	n. (户外)厕所	01
oxidant	n. 氧化物	13
oxide *	n. 氧化物	02
oxygen level	含氧量	02
parameter	n. 参数[量，项]，系数	02
pathogenic organism	病原有机体	10
peat	a. 泥炭的	15
penetrate	v. 渗入	15
peptide	n. 肽，缩氨酸	06
percolate	vt. 渗漏	12
perforate	v. 穿[钻、打、冲]孔	05
permanganate	n. 高锰酸钾	03
permeable	a. 可渗[穿]透的，渗透性的	02
perplexing	a. 使人困惑的	12
persist in	坚持；留在……上	12
pesticide	n. 杀虫剂，农业药	08
phosphate	n. 磷酸盐[酯]	06
phosphoric	a. 磷的，含(五价)磷的	07
phosphorus *	n. 磷；磷光体，发光物质	06
photochemical	a. 光化学的	16
photosynthetic	a. 光合的	07
pilot	a. 中间规模的	04
pilot testing	中间试验	04
pitcher	n. 水罐	09
plating	n. (电，喷)镀	08
polymer *	n. 聚合物[体]，多[高]聚物	04
polymer-processing	聚合物加工	16
polymeric	a. 聚合的	06
pore *	n. 细[毛、微气]孔，孔隙	04
pore size	n. 孔径大小	16
potable	a. 可饮用的	01
potassium *	n. 钾	03
precipitate	v./n. (使)沉淀；沉淀物	02
precipitation	n. 沉降	11
preliminary	a. 初步的，预备的	16
prime mover	原动机	09
probe *	vt./n. 探测，探查；探测器，(试)探(电)极	02
profile *	n. 断[剖，切]面(图)，侧[立]面图	08
propeller	n. 螺旋浆	09
propeller pump	轴流泵，螺旋泵	09
pseudoplastic	n. 假塑性体	08
quantify *	vt. 定量测定	11
quantitative *	a. 定量的，(数)量的	09
radial *	a. 径向的	09
radial flow	轴向流，径向流	09
ram	n. 夯(锤)，锤头，锤体	09
reactive *	a. 反应的	12
reactivity *	n. 反应性	12
recreation area	游览胜地	10
regulatory *	a. 管理的	10
remedial	a. 补救的	12
repercussion	n. 影响	16
repulp	v. 再生浆	15
residual *	a./n. 剩余的，残余[留]的，剩余，残余物	03
residue *	n. 剩余(物)，残余(物)；滤[余，残]渣	06
respectively	ad. 依次地	11
respiration	n. 呼吸	07
rheogram	n. 流变图	08
rheological	n. 流变的	08
rotodynamic	a. 旋转动力的	09
rumble	vi. 发出隆隆声	14
runoff	n. 径流	10
sanitary waste	生活废水，生活废物，卫生设备排出的废物	05
saturate	vt. 使饱和	02
scale	n. 结[锅、管]垢，水垢[锈]	03
scale-up	n. 按比例放大[扩大，升高]	08
scrap *	vt./n. 废弃；废料，碎片	02
seaboard	n. 海岸线，沿海地区	01
sediment	n. 沉积物	10

segregation * n. 分离	15
settle v. （使）沉淀	01
sewage n. 污水；下水道（系统）	05
sewerage n. 污水[排水]口程，排水系统；污水	05
shaft * n. （传动，旋转）轴	09
silt n. 淤泥，泥沙	03
size n./vt. 尺寸，大小；依一定尺寸制造；（管材，轧管）定径	05
slime n. （粘，软，矿，煤）泥	07
sladge n. 污泥，泥状沉积物	03
soften * v. 软化；使[弄，变]软	03
solute n. 溶质；溶解物	16
solution n. 溶液，溶解（状态）	02
solvent * n./a. 溶剂（的）	06
sort v. 分类	15
so to speak 打个比方	12
sparingly ad. 有节制地；缺乏地，少量地	06
specific a. 比（率）的，单位的	02
specific speed 比速	09
spill n./v. 泄油	10
spillage n. 泄露，溢出	01
spore n. 孢子	13
spray n. 雾状物	13
stabilize * vt. 使稳定	03
stack n. 烟道	16
stirrup n. 镫骨	14
strain v. 粗[过]滤	04
strategic a. 策略的；政策的	14
stringent a. 严格的，精确的	03
substrate n. 基质，被（酶作）用物	06
suck out 吸出	16
suction n. 吸力；吸入；空吸	04
sulfate n. 硫酸盐	11
sump n. （集水，污水，排水）坑	09
surcharge vt. 超[过]载，（使负担）过重	05
surly a. 乖戾的	14
surface v. 暴露出来	01
surplus n. 剩余（物），过剩	06
symptom n. 征兆；迹象，症状[侯]	06
synchronism n. 同步	09
synthesis * (pl. syntheses) n. 合成（法）	06
tenuous a. 薄[脆]弱的	02
termination * n. 终止，结束	04
terpene n. 萜烯	13
terrain n. 地带，地形，场所	05
tetraethyl a. 四乙基的	13
thermal fixation 热固	13
thicken v. （使）变厚[粗、浓]	08
thiosulfate n. 硫代硫酸盐	02
thixotropic a. 能变（性）的，摇溶的	08
titrate v. 滴定	02
toluene n. 甲苯	12
toxicity n. 毒性	12
toxin n. 毒素[质]	07
trepidation n. 惊恐，惶恐	01
trickle v. （使）滴（下），一滴滴地流	07
trickling filter 生物（滴）滤池	07
trip v. （使）脱扣[开]；切断；关闭	09
turbidity n. 混浊度	01
turbulence * n. 湍流，紊流，涡流	04
tympanic a. 鼓的	14
tympanic membrane 鼓膜	14
typhoid n. 伤寒	01
uncontaminated a. 未被污染的，无杂质的	03
underflow n. 潜[底，下层]流，地下水流	04
uninhabitable a. 不适于居住的	02
urea n. 尿素	06
utility n. 公用事业公司，公用事业设备	01
variablity n. 易[可，能]变性，变化[异]性	08
vegetative a. 植物的	11

venturi scrubber 文丘里涤气器		16
viable *　　*a.* 活的，有活力的		08
vibration　　*n.* 振［摆］动		09
vice versa　　*ad.* 反之亦然		08
violate *　　*vt.* 违犯［背，反，章］		08
viral　　*a.* 滤过性毒的		01
virgin　　*a.* 原始的；洁白的		15
virus　　*n.*（过滤性）病毒，毒素		04
viscosity *　　*n.* 粘性，粘度		08
void *　　*n./a.* 空隙，孔隙；空的，空虚的		04
volatile *　　*a.* 挥发（性）的，易挥发［散发］的		06
volute　　*n./a.* 螺旋形（的），涡旋形的		09
VSS=volatile suspended solid　挥发性悬浮固体		08
waterborne　　*a.* 水传播的		01
water course　　*n.* 水道，渠道，河道		03
water works　　*n.* 供水设备［系统］；自来水厂		03
windrow　　*n.* 堆料		15
with respect to　　关于；就……而论		10
with the adrent of　　随着……的到来		01

Appendix II Translation for Reference

第 1 单元

美国城市供水系统发展史

　　如今，美国人均日用水量约为 150 至 200 加仑（包括商业用水），家庭人均日用水量约 60 加仑。平均全国日用水量达 370 多亿加仑，其中大部分由公用供水设施进行处理。

　　美国公用供水系统的发展史不仅是供水领域的历史，而且是一个不断发展的国家的历史。水及其诸多的用途一直是美国成长与发展的必不可少的重要方面。根据正式记载，美国从一个乡村化的农业国转变为一个城市化的工业强国，在很大程度上确实依赖于供水和为生活、工业及商业提供大量用水所需的工程建设。

　　美国有记载的最早公用供水系统当属 1652 年麻萨诸塞州的波士顿城。在早先那个年代，人们对建公用供水系统不屑一顾，因为其所提供的服务似乎还不如人们使用自家的水井或蓄水池方便。水只要看上去干净，即晶莹、清澈、凉爽，且无怪异的味道或气味，便是"好水"。这样的水在后院的井里随时可取。大多数人断无想到伤寒、痢疾、霍乱和"夏季易发疾病"会因水而引发。而这水却频频取自离居家户外厕所不太远的井中。

　　直到 1875 年以后，科学知识才确凿地证实了水生细菌可导致伤寒和霍乱，而且直到 1900 年以后，公众才意识到使用不洁水的危险性——无论这水的外观及味道如何。令人遗憾的是，直到过滤技术得到较为普遍采用的十九世纪和二十世纪初，公用供水通常并不比私人水源更安全。在早期的公用供水系统中，人们通常的作法是直接从小溪或河流中取水，不作任何处理或只稍加处理，然后将水用泵打入配水系统。

　　1800 年，美国只有 16 个公用供水系统，其中大部分在最初建造时只是为了"消防和涤尘"，很少有人考虑生活用水。这些系统大多数位于新英格兰，或分布于大西洋沿海地区的一些较大的城市中。

　　到 1850 年，居民区供水系统的数目已增至 83 个；在这些系统中，除了用沉淀池对混浊度做一些基本控制外，没有一个配置其他的净化工艺。然而，1900 年前后的这一时期被称为公用供水的"新时代"，这主要是因为水处理工艺开始提供更优质的水和更方便的用户服务，而这正是私人供水设施，如水井或水池所不能比拟的。在 1880 年，仅有 600 个供水系统；可到 1897 年，已出现了近 3,350 个公用供水系统——其中 1,400 个是在 1891 至 1897 几年间建造的！

　　到了 1950 年，公用供水系统已趋于成熟。早些年间的忧虑和惊恐已随着处理技术的出现而消失，而且从 1900 至 1950 年这 50 年间，公用供水系统的成就显而易见。1950 年，美国城市供水系统已超过 17,000 个。采用絮凝、快速过滤和加氯消毒方法的水处理工艺已将公用供水系统的作用从"消防和涤尘"的概念转变为价值达数百万美元的产业。

美国供水领域过去二百年间的技术进步,在整个公用供水史上也许一直是最重要的。水传播疾病几近消灭,较为廉价的饮用水供应充足,从而给该产业带来一个独特的问题——普通用户对公用供水视若当然!为提供更多、更好的水需要新的科学研究和技术,这可能是十分昂贵的。

虽然供水行业是美国最古老的产业之一,且就容量而言,它是全美单一商品的最大供应者,但是它却面临着其他好几个方面的忧患。水质问题正在美国许多地区出现。国内水受到重金属污染的新闻报道在报端层出不迭。对氯已产生耐药性的病毒生物体使目前所采用的消毒工艺不起作用,从而对健康构成严重威胁。目前很多居民区的设施根本无法应付工业及交通意外泄漏造成的污染。由于管理不善和监督不力,交叉连接和潜在倒流继续困扰着供水系统。

尽管有这些干扰,供水领域总的来说似乎有信心去克服这些难题,并迎接未来的挑战。借助科研手段,技术进步和艰苦不懈的努力,供水行业的人们正表现出美国人著称于世的勇气和决心;而且他们自信能继续提供可为美国公民所享用的最优质的水。

第 2 单元

水 质 检 测

要做到对水污染进行控制,对其污染物的定量检测显然是十分必要的。然而,这些污染物的检测却谈何容易。

第一个难题是引起污染的特定物质有时鲜为人知。第二个困难在于这些污染物一般浓度极低,因此需要极其精密的检测方法。

这儿仅讨论用来检测水污染的许多分析测试方法中的一种。用于水和废水工程的分析技术的全卷被汇编成"标准法"。目前该卷已出第十五版,是应测试技术标准化之需而产生的。它在这一领域具有权威性,其法律地位举足轻重。

许多污染物是以每升水含多少毫克物质(mg/L)来计量的。它是重量/体积计量法。在许多较早的出版物中,污染物被计量为百万分之几(ppm),这是个重量/重量参量。如果所测液体是水,这两种单位是相等的;这是由于一毫升水重一克。由于一些废水可能不具有水的比重,因此 ppm 计量已被废弃,人们偏向于用 mg/L。

第三个通用的参量为百分比,表示为重量/重量关系。很明显,10,000ppm=1‰;只有 1 毫升=1 克的情况下,它才等于 10,000mg/L。

水质最重要的指标或许是溶解氧。氧气尽管难溶于水,但对水生生物来说却是必不可少的。没有游离的溶解氧,我们想得到的大多数水生生物将无法在溪流和湖泊中安居。但是,在常温下,可能溶于水的氧的最大值约为每升 9 毫克;这一饱和值随水温的升高很快减小。因此,饱和同缺氧间的平衡是脆弱的。

溶解于水的氧的数量通常以氧探测器或旧的标准湿测技术,即温克勒溶解氧测定法来测定。温克勒溶解氧测定法,创始于八十多年前,为所有其他方法参照的标准。

温克勒测定法中的简化化学反应如下：
1. 加于水样中的锰离子与有效氧结合

$$Mn^{2+}+O_2 \longrightarrow MnO_2 \downarrow$$

形成沉淀物。

2. 加上碘化物离子，锰的氧化物和碘离子反应形成碘：

$$MnO_2+2I^-+4H^+ \longrightarrow Mn^{2+}+I_2+2H_2O$$

3. 碘量由硫代硫酸钠的滴定测出，其反应式为：

$$I_2+2S_2O_3^{2-} \longrightarrow S_4O_6^{2-}+2I^-$$

值得注意的是，由于所有的溶解氧和 Mn^{++} 给合，以致 MnO_2 的量和溶解氧成正比。同样，碘量和用来使碘氧化的氧化锰成正比。尽管是滴定法测碘，但碘量却因此直接与氧的初始浓度有关。

温克勒测定法有明显的缺陷，如化学干扰和受限于携带湿法实验设备到现场或把试样带到实验室从而冒在运带过程中水样损耗（或获得）氧气的风险。所有这些缺陷均可使用一个常被称为探测器的溶解氧电极来克服。

最简单的（也是历史上的第一个）探测器的工作原理和原电池工作原理相同。如将铅电极和银电极置于电解液中，且两极之间连一微安计，那末在铅电极的反应会是：

$$Pb+2OH^- \longrightarrow PbO+H_2O+2e^-$$

在铅电极，电子被释放，经微安计到达银电极，会发生如下反应：

$$2e^-+1/2O_2+H_2O \longrightarrow 2OH^-$$

除非有游离溶解氧，否则这个反应不会进行；这时微安计也不会显示任何电流。其技巧在于制造并标定一种仪表，其工作方式应能使所记录的电荷和电解液中的氧的浓度成正比。

在民用型号中，使用不导电的塑料将电极彼此绝缘，而且用一渗透膜覆盖电极；在渗透膜和电极之间加几滴电解液。穿过渗透膜的氧的数量与溶解氧的浓度成正比。水中的高浓度溶解氧可产生一个很强的渗透力穿过膜，而低浓度溶解氧只能迫使有限的氧透过膜参加反应，从而产生了电流。因此，所测的电流就与溶液中的含氧量成正比。

第 3 单元

水 处 理

市政给水处理的目的是向人们提供化学指标和细菌指标合格的生活饮用水。为了生活饮用，处理过的水必须感官性状合格，即浊度、色度适当，无异臭异味。工业用水的水质要求往往比生活用水更严格。因此，工业用水可能要求附加处理。例如，锅炉用水必须除盐以防产生水垢。

通常，市政供水水源为深水井、浅水井、河流、天然湖泊和水库。井水一般水温低，水质清澈、均匀，易处理为城市用水。处理中须去除溶解气体和不宜的矿物质。最简单的处理为消毒和加氟。深井水要加氯以提供余氯保护，防止在配水系统中可能被污染。至于靠地表水来补充的浅水井，加氯既对地下水消毒又提供余氯保护。加入氟化物是为了减少龋齿发病率。溶于井水中的铁和锰，接触空气时，就被氧化，形成微小的锈粒子，使水变色。去除工艺是用氯或高锰酸钾来氧化铁和锰，再经过滤去除沉析物。硬度过大的水一般靠沉析软化。如有必要，将石灰和纯碱与原水混合即可去除可沉降的析出物。在终滤前，用二氧化碳来稳定水。曝气通常是对大多数地下水体处理的第一步，以去除其中的溶解气体和增加溶解氧。

地表水水源主要让人担忧的是污染和富营养化。其水质取决于流域内的农业耕作，市政和工业排水管道的布局，诸如水坝之类的河流开发，季节变化以及气候条件。长时期的暴雨冲走耕地和林区的泥沙和有机物；而枯水流则会导致下水道排放的废水污染物浓度大大提高。冬夏之间，河水温度变化显著。湖泊和水库的水质主要取决于季节。城市水质控制实际应从河流流域的管理开始，以便保护原水水源。严重污染的水体处理起来既困难，成本又高。尽管一些地区能勘测到地下水，或者在泵送能及的范围内以污染较轻的地表水源来替代，然而本国人口的大多数是从附近的地表水水源取水。给水厂的运作任务则是将原水处理成家用合格的安全饮用产品。

地表水的一级处理是用混凝、沉淀和过滤等方法对水进行化学澄清。比起河水来，湖泊和水库全年水质更均匀且要求的处理级别也低些。自然净化可使混浊度、大肠菌数、色度下降并能消除水质逐日间的差异。另一方面，在夏秋两季，藻类的繁殖可能提高混浊度和产生难以去除的味道和气味。加氯通常是水处理的最初和最后的工序，它对原水消毒并使处理后的水保持余氯。过量的预加氯和活性碳吸附被用来去除那些产生味道和气味的化合物。要根据水的特性和处理费用来选择用于混凝的特定的化学药品。河水，作为原水，总是需用具有极大操作伸缩性的最齐全的处理设施去应付原水质的逐日变化。在化学处理之前，预备工序常为预沉淀以减少泥沙和可沉有机物。许多河水处理厂有二级化学混凝和沉淀以提供更大范围的处理深度及机动。其处理单元可能是连续操作，或是分级处理，即一级进行软化，另一级进行混凝。多达十几种的化学药品可在不同的运行条件下使用，以提供令人满意的成品水。

来自水处理过程中的两种主要废物为污泥和冲洗废水：前者来自沉淀池，由化学混凝和软化反应所产生；后者来自反冲洗滤池。这些排放物的成分变化很大，含有从原水中去除的浓缩物质和在水处理过程中添加的化学药品。这些废料源源不断地产生，但却间歇地被排放。从历史上看，废物处置方法就是不加任何处理地将其排放到河道和湖泊中。如果出于这么一种观点，即滤池的反冲水和沉淀固体物质被排回水系并没增添新的杂质，送回的不过是水中原先就存在的物质，上述做法是合理的。这个论点现在已无市场，因为水体水质已降到部分水回抽的程度，并且用于水处理的化学药品带来了新的污染物。因此，联邦政府和各州不断推出更加严格的控制污染规定，要求处理从水净化和软化设施中排放的废物。

第 4 单元

过 滤

过滤用来使水和废水透过多孔介质而将其中的非沉降性固体物质分离出来。最普通的过滤系统是使水透过一粒状介质组成的层状滤床进行过滤。滤床通常是上面为粗无烟煤,下面为细砂。

穿过粒状介质床进行重力过滤是给水处理和废水三级处理中去除胶体杂质最常用的方法。

有关在粒状介质滤池内去除悬浮固体的机理是复杂的,这一过程由截流、隔滤、絮凝和沉淀等组成。起初,表面隔滤和孔隙筛滤造成在滤池滤料上部的沉淀物蓄积。由于孔隙面积减小,穿过现有孔隙的水流速度加快,致使一块块截留的絮凝体被剪碎,将杂质携带至滤床深处。滤床内去除杂质的有效范围越来越深。湍流和因此而增大的颗粒在孔隙的接触,促进了絮凝,导致了较大絮凝颗粒被捕集。最后,清洁滤床层不复存在,遂泄漏发生。杂质由滤后水带出,并使滤池运行终止。

未经化学处理过的原水中的微小颗粒物质会穿过滤床内较大的孔。另一方面,进入滤池的悬浮固体与化学处理带来的过量混凝剂会堵塞滤床表面的孔隙。当水中的杂质和混凝剂浓度形成"深层"过滤时,即达最佳过滤状态。杂质既不穿透滤床,也不在滤床表面全部被隔滤掉,而是数量可观的絮凝固体在滤床整个深度上得到去除。

一个处理地表水使其达到饮用水水质的典型流程包括在过滤前使用化学混凝剂的絮凝和沉淀工艺。在重力作用下,常常是借助正水头和来自下面吸力的结合,水向下透过截留絮凝体和杂质颗粒的介质。当介质被塞满或发生固体漏泄,滤床则要被反冲水清洗,向上的水流使介质流态化并带走积聚在滤床里的杂质。细菌和病毒消灭取决于令人满意的混浊度控制从而增强氯化反应的效率。

在絮凝和沉淀之后的过滤速率,其数值范围为 2~10 加仑/(分·英尺^2)[1.4~6.8L/(m^2·s)];通常,最大设计速率为 5 加仑/(分·英尺^2)[3.4L/(m^2·s)]。

直接过滤过程不包括滤前沉淀。从水中除去的杂质被收集和存贮于滤池中。尽管必须对化学药品进行快速混合,但絮凝阶段或者取消,或者被减少到不足 30 分钟的混合时间。水中经化学凝聚的颗粒在粒状介质中发生了接触絮凝作用。在直接过滤方面的成功进展当推具有更大容量、进行深层过滤的、由粗到细多层滤料滤池的研制,使用机械或空气搅动以帮助清洗介质的反冲洗系统的改进和更好的聚合物混凝剂的使用。

低浊和低色度的地表水,最适合用直接过滤工艺进行处理。根据文献中引用的经验,色度低于 40 度、浊度一直在 5 度以下,铁和锰的浓度分别低于 0.3 和 0.5mg/L,藻类计数在每毫升 2000 之下的原水可成功地进行处理。当水的色度超过 40 度或浊度持续高于 15 度时,直接过滤的运转会出现问题。在短期间内,追加聚合物,可能出现的问题往往可以缓解。生化处理之后,需经三级过滤的废水,其悬浮固体的含量为 20~30mg/L,直接过滤法可将其降到 5mg/L 以下。要使病毒灭活和大量灭菌，经化学处理的废水应先过滤，然后用氯气消毒。

未经絮凝和沉淀而进行过滤的可行性取决于水质数据的综合权衡。由暴雨径流和藻类大量增殖造成的高混浊度状况必须予以评定。直接过滤与常规处理、滤池介质的设计以及化学处理的选择相比较，确定其效率高低的有效手段往往是中间试验。

直接过滤的滤速通常为每平方英尺 1~6 加仑/分 [0.7~4.1L/(m²·s)]，这比前面进行传统预处理的过滤速率稍低。

第 5 单元

废 水 收 集

在古老城市，造排水沟的唯一目的不过是将雨水排出城外。这些沟最终被加上盖板，成为我们今天所说的雨水管道。

随着供水事业的发展和室内卫生间使用的增多，对排放被称作生活污水的家庭污水的要求呼声日高。污水排放可由两种途径中的一个来完成：(1) 生活污水排放进雨水管道，于是雨水管道既排放污水又排放雨水，被称为合流排水管道；(2) 敷设新的地下管道系统用以排放污水，这些管道称为生活污水管道。

新建城市和老城中较近时期（1900 年后）兴建部分几乎都分别建有生活污水管道和雨水管道。在这一课里，雨水管道的设计不作详述。这儿要强调的是：对生活和工业废水量的估计，而在处理这些废水的污水工程系统的设计中就应作出此估计。

"Sewage" 这一术语这里用来仅表示生活污水。然而，除了生活污水，下水道还须输送工业废水，渗透水和入流水。

工业废水量通常可以由用水记录确定。其流量也可在仅为专门工业服务的检查井内用小型流量计测得。一般使用巴氏槽，计算所得流速和水流深度成正比。工业用水流量，全天变化幅度很大，必须进行连续记录。

流入生活污水管道的地下水为渗透水。污水管敷设常低于地下水位，而管道的任何裂隙会使水渗入。对新的、敷设质量高的污水管道来说，其渗透量最小，可达 $500m^3/(km·day)$ [200,000 加仑/（英里·天）]。通常，对旧管道系统，则应估算的渗透量为 $700m^3/(km·day)$ [300,000 加仑/（英里·天）]。既然有额外的水必定要通过污水管和废水处理厂，渗透水当然是不利的。因此，尽可能减少渗透量是有意义的；这就必须要管理维修好污水管道，并使下水道附属建筑物避开大树；其树根会扎入污水管，使之严重损坏。

生活污水管的第三个进水来源被称为入流水，即被生活污水管无意收集的雨水。一般入流水来源于低洼地带的多孔检查井盖板处，由此雨水流进了检查井。污水管紧靠小河和排水管渠；而后二者的高程高于污水管的检查井，或检查井有破裂处，这也是入流水的主要来源。最后，生活污水管的非法连接物，如屋顶雨水管，可明显增加雨季流量和旱季流量之比。一般，旱季流量和雨季流量之比在 1:1.2 和 1:4 之间。

生活污水流量在不同季节，一周内的每一天和一天内的每一小时都在改变。设计污水管时，三个关系紧要的流量为平均流量，高峰（即最大）流量和极小流量。平均流量对最大流量和最小流量之比为总流量的一个函数。这是由于一个较高的日平均排水量就意味着有一个较大的社区，其极值水量的变化幅度要平稳一些。

从住宅区和工厂企业收集废水的污水管道，几乎总是采用明渠或重力流管道。在一些地方用压力污水管，但其维修费用高，且用武之地仅限于严格限制用水或重力流管道无法有效敷设的地形。

建筑物连接管道通常用直径为 6 英寸的陶土管或塑料管，与一般敷设于街道下面的污水支管相连接。污水支管的口径要大到足以输送可能出现的最大高峰流量而不至超载（充满）；支管通常由陶土、石棉、水泥、混凝土制成，或用铸铁管。污水支管将废水顺次排放到俗称为"截留器"的污水截流管里。这些截流管集水面积很大，最后将废水排放到污水处理厂。

用于收集和截留的污水管在敷设时，须有足够大的坡度以便在枯水期保持足够的流速；但当流量处于最大值时，不要大到造成过高的流速。此外，污水管必须要有检查井，一般井距为 120～180m（400～600 英尺），以便于清通和检修。每当污水管改变坡度、大小或方向时，也需设检查井。

在有些情况下，使用重力流管道几近不能或不划算，则污水须用水泵排放。

第 6 单元

废水的组成

表 6-1 中的数据表示出在初步沉淀前后生活污水的近似组成。生化需氧量和悬浮固体（非过滤残渣）是确定生活污水特性的两种最重要的指标。浓度为 240mg/L 的悬浮固体相等于 120 加仑中 0.24 磅的悬浮固体，而 200mg/L 的 BOD 相当于 120 加仑中 0.20 磅的 BOD。在初步沉淀中，悬浮固体和生化需氧量分别减少约 50% 和 35%；大约 70% 的悬浮固体是挥发性的，这指那些摄氏 550℃ 烧失的悬浮固体。

普通生活污水的近似组成　　　　　　　　　　　　　　表 6-1

	沉淀前	沉淀后	经生化处理
全部固体	800	680	530
全部挥发性固体	440	340	220
悬浮固体	240	120	30
挥发性悬浮固体	180	100	20
BOD	200	130	30
氨氮中含氮	15	15	15
总氮中含氮	35	30	26
溶解磷中含磷	7	7	7
总磷中含磷	10	9	7

全部固体（蒸发残渣）就包括有机物和溶解盐；后者的浓度在相当程度上取决于城市废水的硬度。在生活污水中氮的浓度直接和有机物（BOD）的浓度有关。总氮的40%左右为溶解氨。如果原废水在集水污水管中被长时间滞留，占较大百分比的氨氮会由废水中的蛋白质和尿素的脱氨基作用生成。每升废水中含10毫克的磷大约相等于人均每年3磅磷的排出量。其中约两磅来自合成洗涤剂中的磷酸盐助洗剂。

在经生物处理过的废水中氮和磷的过剩表明：生活污水中，营养物的含量超过了生物的需求。生物处理需求的生化需氧量、氮和磷（BOD/N/P）的重量比约为100：5：1。处理所需的这三者的准确比例取决于处理工艺和废水中氮、磷化合物的生物有效性。100：6：1.5这一最小比值一般和未经沉淀的生活污水的处理相关，而100：3：0.7这一比值适合于氮和磷呈溶解状态的废水。表6-1所列普通生活污水在沉淀前后的比例分别为100：17：5和100：19：6，两者皆超过100：6：1.5这一最小比例。对缺乏营养物的工业废水的生物处理而言，可溶性磷靠添加H_3PO_4获得；而可溶性氮靠添加NH_4NO_3获得。

废水中的生物可降解的有机物质一般可分为三类：碳水化合物、蛋白质和脂肪。碳水化合物为碳的水合物，其通式为$C_nH_{2n}O_n$或$C_n(H_2O)_n$。

形式简单的蛋白质为肽键连接的氨基酸组成的长链分子。这样的蛋白质在活性物质的结构（如肌肉组织）和动力学（如酶）两方面都是重要的。二十一种普通氨基酸，当在长肽链上被连结在一起时，就形成大部分自然界中见到的简单蛋白质。由于蛋白质包含所有的基本营养素，作为一种细菌基质的蛋白质混合物是一种绝好的生长媒介。另一方面，由于纯碳水化合物不包含合成所必需的氮和磷，所以它们不宜作为一种生长媒介。

类脂物，连同碳水化合物与蛋白质一起，形成大部分活细胞的有机物。该术语指生化物质的多相聚集，而这些物质又具有在不同程度上溶于有机溶剂（如乙醚、乙醇、己烷和丙酮）、同时仅微溶于水的共有特性。类脂物可按它们共同的化学和物理特性分为脂肪、油和蜡。简单脂肪，当被水解作用分解时，将产生脂肪酸。在卫生工程学中，fats（脂肪）这个词，按目前用法，显然表达了类脂物这个意思。Grease（油脂）一词适用于广义的类脂物。

实际上，并非所有的可生物降解的有机物都可被分成这三种简单的类别。许多天然化合物，如脂类蛋白质和核蛋白都有碳水化合物、蛋白质和脂肪组合结构。

废水中，约20%～40%的有机物可认为是非生物可降解有机物。有些有机化合物，尽管在特殊细菌可使它们分解这个意义上是生物可降解的，但由于废水处理过程中时间的限制而必被环境卫生工程师认定是部分生物可降解的。例如，木质素，一种在木材纤维中和纤维素有联系的聚合非碳水材料，在实际应用上，是非生物可降解的。纤维素本身易被生活污水细菌的全体种群排斥。饱和碳氢化合物，因其物理特性及对细菌作用的排斥性，所以是处理中的一大难题。

第 7 单元

生物处理系统

　　生物处理法是去除城市废水中有机物的最有效途径。这些生物系统依赖混合微生物培养物质进行分解，并从溶液中去除胶体和溶解有机物质。接收微生物的处理室可提供一可控环境；例如，给活性污泥提供充足的氧气以维持好氧状态。废水包含生物食料，生长营养物质和微生物的培菌液。不熟悉废水处理的人经常问这些"专门的"生物培养物质来自何处？其答案是，用生活污水中各种各样的细菌和原生动物向各处理单元接种。然后，通过仔细控制污水流量、再循环沉降的微生物、供氧和其他因素，所需的生物培养物得以生成和维持，被用来处理污染物。生物滤池中，介质表面的粘泥层是靠将废水洒布滤床而形成的。在几周之内，滤池处于工作状态，将有机物从滴滤过滤床的液体中除去。机械或空气扩散系统中活性污泥的生成始于启动曝气器和喂给废水。开始，为保持足够的生物培养物质，有必要从二次沉淀池底部进行高速再循环。然而，短时期内，一种可沉淀的生物絮凝体即可成熟，它能有效地絮凝废水中的有机物。由于在未处理的污水中，消化作用所必需的、用以形成甲烷的细菌不足，所以厌氧消化池是最难启动的处理装置。再者，这些厌氧菌生长很慢，需要最佳的环境条件。可以用污水注满池子和用大量来自附近处理厂的消化污泥接种的方法相当显著地加速启动厌氧消化池。然后，以降低的初始速率加入生污泥及维持 pH 值所必需的石灰。即使具备了这样的条件，要使处理过程充分进行也得需要几个月的时间。

　　影响生物生长的最重要的因素是温度、营养物的可得性、供氧量、pH 值、毒素的存在和阳光（如有光合植物）。细菌按其生长最佳温度范围分类。中温细菌在 10~40℃ 温度范围内生长，最佳温度为 37℃。曝气池和生物滤池的工作温度一般在上述范围的下半区。由此可知，北方地区污水温度在温暖季节当在 20~25℃，在冬季当在 8~10℃。

　　城市污水通常含有足够浓度的维持微生物生长的碳、氮、磷和微量营养物质。从理论上讲，生化需氧量、氮、磷三者之比为 100:5:1；这对好氧处理已绰绰有余，但视系统类型和运行方式可略作调整。一般生活污水多呈过量的氮和磷，其生化需氧量、氮、磷三者之比约为 100:17:5。如果城市废水含有大量的缺乏营养物质的工业废水，一般要按需添加无水氨（NH_3）或磷酸（H_3PO_3）来补充氮。

　　扩散式或机械式曝气池必须提供充足的空气维持溶解氧以便供生物群代谢废水有机物所用。微生物活动的速率，在溶解氧浓度超过最小临界值的情况下，不受溶解氧的浓度的影响；如低于这个值，速率则会受呼吸用氧的制约而降低。确定这一最小值则取决于活性污泥工艺的类型及被处理污水的特征。临界溶解氧最常用的设计指标为 2.0mg/L，但在实际运作中，低达 0.5mg/L 的指标已被证明是可行的。自然，厌氧系统必须在完全无溶解氧的状态下运转；因此，消化池用漂浮的或固定的盖密封以隔绝空气。

　　氢离子的浓度直接影响到在中性环境下运行最佳的生物处理系统。通常曝气系统运行的 pH 值范围为 6.5 到 8.5。在这个范围之上，微生物活动受到抑制；pH 值在 6.5 以下，真菌在代谢废水有机物方面和一般细菌相比，则更受青睐。厌氧消化的 pH 值所容许范围很小，为 6.7 到 7.4 之间，最佳运行范围值为 pH7.0 到 7.1 之间。生活污水污泥许可在这一狭窄的范围内运作，但启动期或有机物超负荷期除外。随原污泥的馈入，经心添加石灰，消化器中 pH 值的控制已获得一定效果。可惜，酸性的增加和 pH 值的降低可能是其他消化问题出现的征兆，例如，会导致有毒重金属的积累，对此添加石灰也无济于事。

生物处理系统受抑于有毒物质。来自金属精炼企业的工业废水常含诸如镍和铬这样的有毒离子；化学加工产生了可负面影响微生物的各种各样的有机化合物。在城市废水处理过程中，既然对去除或中和有毒化合物无能为力，那末在把废水排入城市下水道之前，应由企业对其进行预处理。

第 8 单元

污泥的特征

污泥值得考虑的特征完全取决于污泥的用途。例如，如果利用重力将污泥增稠，它的沉降和压缩特性是重要的。另一方面，如果将污泥厌氧消化，挥发性固体的浓度、重金属等则不可轻视。

另一在设计污泥处理和处置操作中极其重要的事实是污泥的变异性。事实上，这种变异性用以下三条"定律"表述：

1. 没有哪两种废水污泥在所有方面都相同；
2. 污泥特性随时间变化；
3. 没有所谓一般的污泥。

第一条反映了没有两种废水是相同的这一事实；如果增添处理变量，所产生的污泥会有显著不同的特性。

第二条常被设计者忽视。例如，电镀废水[例如，$Pb(OH)_2$，$Zn(OH)_2$ 或 $Cr(OH)_3$]处理中产生的化学污泥的沉降特性之所以随时间变化，就是因为不可控 pH 值的变化造成的。生物污泥当然在不断变化，当污泥由好氧变至厌氧状态时，此变化最大（反之亦然）。因此，设计污泥处理设备是相当困难的；这是由于仅仅几小时后，污泥的某个重要指标就可能发生变化。

第三条"定律"一直被违反。列出的一般污泥的"平均值"的表格仅可用以进行描述和比较，不应作设计之用。

有了以上的导向说明，我们现在可进一步讨论"一般污泥"的一些特征。

第一个特征，固体浓度，或许是最重要的变量；它限定待处理的污泥量并确定该污泥是呈液体状或固体状。当然，挥发性固体的重要性在于污泥的可处理性。由于挥发性物质含量高，污泥会难以处理使之符合环境要求。随着挥发物被降解，产生了气体和气味；因此，挥发性固体的高浓度会限制处理方法。

污泥流变特性值得注意，由于这是描述污泥的物理性质的、为数不多的基本指标之一。然而，象污泥这样的两相混合物几乎毫不例外的属于非牛顿的和触变性的。污泥趋于表现为假塑性，具有明显的屈服应力和塑性粘度。假塑性液体的流变性可用一流变图来确定。阶段触变性对时间的关系取决于流变特性。

随着固体浓度增加，污泥趋于表现为更象塑性液体。真正的塑性液体可由如下公式表示：

$$\tau = \tau_y + \eta \frac{du}{dy}$$

其中　τ＝剪应力；

　　　τ_y＝屈服应力；

　　　η＝塑性粘度；

　　　du/dy＝切速，即速度梯度，(u) 深度，(y) 纵向尺寸。

屈服应力变化范围很大：从 6％的原污泥为 $40 dyn/cm^2$ 以上到被增稠的活性污泥的仅 $0.07 dyn/cm^2$。这一极大反差表明流变参量完全适用于比例放大之需。可惜，极少有研究者肯倾力去度量流变特性（这样的分析甚至不包括在"标准检测方法"中），以致在现有数据中存在许多空白。

化学成分的重要可举数条理由说明。首先，污泥的肥料价值取决于氮、磷、钾以及微量元素的可用性。然而，更重要的检测指标是重金属浓度和会使污泥毒害环境的其他有毒物质。重金属浓度的变化范围是很大的（例如，镉的含量可从小到几乎为零，大到超过 $1,000 mg/kg$。由于这些有毒物的主要来源是工业排放，仅一个疏于管理的工业公司排放的有毒物就足以使污泥不能作肥料使用。大多数工程师一致认为，尽管在污水处理厂里将污泥进行处理以去除其有毒成分会是非常切实可行的，但目前尚无有效办法从污泥中去除重金属、农药和其他潜在有毒物；他们还认为，必须对渗流水加以严格控制（即实行不漏水污水管条例）。

除了物理和化学特征，污泥的生物指标也可能是重要的。挥发性固体参数实际上经常被认为是生物特征，其前提是挥发性悬浮固体是活生物量的总度量。另一个重要指标为细菌和病毒的二种病原体的浓度，特别是涉及到最终处理时尤其如此。初级澄清池似乎起着类似病毒和细菌浓缩池的作用；这样，相当大一部分微生物存在于污泥之中而不是在流出的废水中。

第 9 单元

泵和泵站

在供水系统中，泵和泵送机械有以下的服务目标：(1) 从水源（地表水或地下水）提水，或者通过高扬程泵把水迅速送到居民区，或者用低扬程泵将水打入净水厂；(2) 将水从低压供水区增压至高压供水区、单独的消防用水源和高层建筑物上层；(3) 令水进出处理厂，在此过程中，反冲过滤池，使水由沉淀池和其他处理构筑物流出，抽排沉淀固体和向运行设备供水（特别是压力水）。

如今大多数给水和废水的泵送都是由离心泵或轴流泵来完成的。水穿过叶轮时的流向确定了泵的类型：（1）在开式或闭式叶轮泵中表现为辐向流，该泵具有螺旋形或涡轮式外壳和水单吸或双吸进入叶轮的方式；（2）在轴流泵中表现为轴向流；（3）在开式叶轮混流泵中表现为混流。轴流泵不是离心泵。这两种泵都可称为旋转动力泵。

开式叶轮泵的效率不如闭式叶轮泵，但其可令相当大的漂浮物通过而不致被堵塞。因此，它们在提升废水和污泥时是大有用场的。单级泵仅有一个叶轮；而多级泵则有两个或两个以上的叶轮，且每一级叶轮都将水打入下一级叶轮中。多级叶轮井泵可本身带有潜于水下的电动机或由位于泵站地面上的原动机的轴驱动。

除离心泵和轴流泵外，水和废水系统可包括：（1）活塞泵，其大小从手压罐形泵到上一世纪装有蒸汽驱动装置的大型泵机不等；（2）装有两个或两个以上转子的旋转泵，（其形状从网式瓣轮到齿轮多样，多被用作小型灭火泵）；（3）水锤泵，利用大量低压水形成的冲击来驱动少量的水（为冲击水的二分之一到六分之一），使其通过输水管到达较高高程，这一过程同水锤引起的压力波及其操作程序相一致；（4）射流泵，或称喷射器，用于井中和脱水操作中，引带高速空气射流或水射流通过喷嘴进入管子狭窄部分；（5）气升泵，其内由朝上的空气管释放的气泡通过喷射管提升井水或排水坑的水；（6）往复式喷射器，被置于压力容器内，水（特别是废水）在容器内积蓄，而当浮球阀被上升水推开并使压缩空气进入容器内时，水就会从容器中通过一喷射管被喷出。

抽水机组的选择要和系统水头及泵的特性相一致。系统水头是相对于泵的静水头和动水头之和。因此，它随着所需流量及贮水量和吸水水位的变化而变化。当配水系统位于泵和配水库之间时，系统水头也和所需水位涨落相呼应。泵的特性取决于泵的大小，转速和设计。对每分钟一定转速为 N 的泵来说，其特性由排放流量 Q（通常用每分多少加仑表示），分别与水头 H（用英尺表示），效率 E（用百分率表示）和输入功率 P（用马力表示）之间的关系来确定。为了便于比较，几何设计已定的泵，其特点也可由其比速 N_s，即同一系列的（几何上相似）叶轮直径为 D 的泵的假设速度表示出来；在该转速下，泵能将每分一加仑的流量提升一英尺水头。因为排放流量和过水面积与流速的乘积成正比，流速和 $H^{1/2}$ 成正比，Q 和 $D^2H^{1/2}$ 成正比。但是，流速也和 $\pi DN/60$ 成正比。因此，$H^{1/2}$ 和 DN 成正比，或 N 和 $H^{3/4}Q^{1/2}$ 成正比。

一般地说，泵的尺寸和流量大，泵的效率就高。比速低于 1000 单位，效率急剧下降。辐向流泵在比速 1,000 到 3,500 单位之间性能上乘，混流泵比速最佳范围为 3,500 至 7,500 单位；而轴流泵出其右，可达 12,000 单位。对给定的 N 来说，高流量、低水头泵具有最高的比速。对双吸泵来说，比速用一半的容量来计算。至于多级泵，水头分布各级之间。这可保持高比速，由此也可保持高效率。

比速也是一个重要的抗气蚀的安全标准。气蚀是由振动、噪音和泵叶轮快速毁坏相伴随的一个现象。当相当多的势能被转化成动能降低了叶轮表面的绝对压力使之低于常温下水的蒸汽压时，就发生气蚀。此时，水就汽化并形成蒸汽泡，当蒸汽泡被带入高压区时，它们会突然溃灭。当进口压力太低或泵容及转速增加而进口压又无补偿升高时，气蚀就出现了。因此，降低泵与水源的相对高度可减少气蚀。

第10单元

水污染物的分类

为了对水污染的影响以及对其控制所应用的技术有所了解，将污染物分门别类是有用的。首先，污染物可以根据它来源的特性分为点源污染物或分散源污染物。

点源污染物是指从管道，沟渠或其他任何限制的或局部地点注入水中的污染物。点源污染物最常见的例子是管道向溪流或河流排放污水。多数是污水处理厂排放出的处理过的污水，这些水在一定程度上仍含有污染物，但在少数个别事例中，未经处理的原污水被排放出来了。

分散源或非点源是指广阔的，无限制的区域，污染物从这一区域进入到水体中。例如：从耕种地区流出的地表径流带着泥沙、肥料、农药及动物粪便流入河流。这些都不是来自具体的某一地点。这些物质都可能从流经这一地区的河流的整个沿线进入该河流的水中。来自矿区的酸性径流是一种分散源污染物。都市和城镇雨水排放系统也可认为是许多污染物的分散源。尽管这些污染物常由排水管或雨水下水道排入河流或湖泊中，但通常有许多排入点分散在一片广阔的区域。

点源污染物比分散源污染物更容易处理。来自点源的污染物已经集中起来并被输送到一定的地点，在那儿经过处理厂的处理，将它们从水中除去。处理厂的点排放物易于受到管理机构的监督。

控制来自分散源的污染物就困难多了。许多人认为污水是水污染问题的罪魁祸首，但是在美国，多数水污染是分散源造成的。也许，控制分散源最有效的办法是在土地使用方面建立合理的限制法规。

除对水污染物按其来源分类以外，也可以主要根据它们对环境和健康的影响分为几类物质。例如：将污染物分为以下九种类型。

1. 病原有机体　　2. 耗氧物
3. 植物营养物　　4. 毒性有机物
5. 无机化学品　　6. 沉积物
7. 放射性物质　　8. 热污染
9. 油类

生活污水是前三种污染物的主要来源。病原体，或致病微生物是传染病患者通过粪便排泄出来的，并且有可能被带到接纳污水的水域。人口稠密的大社区所排放的污水很可能带某些病原体。

污水中也有耗氧物质，即有机废物。这种有机废物被微生物分解时，产生一定的生化耗氧量，可简称为 BOD。BOD 通过消耗溶解氧量而改变水体中的生态平衡。氮和磷是主要的植物营养物，既存在于污水中，也存在于农田或近郊草地的径流中。

常规的污水处理过程能有效地减少污水中的病原体和 BOD，但却不能彻底地将它们消除。特别是有些病毒，对污水消毒过程有一定的抵抗性。（病毒是一种极小的病原有机体，只有在电子显微镜下才能看清。）为了降低污水中氮和磷的含量，通常必须要用一些高效的污水处理法。

毒性有机化学品主要是农药，一般进入耕种区地表径流水中。也许在化学品家族中，最危险的一种是氯化烃类，如氯丹、狄氏剂、七氯以及臭名昭著的滴滴涕。这些是杀灭毁坏农作物害虫的非常有效的毒物。然而，不幸的是，它们也能杀死鱼类、鸟及包括人类在内的动物。而且它们的生物降解性能很差，在某些情况下，需要三十多年才能从环境中消失。

当然，毒性有机化学品也能从工业生产中直接进入水中。这种情况很可能是由于某些工厂对化学品管理不当，或更常见的是由于对化学废物不恰当或非法的处理造成的。正确地管理有毒及其他有害废物是八十年代关键的环境问题之一，特别是地下水质的保护。毒性无机化学品，特别是"重金属"类，如铅和汞，通常也产生于工业生产，并且也属有害废物。

油类是雨水冲刷路面及停车场而排入地表水中的。海上大型油轮意外地泄油事件时有发生，引起极大的环境破坏。近海油田喷井事故往往会在短时间内泄漏出数千吨的原油。海洋石油最终会向沿岸地带转移，影响生物，破坏游览胜地的风景。

第 11 单元

空气污染对水质的潜在影响

无论是自然界的，还是人类造成的污染源都会导致水污染。人为的主要污染源已尽人皆知，而对于天然的污染源，尽管有所认识，但就其对水污染所起作用的程度却并未得到正确了解。空气污染物对水质的潜在影响仅仅引起人们粗略的注意。至于其影响的程度及大小则仍然存在着争论。

除了对环境化学循环本身的兴趣以外，为了发展区域水质管理计划的需要，促使目前需要一套大气对水污染影响的评估方法。其他的计划和工程也要求对各种各样水污染源鉴定和定量测定。

有些研究人员得出结论，认为大气对水质的影响不大。然而，许多研究支持这样的观点：大气对水质有着极其重大的影响。这些研究表明，在某些情况下，大气中某些物质对水体的影响比水流中这些物质对水体的影响还要大。

空气环境与水环境的联系一般可以从以下几个方面考虑。首先，大气污染物对水质的影响可分为几个部分，主要部分是地表污染物的通量或沉积速率、最终进入水体中沉积物的分量和沉积物到达水体的速率。因此大气是水污染物的一大潜在的来源。但是，它对水质的影响是由落入水体中沉积物分量和沉积速率所决定的。为了对每种空气污染物导致水质恶化的相对重要性有一个全面的评价，有必要对上述几个部分进行估测。另外，人们还必须考虑某一种特定的空气污染物在空气、土地和水环境中，以及与空气、土地和水环境之间所有重要的反应和作用。

一种空气污染物能直接和间接地传递到水体的表面。所谓直接的从空气到水的传递，是指无论在干燥或潮湿的天气季节中在空气与水的界面上都可能发生的气体、液体及固体的交换。这些交换被称为干沉积或湿沉积。干沉积包括在干燥天气季节里,大气中微粒由于重力而形成的回降和微粒及气体的湍动沉降。湿沉积是指雨洗、冲洗、雪洗及清除。所谓雨洗和雪洗,是指发生在云层内部将污染物依次凝结的过程。冲洗及清除是分别通过降雨或降冰状物,去除云层以下的物质。(如果某一水体表面有冰覆盖,这几种交换依然可能发生。不过覆盖的冰如同一个蓄积器起着延缓时间的作用。)

来自空气中的污染物间接地传递到水中,可以因污染物在地面上的迁移,转化及蓄积而得缓和。蓄积能使污染物到达地面和污染物出现在水中的时间之间有一段明显的时间延缓。例如:如果径流水与地下水的含水层没有直接的联系,那么地下水的污染要经二十年才会显示出来。雪也能带来时延。在这种情况下,沉降对河流的影响也能有所滞延。

在空气、水及地面环境中,污染物的转化(生物的,化学的及物理的)总在发生。例如:进入空气中的硫化氢最终总是以硫酸盐的形式存在于水环境中。一旦到了水中,硫酸根离子在厌氧的环境中转化回硫化氢并向空气中释放。空气中的氨以 NH_4^+ 或亚硝酸根离子或硝酸根离子形式进入水中。在水中,氮元素与动植物相结合,最后形成氨气或氮气,并向空气中释放。

沉积于地面的空气污染物蓄积给这些污染物提供了充分的机会,在它们进入水体之前转化成其他的化学形式。沉积于各种植物表面或固体上的物质也能进行化学转化,并且,沉积速率因不同的表面而有差别。许多事实证明,污染物的转化及其速率对水质问题的改善或恶化起着重要的作用。

第 12 单元

有害废物

通常人们认为一般家庭或商业机构所产生的城市固体废物不存在危害。但是,在现代社会里,化学物品制造业及相关的工业制造出大量的危险物质。这些危险的或有害的废物能带来严重的疾病、伤害或死亡。如果运输或倾倒不当,也会给环境造成严重的威胁。

近来,已有数百件有案可查的事件都是由于对有害废物非法或不当的处理而给公众及环境造成了危害。大多数案例涉及到作为公众水源的地下水的污染。对有毒废物不加区别地处理也给河流和湖泊带来污染。七十年代后期,在美国的肯德基发生过新闻媒体称之为"圆桶谷"的事件。大约六千只破损和渗漏的装有有毒物质的金属桶在它们的堆放地泄泌所装物质。因此,该地区的土壤及地表水受到了二百三十种有机化学品和金属的污染。

美国另一桩臭名昭著的有毒废物泄漏事物也发生在七十年代后期,在纽约州的尼加拉瀑布附近。早在二十五年多前掩埋的化学废物渐渐地泄漏出金属包装,以此作为确定受污染地区相应的反应来进行评定。目前,这些地区的土壤里只要超过 $1\mu g/L$(十亿分之一)的二噁英就要采取补救措施以保护公众的健康。

反应性废物是指那些不稳定,且易与空气、水或其他物质起强烈反应的废物。这些反应不是导致爆炸就是生成有毒的蒸气烟雾。包括有机溶剂，如苯或甲苯在内的可燃烧性废物燃点相对较低，是直接的火灾源。包括强碱强酸性物质在内的腐蚀性废物通过化学反应损坏材料及活体组织。反应的、可燃的、腐蚀性的废物都给生命有机体或自然环境带来直接的危害性影响。这些废物给有关运输、储存及处置方面产生了极为棘手的问题。所以处理时必须特别小心仔细。

传染性或生物废物包括外科手术的人体组织，用过的绷带和皮下注射针头，微生物及其他医院及生物研究中心的废物。这一类有害废物必须正确地处理和处置，以防传染病在公众中传播。

放射性废物，尤其是来自核电站的废物也应受到特别关注。过量地受电离辐射能的照射给生命有机体造成危害。放射性物质只要不发生明显的衰变，就会一直长期地存留在自然环境中。但是由于这个问题的范围及工艺的复杂性，放射性物质的处置通常要与其他有害废物分开。

根据美国环境保护局估计，美国全部非放射性工业废物中的约百分之十是有害物质。粗略算来每年约有六千万吨有害废物。到八十年代中期，仅仅百分之十左右的这些废物得以按照环保要求的正确方法进行处理，而大部分的废物处理，打个比喻说，都只是"隔靴搔痒"，从而给公众的健康及环境质量造成了延续性的威胁。据估计目前约有四万只之多的有毒废物桶，这些废物桶内的废物通过土壤渗透到建在这个区域的住宅的院落和地下室。许多家庭在目睹居民中无数奇异古怪的病症后，都远走他乡。该区域约有八十种之多的不同化学品得到鉴定，被怀疑是人体致癌物。

有害废物与其他固体废物的性质不同。有害废物常为液态，但也有固态，泥浆状或气态。通常这些废物存放和封闭于金属桶或钢瓶内。根据毒性，反应性，可燃性及腐蚀性等特征，有害废物主要分为这四类。另外还有两种，即传染性和放射性废物。

有毒废物，即使是少量或痕量，均具毒性。有些毒性废物可能对人畜造成急性中毒，成直接影响而导致死亡或患暴病。另一些毒性废物对人畜有慢性或长期的影响，使受害者遭受无法拯救的伤害。有些毒性废物是公认的致癌物，使受毒害的人在最初中毒多年后患癌症。还有些毒性废物属于致突变剂，给儿童或那些已中毒人畜的后代带来生理畸变。

大多数毒性废物是工业生产造成的，这些工业包括化学品，农药，油漆，石油副产品，金属，纺织品及许多其他产品的制造业。环境保护局已明确地鉴定并列举出数百种不同的化学品为有毒物，而毒品的品种还在不断地扩大。

农药二噁英已被环境保护局列为"永远会对环境造成污染的最令人头痛且有潜在危险的化学品之一"。对这种特殊的物质已经采取了一项特别的控制措施，其中包括一项系统的调查工作，以确定受二噁英污染的地区和范围。在美国，公众健康的大敌将是那些危险的废物"堆"，其中许多正在给人体健康和环境带来严重的问题。净化污染的环境预计将需要几百亿美元之多的费用。

第13单元

空气污染

关于对空气污染的定量研讨，由于缺乏对"洁净空气"的明确定义而有所困难。大多数科学家认为"空气"应是表1中所列气体的混和物。如果这种空气就是洁净空气，那么空气中的任何成分都可以称为污染物。然而，大自然中永远找不到如此的"洁净空气"。因此将那些以足以产生有害影响的浓度而存在的物质定义为空气污染物也许比较恰当。这些污染可能来自自然界（如森林火灾的烟雾）或者来自人类自己（如汽车废气）。它们可能是气态，或是颗粒状（大于一微米的液态或固态微粒）。

标准干空气的成分（ppm） 表 13-1

氮	780.900
氧	209.400
氩	9.300
二氧化碳	315
氖	18
氦	5.2
甲烷	1.0 到 1.2
氪	1.0
一氧化二氮	0.5
氢	0.5
氙	0.08
二氧化氮	0.02
臭氧	0.01 到 0.04

在空气污染的控制中，气态污染包括常温常压状态的气体物质，也包括常温常压下呈液态或固态物质的蒸气。目前所知的最主要的气态污染物有一氧化碳、碳氢化合物、硫化氢、氮氧化物、臭氧和其他氧化剂及氧化硫。二氧化碳因其对气候的潜在影响也是主要的气态污染物。

颗粒状污染物可分为：尘埃、烟尘、烟雾、烟及雾状物。大气中和来自污染源的颗粒状污染物的化学成分复杂，可能含有许多金属和非金属成分。

许多引起人们关注的污染物是大自然自身产生和散发的。例如：自然界固有的微粒就包括花粉粒，霉菌孢子，盐雾，森林火灾所散发的烟尘以及火山爆发时喷出的火山灰。来自天然污染源的气态污染物有血红蛋白降解过程中产生的一氧化碳，松树的萜烯烃，由于细菌作用而导致半胱氨酸及其他含硫的氨基酸分解时生成的硫化氢，氮氧化物及甲烷。

人为造成的污染源可简单地归为以下几种：固定燃烧炉，运输工具，工业生产及固体废物处置污染源。固定燃烧过程中主要释放出的污染物是颗粒状污染物，如飞灰和烟尘以及硫和氮的氧化物。当然，二氧化硫的排放量是由燃料中的含硫量而决定的。煤和油的燃烧中含硫量相当可观，因此，二氧化硫的排放量也就相当惊人。大气中的氮在高温过程中热固定,就会产生氮氧化物。由此可见,几乎任何一个燃烧过程都会产生一氧化氮(NO),接着继续氧化成二氧化氮(NO_2)。由燃烧而产生的其他重要污染物有：有机酸、醛类、氨及一氧化碳。一氧化碳的排放量与燃烧过程的效率有关,即：较高效率的燃烧过程能氧化较多的碳,产生二氧化碳而降低一氧化碳的排放量。从空气污染的角度来看,所有用于固定燃烧的燃料中,天然气或许是最理想的燃料。实际上,天然气不含硫,并且颗粒状污染物的排放量几乎是零。

运输工具污染源,尤其是用内燃机的汽车,是最主要的空气污染源。汽车的颗粒排放物有烟尘和铅尘,而后者都通常是卤化合物。正如其他任何一种燃烧过程一样,烟尘应归咎于含碳物的不完全燃烧。另一方面,所排放出的铅直接与在燃料中加入的抗爆剂四乙铅有关。运输工具所排放的气态污染物有二氧化碳、氮氧化物和碳氢化合物。燃料在曲轴箱,汽化器及汽油箱里的不完全燃烧和气化,导致了碳氢化合物的排放。

人类在控制汽车污染方面已作出了重大的成就。目前排放废气的洁净度较1963年模式提高了百分之九十多,在今后的五年内显然还会有更大的改进。

由工业生产所排放的污染物反映了现代工业技术的创新。因此,工业生产过程中排放了一定量的几乎每一种可以想到的污染物。

固体废物处置常常是城市主要的空气污染源。尽管固体废物处置过程并不一定是主要的污染源,但许多社区仍然允许在庭院或露天焚烧垃圾作为固体废物处置的办法。这些试图减少废物的方法却制造出种种难以控制的污染物。这些污染物是难闻的气味、一氧化碳、少量的氮氧化物,有机酸、碳氢化合物,醛类以及大量的烟尘。(在庭院和露天焚烧垃圾都是无效燃烧最典型的例子。)

第14单元

噪声对健康的影响

强噪声对健康最直接的急性危害是听力下降,其原因是耳组织的某些部分受到损害。

振荡引起的声压波使中耳(鼓膜)发生运动,这使中耳的三根耳骨活化。锤骨、砧骨和镫骨实际上增强了来自中耳的运动,并将这一运动传送到内耳。内耳是一个充满液体的空腔,内有耳蜗。在这蜗形结构中,物理运动传送到极微小的毛细胞上。这些毛细胞转向,很象水流中漂动的海藻,而一定的细胞只与一定的频率相响应。这些毛细胞的机械运动可转换成生物电信号,通过耳神经传送到脑。

急性损害能波及到中耳,但这只在骤然出现很响的噪声时才会产生。更严重的损害是对内耳中微小的毛细胞的慢性损害。长久地暴露于一定频率的噪声能导致或是几天即可消失的暂时失聪,或是永久性的失聪。工业中中等频率的噪声会使许多人失聪。不幸的是,语言的频率也是中等,因此语言听力常受到阻碍。许多老人,当他们还能听到喷气式飞机的声音及隆隆的火车声时,却抱怨"人们都在耳语"。他们的某些毛细胞受到了损害,妨碍了对特殊(语言)频率声音的接受。

年龄的增长也会引起失聪,因此难以建立表明失聪是由强噪声引起的流行病学数据。但是研究表明,噪声可引起失聪是确实的,不是人们想象出来的。

噪声的另一个问题是它对人体的其他功能,如心血管系统的影响。已发现,噪声可改变心跳的节律,使血液粘稠,血管扩张,并使之难以调节。毫无疑问强噪声会引起头痛及烦燥。做精密工作的人们,如钟表制造工对噪声尤其头痛。

噪声所产生的上述所有反应都是我们的祖先原始人也曾经历过的。对于原始人噪声意味着危险,他的感觉和神经总是"警觉"着,随时准备驱除这种危险。在当代,噪声充满世界,我们总是"警觉"着,这引起了多少我们的生理疾病还值得探讨。

我们也认识到,人类不能适应噪声,也就是说人体功能不再能经受强噪声,因此人们在生理官能上不能"习惯于"噪声。

除噪声问题之外,还必需适当地指出在我们通常的 20～20,000 赫兹(Hz)听觉范围外的超高和超低频率声音的潜在危害问题。它们对健康的危害仍有待进行研究。

对在喧闹的和安静的医院内患者的比较的大量既往事实表明,当医院环境喧闹时,患者的恢复期增长(不论是由于内部的或外来的噪声)。这可能带来直接的经济影响。

近来的法庭案例中,劳动者在工作中遭到失聪要求赔偿费,赢得胜诉。美国退役军人管理局每年为照顾患听觉疾病的病人耗费上百万美元。

其他费用,如安眠药丸,工业上损失的时间,以及建造隔音的公寓等难以估算。华盛顿的约翰,F肯尼迪文化中心因附近的国家机场时有飞机起落而需隔音设施而花了500万美元。

要测定噪声对生活质量的影响更为困难。对丈夫的发怒,妻子的暴燥,出租车司机的愠怒和店员的乖戾,噪声应负多大的责任?

在喧闹的环境里成长起来的孩子,必须教会他们去听。他们不能将听觉集中于一个声音,如老师的讲话声。

在纽约肯尼迪机场周围 80～90 分贝的范围内有 22 所学校。每当一架飞机经过时,教师必须停止讲话,过后再努力重新引起学生的注意力。

噪声是一种真正危险的环境污染,既然人们在生理上无法适应它,我们也许在心理上要适应它。噪声使我们感官处于"紧张"状态,没法放松。因此必须用我们的心理能力来控制噪声对人体的伤害。因为在人类进化的过程中,噪声是最近才发展起来的,我们还没有适应它,因而必须靠我们的缓冲能力而生活。人们以惊奇的发现这种能力有多么巨大。

第 15 单元

资源回收

从固体废物中回收资源,通常称之为重复利用,理论上是很诱人的。遗憾的是,我们当今的经济体系难以做到有效(赚钱)的重复利用,尽管实际情况正在迅速改变。在不久的将来资源回收会成为处理固体废物最理想的办法。

当人们热切地关注环境问题时，对于资源回收的整个必要过程却很少问津。事实上，"重复利用"已经与"收集"相混淆，而收集仅是个回收过程的一个步骤而已。从消费者那儿收集到某种物质后，必须清洗，卖给某制造厂家，运输，再制造，然后（最重要的一步）再一次卖给消费者。最后一个步骤事实上决定了整个过程的运行。一旦再制造的产品无法出售，所做的其他一切都毫无意义。因此，我们不应该将回收报纸称为"重复利用"。因为，只有当纸张被消费者重新使用时，这个过程才得以完成。

重复利用有两个基本理由：（1）节约资源；（2）减少有待处理的废物量。目前已提出的一些常见的可重复利用的物质是：纸、金属、玻璃及有机物。

纸是一种供应量大而且相当清洁的产品。但是得到重复利用的纸约占目前供应量的百分之二十，因为，令人遗憾的是，制造原生纸简直太便宜了。人们认识到每重复利用一吨纸，可以从砍伐下拯救十七棵树，这种认识常常会促进公众的废纸回收热。这种无偿劳动十分必要，它可以让许多再生纸浆厂有利可图。

很可惜，如此精心收集起来的一吨废纸难以使十七棵树免遭砍伐。仅有很少部分的回收纸最终成为再生纸，而大部分回收纸被运往海外。将回收纸制成再生纸比生产原生纸确实要贵。

要使回收纸得到重复利用而能真正地挽救我们的森林，唯一的办法是开辟再生纸的市场，人为地将原生纸的价格提高。要达到这个目的，既可以通过公众舆论的支持、立法，也可以采取税收的办法。

从工业废料中能轻而易举地回收金属，这也是"再生金属"最大的来源。废金属其次的来源是报废的汽车。很遗憾，当前金属生产中的炼钢工艺仅能承受有限的废料，因此废钢的市场价值较低。

有些铝制品公司已成功地回收了大量的铝制罐头盒。这些罐头盒是极为令人头痛的废品，因为这些废罐头盒被丢弃后，它们不会腐烂，而只会成为显眼的垃圾，几乎永久地存在着。

玻璃是完全可以重复利用的产品。它清洁、量大、极易再加工，而且用途极广。令人遗憾的是，它也太便宜了。制造一只新玻璃瓶与重新制造或重灌一只旧玻璃瓶的花费几乎一样。此外，生产玻璃的原材料极为丰富，以致于人们从重复利用回收玻璃中似乎一无所获。

各种有机物能转化成一些有用的产品。最常见并在许多国家广泛地采用的处理方法是堆肥。

与掩埋不同，堆肥是一种需氧分解固体废物的方法。典型的堆肥过程包括：（1）将废物（包括生活垃圾及工业垃圾）的有机成分和无机成分分离开；（2）将有机成分碾碎；（3）无论是露天料堆或在机械"消化堆"中进行稳定化处理。

这种过程中，分离是一个薄弱的环节。大多数居民区都无法要求居民将纸和厨房垃圾与玻璃和金属罐头盒分开，堆肥工厂里的手工分拣是费用大又往往不可靠的方法，但却十分必要。

目前许多科研项目直接的目的是寻求更好的分离方法。因为人们已认识到，一旦这个问题得以解决，堆肥将是资源回收中一个极其诱人的方法。

碾碎以后，通常是在将金属分开以后，这些有机材料常常堆放成长形堆状，称为料堆，有 8 至 10 英尺宽，4 至 6 英尺高。在这种情况下，足量的湿度和氧可以保证需氧生活条件。必须对这料堆进行定期的翻搅，让料堆所有部分都能有足够的氧气渗入。

完全由于生物的活动料堆的温度接近 140°F。料堆在最初堆积后，pH 值近似中性。对于大多数的废物，不需要补充营养物。然而，树皮和其他材料堆肥时成功的办法是添加氮和磷的营养物。

通常必须控制湿度。湿度过大难以维持需氧状态，而缺氧状态会抑制生物活性。理想的含湿量为 40%～60%。

对于运用接种剂、冻干培养物加速堆肥过程仍有一些争论。一旦堆肥料堆形成，约需要两个星期，尚不能证实接种剂能起任何决定性的作用。许多城市废物含有有效堆肥所需的各种有机物，因此就无需"神秘的细菌培养物"了。

堆肥过程的终点可由记录温度下降来测定。堆肥一般会散发出类似泥炭沼的土腥味，且呈深褐色。

在美国目前有好几家堆肥厂在运行，大部分厂家有某种"自动调节料堆"。这些料堆常归类为"消化堆"，可以对混合物充气，并有助于保持合适的湿度。堆肥的时间可由几星期缩短为几天。

尽管堆肥是一种极为好的土壤调节剂，但并没有被美国农民广泛使用。无机肥料既便宜又容易使用，而且大多数农庄所处地区的土壤条件良好。众多发达国家粮食供给丰富，并不要求利用不太好的土地，而这些土地使用堆肥才真正有价值。

第 16 单元

排放气中有机蒸气的去除

有许多工业过程，排放大量的有机蒸气进入大气层。炼油操作、胶布厂、聚合物加工、合成纤维工业、溶剂萃取、皮革加工、纸和塑料加工、锅炉和熔炉中矿物燃料的燃烧、内燃机的运行等等都会增加大气污染。人们可能已注意到：一旦有机物质逸出而进入大气中，几乎没有一种方法能使它们固定，它们甚至可能进入地球大气层以上的区域，耗尽能防止一些有害的射线到达地球表面的臭氧层。有机物质的光化学反应能导致一些化合物的形成，这些化合物能直接危害生物体或改变大气层的能见度及形成烟雾。有机物质造成的污染不是地区性的，它跨越国界并对所有生物都有影响。

使用一个能从加工区域随空气一道吸出有机蒸气的通风橱这一点是非常重要的。可用下列方法在具有合适的收集体系的情况下对含有有机蒸气的气体进行处理：

1. 在合适的液体中吸收蒸气。
2. 在低温下冷凝蒸气。
3. 在合适的介质中吸附蒸气。
4. 利用燃烧来销毁蒸气。

对于气体的吸收，吸收设备的效率依赖于这样几个因素（如果有这些因素存在的话）：

接触的有效界面积、相接触的时间、吸收液中溶质的浓度、相之间的反应速度。液体吸收剂可与所涉及的污染物发生反应或不发生反应。反应类型的吸收剂是通过化学反应将污染物转变成相对低毒性的形式而除去污染物的。反应或不反应类型的吸收剂在处理以后通常使其再生而再用于该过程。

对于吸收设备的良好的操作来说，含有蒸气的气体温度通常最好在100℃以下。所以需要冷却尾气和烟道气。如果存在其他的污染物也要吸附的话，在它们进入吸附系统之前也需冷却。可使用直接接触的冷却器来达到这一目的。这类冷却器可用喷淋式、填床式和文丘里式。最后一种更有效却有着较大的压降。然而由于它体积紧凑、操作简单而仍然常被使用。不过，有必要在文丘里涤气器之后使用除雾器。当要求非常高的气体流速和较小的压力损失时，可使用喷淋式和填床式设备。在蒸气和其他污染物的吸收过程中，总有细小的吸收剂液滴被携带。在高效接触器中这种携带更严重。

要使蒸气冷凝下来并能被收集，蒸气和气体的混合物需冷却到它的露点温度。然而，蒸气-气体的露点温度是随着蒸气在气体中的浓度的下降而持续下降的。所以，有必要逐渐地降低气体混合物的温度以便有越来越多的物质回收。物质回收的程度或排放气中蒸气的最终浓度依赖于气体冷却的最终温度。如果冷却是在管壳式冷凝器中进行的，那么在冷凝器中所得到的物质则是纯净的。由于冷却气体的费用很高并且气体的最终浓度较强地依赖于蒸气-气体混合物的温度，因此不可能仅通过冷凝就将物质全部回收。所以，从气体中冷凝蒸气作为一种回收方法仅应用于这样的情况：蒸气-气体混合物中富集蒸气或被蒸气饱和。事实上，通过将气体冷却到经济上可行的温度来冷凝回收尽可能多的物质，这是很合乎需要的。所以，有机物质的冷凝最好把它当作一种在像吸附和燃烧这样的处理之前的初步去除方法。

正如早已讨论过的，蒸气-气体混合物的冷凝和吸收的方法只是当蒸气的浓度高的时候经济上才是可行的。这些方法的一种或两种可用于初步的回收和去除大量的蒸气。剩下的量对于排放到大气层中来说可能仍然太多。对于排放气中残留的蒸气量需要进一步清洗。当气体中有机蒸气的量很小（500ppm 或更少）并出于经济上的考虑而不能使用吸收和冷凝的方法时，吸附显然是最好的方法。

对于吸附，具有适当的孔径大小和表面积的活性炭可用于固定床和流化床。对于较高气体流速流化床是较便宜的、具有低的总操作费用，并由于高的溶剂载荷而具有低的蒸气消耗，从而也使得着火的危险性较小。

用燃烧来销毁有机蒸气，称作焚烧。可根据蒸气成分的性质、组成和浓度采用下列三种方法中的一种：

1. 直接火焰燃烧。
2. 热焚烧。
3. 催化焚烧。

Appendix III   Key to Exercises

UNIT ONE
Reading Comprehension
  I.   1. T   2. F   3. F   4. T   5. T
  II.   1. B)   2. C)   3. D)   4. B)   5. D)

Vocabulary
  I.   1. install   2. established   3. surfaced   4. settled   5. pump
  II.   1. b   2. d   3. a   4. e   5. c

Translation
1. 进入河床的水流，大部分源于地下水。
2. 不管对"可靠出水量"有何种理解，都必须将各种因素考虑在内。
3. 无论地表水还是地下水都可直接送至生活区。如水质条件需要，可先输至水处理厂。
4. 配水库在输水系统中也很有必要，有助于平缓洪峰负荷。
5. 地下水是一重要的直接供水水源，由水井采出。

UNIT TWO
Reading Comprehension
  I.   1. T   2. F   3. T   4. F   5. T
  II.   1. D)   2. D)   3. D)   4. A)   5. A)

Vocabulary
  I.   1. saturated   2. precipitate   3. Specific   4. solution   5. permeability
  II.   1. c   2. d   3. a   4. b   5. e

Translation
1. 耗氧率很低往往表明不是水至清就是有效微生物不能消耗可用有机物。
2. 含氧量多少之差就是 BOD，即需氧量，以每升水样用氧的毫克数来计算。
3. 既然大多数天然水含有藻类，而且如果光线充足，氧气在瓶中也可得到再补充，光线也是一重要的变量。
4. 水能传播多种疾病，包括伤寒和霍乱。
5. 这简直如同谚语中所说的大海捞针。

UNIT THREE
Reading Comprehension
Ⅰ. 1. F 2. F 3. T 4. T 5. F
Ⅱ. 1. B) 2. C) 3. A) 4. C) 5. B)

Vocabulary
Ⅰ. 1. soft 2. stabilization 3. algae 4. sludge 5. disinfected
Ⅱ. 1. d 2. c 3. b 4. a 5. e

Translation
1. 具有这种性质的水被称为"硬水"。
2. 我们知道钙和镁是水的硬度的起因，碳酸氢盐是水暂时硬度的起因，而硫酸盐和氯化物是水的永久硬度的起因。
3. 水的硬度可由水的"肥皂破坏力"来测定，但更准确的方法是用能生成组成物的硬度的总量来测定。生成的组成物用化学上等量碳酸钙来表示。
4. 氯胺法可防止由游离氯而引起的异味。
5. 滤床变脏，水头损失就增大。

UNIT FOUR
Reading Comprehension
Ⅰ. 1. T 2. F 3. T 4. F 5. T
Ⅱ. 1. C) 2. C) 3. D) 4. A) 5. C)

Vocabulary
Ⅰ. 1. porous 2. filterrun 3. strain 4. viruses 5. fluidized
Ⅱ. 1. c 2. a 3. d 4. e 5. b

Translation
1. 直到有足够的肥皂溶解和所有这些物质起反应时，才会出现泡沫。
2. 除非有游离溶解氧存在，反应不会进行。
3. 正常情况下，大肠杆菌一般无害。
4. 这两种物质并不都溶于水。
5. 并不是每一点细微差别都注意到了。

UNIT FIVE
Reading Comprehension
Ⅰ. 1. F 2. F 3. F 4. T 5. T

Ⅱ.　　1. C)　　　2. A)　　　3. D)　　　4. B)　　　5. B)

Vocabulary
 Ⅰ.　　1. kept clear of　2. detrimental　3. sanitary wastes　4. Collecting sewers
   5. sewerage
 Ⅱ.　　1. d　　2. e　　3. a　　4. c　　5. b

Translation
1. 为了便于维修,对污水集水系统的设计标准作了许多规定。
2. 街道坡度、路缘设计和路沟凹度限定了最佳进水口的选择。
3. 管线沿地面的总体坡度敷设以便进水可以向下流至合适排放点。
4. 生活污水管的设计和施工应考虑防止超载。
5. 须有专门措施来保护管道和检查井免遭由冲刷和水力冲击负荷造成的位移。

UNIT SIX

Reading Comprehension
 Ⅰ.　　1. T　　　2. T　　　3. T　　　4. F　　　5. T
 Ⅱ.　　1. D)　　2. D)　　3. B)　　4. D)　　5. C)

Vocabulary
 Ⅰ.　　1. nutrients　　2. phosphates　　3. solvent　　4. polymeric　　5. grease
 Ⅱ.　　1. b　　2. c　　3. a　　4. d　　5. e

Translation
1. 几乎所有的新厂都使用了机械化清洁设备。
2. 沉淀池若位于像筛滤、去除粗砂一类的预处理设施之后,叫做初级澄清池。
3. 由初级澄清池排出的水,尽管已有许多固体有机物被滤出,但对氧的含量仍有一个较高的需求。
4. 岩石上生物生长得十分活跃。
5. 一般来讲,有臭味和水分大是生污泥难以处理的两个特点。

UNIT SEVEN

Reading Comprehension
 Ⅰ.　　1. F　　　2. T　　　3. F　　　4. T　　　5. T
 Ⅱ.　　1. C)　　2. D)　　3. C)　　4. D)　　5. C)

Vocabulary
 Ⅰ.　　1. metabolize　　2. critical　　3. digesters　　4. diffusing　　5. decomposition
 Ⅱ.　　1. c　　2. a　　3. e　　4. b　　5. d

Translation
1. 这种方法，如果有效，既简便成本又低。
2. 澄清水由 V 形堰逸出。
3. 使用臭氧化法，起作用的是氧不是氯，且没有余味。
4. 街道进水口下面的集水坑通过较短管线与雨水主管相接。雨水主管位于街道管带内，常沿街道中心铺设。
5. 除非污泥要焚化，脱水很少被用作中间处理环节。
6. 并非所有的污水管都可作重力管道用。
7. 第三个处理步骤就是去除砂粒。
8. 所谓活性炭，就是一种带有大的吸收表面积的细粉碎的碳。
9. 从设计原理方面来看，生活污水管同雨水管的主要差别是：后者被假定会发生周期性的超载和溢流。
10. 许多人认为：由白垩层采出的矿泉水，水质硬，晶莹清澈，为首屈一指的饮料。

UNIT EIGHT

Reading Comprehension

Ⅰ.　　1. T　　　2. T　　　3. F　　　4. T　　　5. F
Ⅱ.　　1. B)　　 2. B)　　 3. A)　　 4. C)　　 5. A)

Vocabulary

Ⅰ.　　1. pathogens　　2. biomasses　　3. compacted　　4. thickening　　5. viscosity
Ⅱ.　　1. a　　　2. d　　　3. b　　　4. e　　　5. c

Translation
1. 如果消化池变"酸"，说明产甲烷菌在某种程度上受到了抑制。
2. 要脱水的污泥被倾倒在约 15cm 深的砂滤床上。
3. 如果用砂滤床脱水被认为是不现实的，就得使用机械脱水。
4. 这些有机酸依次受到一组叫做产甲烷菌的绝对厌氧菌的进一步降解。
5. 参照水泵的比速对各水泵之间加以比较是很方便的。

UNIT NINE

Reading Comprehension

Ⅰ.　　1. T　　　2. F　　　3. F　　　4. T　　　5. T
Ⅱ.　　1. B)　　 2. B)　　 3. D)　　 4. C)　　 5. A)

Vocabulary

Ⅰ.　　1. radial　　2. specific speeds　　3. impeller　　4. dewater　　5. firesupplies
Ⅱ.　　1. e　　　2. a　　　3. c　　　4. b　　　5. d

Translation

1. 六百米以下几乎找不到水。
2. 给初级消化池加盖、加热并搅拌,以增加反应速率。
3. 经验表明,在水中添加足量的氯,使游离氯剩余量超过水中有机物和植物性物质的吸收量,即可降低味嗅。
4. 有人建议,在水源和城市之间建造一座水泵站。
5. 在美国,虽然空气冲洗很少用,但某些水厂已发现用向砂床表面喷射水的方法搅拌和清洗那些常常是最脏的砂层来增加反冲洗的效果是必要的。

UNIT TEN
Reading Comprehension

I. 1.F 2.F 3.T 4.T 5.T 6.F 7.T 8.F 9.T 10.T

II. 1. a point source, a dispersed (or nonpoint) source
2. pathogenic organisms, oxygen—demanding substances, plant nutrients, toxic organics, inorganic chemicals, sediment, radioactive substances, heat, oil
3. sewage
4. cholorinated hydrocarbons

Vocaburary

I. 1. dissipate 2. regulatory 3. depleting 4. culprit 5. identified

II. 1. c 2. a 3. e 4. d 5. b

Translation

1. 我们平均每分钟说150个字,比大多数打字员打字的速度快一倍。
2. 二十世纪六十年代以来,计算机的工作速度已提高近一百万倍。
3. 上海人口是无锡人口的十倍。
4. 那家工厂排出的废水比这家工厂的多四倍。
5. 机械工具的生产已增加了六倍。

UNIT ELEVEN
Reading Comprehension

I. 1.T 2.F 3.F 4.T 5.T 6.T 7.F 8.F 9.T 10.T

II. 1. fallout, deposition
2. rainout, washout, snowout, sweepout
3. directly, indirectly, transport, transformation, storage
4. air, water, land

Vocaburary

Ⅰ. 1. intrinsic　2. impact　3. cursory　4. respectively　5. controversy

Ⅱ. 1. b　2. e　3. a　4. c　5. d

Translation

1. 新型晶体管的开关时间缩短了一半。
2. 待冷却气体的总热函也会减少到原来的 $\frac{1}{5} \sim \frac{1}{4}$。
3. 今年的钢产量比去年少三分之二。
4. 信号增大十倍，增益则可能降低到八分之一。
5. 电子质量为氢原子质量的 $\frac{1}{1851}$ 倍。

UNIT TWELVE

Reading Comprehension

Ⅰ. 1. F　2. T　3. T　4. T　5. F　6. F

Ⅱ. 1. poisons

2. those that are unstable and tend to react vigorously with air, water, or other substances

3. ignitable waste

4. strong alkaline or acidic substances

5. infectious or biological waste

6. those particularly from nuclear power plants

Vocaburary

Ⅰ. 1. ignitable　2. acute　3. indiscriminate　4. evacuate　5. remedial

Ⅱ. 1. d　2. a　3. e　4. b　5. c

Translation

1. 给水染污物定的限度可能有不同的名称。
2. 当然有淤泥，这些淤泥是水处理而产生的。
3. 在过去的 30 年中，大量的文章指出怎样使用自然程序来处理各种各样的废物。
4. 差不多所有城市都有处理厂，这些工厂能处理生活废物。
5. 可使用土处理法，这种土处理法与填土法不同。

UNIT THIRTEEN

Reading Comprehension

Ⅰ. 1. T　2. F　3. T　4. F　5. T　6. T

Ⅱ. 1. natural pollutants
2. fly ash, smoke, sulfur and nitrogen oxides, automibile exhaust, etc
3. carbon monoxide, hydrocarbans, hydrogen sulfide, nitrogen oxides, etc
4. particulate pollutants

Vocaburary
Ⅰ. 1. ingenuity   2. better than   3. concentration   4. nil   5. metallic
Ⅱ. 1. e   2. d   3. a   4. c   5. b

Translation
1. 逆温是高处的一层热空气，它可以阻制污染物的逃脱。
2. 工业每年都在产生大量的新化学品，所有这些化学品最后都进入水中。
3. 最简单的物理过程是蒸发，这可由机械喷雾器来实施。
4. 盐有很高的热导性，这有助去除废物容器中的热量。
5. 太久地暴露于噪声中会引起几天就可能消失的暂时性耳聋，或者是永久的失聪。

UNIT FOURTEEN
Reading Comprehension
Ⅰ. 1. T   2. T   3. F   4. T   5. F   6. F
Ⅱ. 1. ear drum, hammer, anvil, stirrup, inner ear, cochlea, hair cells, frequencies, bioelectrical signals, brain
2. heartbeat, blood, blood vessels, focusing

Vocaburary
Ⅰ. 1. convalescent   2. necessitate   3. deflect   4. ancestral   5. irate
Ⅱ. 1. e   2. a   3. b   4. d   5. c

Translation
1. 例如，原来含有氢、氯和液态水的气液混合体系，就水蒸气与液态水而言，会很快趋达平衡，直到气相中水蒸气的分压基本上等于在该体系温度下液态水的蒸气的分压时为止。
2. 当普通的棒硫溶解于少量称为二硫化碳的不可燃液体中，并且将这溶液倒入结晶皿内时，我们发现溶剂慢慢蒸发，遗留下呈细小晶体形状的硫。
3. 在许多情况下，一些比较老的操作方法由于不能控制污染而过早地停止使用了；例如美国钢铁公司的费耳斐尔德钢铁厂用底吹氧气转炉炼钢法代替平炉法，就是地方当局为反对大量污染而采取干涉行动的直接结果。
4. 总产品回收率随着单位耗电量的增大而减小这一趋势，是由下列两点造成的：在较为强烈的反应条件下脱氧量有所增加，以及整个收尘系统中气体流速一般较高。

UNIT FIFTEEN
Reading Comprehension
Ⅰ. 1.T   2.T   3.F   4.F   5.T   6.T   7.T   8.F   9.T   10.F
Ⅱ. 1. recycling
   2. metals, glass, organics
   3. recycled, virgin, legislation, taxes
   4. Composting
   5. segregation, inorganic, grinding, stabilizing

Vocaburary
Ⅰ. 1. discarded   2. sorted   3. dearth   4. dictate   5. obnoxious
Ⅱ. 1.b   2.e   3.d   4.c   5.a

Translation
1. 尽管警察都已接到命令，要做好准备以应付紧急情况，但人们还是不敢出门，因为警察也同其他任何人一样感到不知所措和无能为力。
2. 因为铝总和其他元素——最常见的氧（因为铝对氧有很强的亲和力）——结合在一起，所以在自然界任何地方都找不到处于游离状态的铝，因而直到十九世纪铝才为人们所知道。
3. 在他生命的七十三年时间里，通讯事业发生了一些非同寻常的大变化，他为这种情况的可能出现做出了很大的贡献。
4. 在铜精矿的情况下，从流床反应器得到的焙砂应当是处于适合化学浸出或离析处理的物理状态：化学浸出的目的是回收铜，离析处理则是用新近研究成功的固态离析法来回收铜与贵金属。

UNIT SIXTEEN
Reading Comprehension
Ⅰ. 1.F   2.T   3.F   4.F   5.T   6.T   7.T   8.T   9.T   10.F
Ⅱ. 1. Refinery operations, coated-fabric units, polymer-processing, synthetic-fibre industry, solvent extraction, leather processing, paper and plastic processing, combustion of fossil fuels in boilers, furnaces and internal-combustion operations
   2. absorption, condenstion, adsorption, destruction
   3. dew point
   4. incineration
   5. direct flame combustion, thermal incineration, catalytic incineration

Vocaburary

Ⅰ. 1. residual   2. incineration   3. preliminary   4. repercussion   5. suck out

Ⅱ. 1. b   2. d   3. c   4. a   5. e

Translation

1. 虽然避免在天然溪流和处理厂里可能有的需氧环境很重要，但厌氧微生物也能提供一些有用的处理。
2. 这种固体废物的处理方法在化肥不能保证供应的国家尤其成功。
3. 废物的处理是一个特别困难的问题，因为废物的增加速度比人口增长的速度要快。
4. 一九七五年，上海重工业的产值是1949年的18倍。
5. 如果两个氯原子结合，就会产生一个氯气分子，自由的氯元素就是这样存在于自然界中的。
6. 你可能会把原子看作是极小的建筑材料，认为任何元素在化学上都是无差异的，而各种不同元素的原子是不同的。
7. 过滤材料得常常清洗。清洗时可采用让水逆流的方法，这样可以让清水来清洗过滤材料。也可使用压缩气泡来搅动过滤材料，使积聚的脏物分离，上升最后被去除。
8. 因为使用了先进的水处理技术，这个城市的污水排放已减少了$\frac{4}{5}$。

图书在版编目（CIP）数据

建筑类专业英语. 第2册，给水排水与环境保护/傅兴海，褚羞花主编. —北京：中国建筑工业出版社，1997（2022.8重印）
高等学校试用教材
ISBN 978-7-112-03033-0

Ⅰ. 建… Ⅱ. ①傅…②褚… Ⅲ. ①建筑工程-英语-高等学校-教材②给水工程-英语-高等学校-教材③排水工程-英语-高等学校-教材④环境保护-建筑工程-英语-高等学校-教材　Ⅳ. H31

中国版本图书馆 CIP 数据核字(2005)第 077578 号

本书按国家教委颁布的《大学英语专业阅读阶段教学基本要求》编写的专业英语教材。本册内容包括供水、水质检测、水处理、废水污水收集和处理、管网、生物处理系统、泵和泵站、大气污染、水污染、噪声污染、有害废物及其处理等。全书安排 16 单元，每单元除正课文外，还有两篇阅读材料，均配有必要的注释，正课文还配有词汇表和练习，书后附有总词汇表、参考译文和练习答案。全书的语言难度大于第一册，还对科技英语翻译技巧作了简要说明，并增加例句和翻译练习题。

本书供高等院校给水排水和环境保护专业三年级下半学期使用，也可供有关人员学习参考。

高等学校试用教材
建筑类专业英语
给水排水与环境保护
第二册
傅兴海　褚羞花　主编
耿建琴　张　萍
史长远　刘　澍　编
迟国基　　　　主审

*

中国建筑工业出版社出版、发行（北京西郊百万庄）
各地新华书店、建筑书店经销
北京云浩印刷有限责任公司印刷

*

开本：787×1092 毫米　1/16　印张：12¼　字数：292 千字
1997 年 6 月第一版　2022 年 8 月第十六次印刷
定价：22.00 元
ISBN 978-7-112-03033-0
(20770)

版权所有　翻印必究
如有印装质量问题，可寄本社退换
（邮政编码 100037）